THE GREAT
DELEVERAGING

THE GREAT DELEVERAGING:

Economic Growth and Investing Strategies for the Future

CHIP DICKSON AND ODED SHENKAR

Vice President, Publisher: Tim Moore
Associate Publisher and Director of Marketing: Amy Neidlinger
Executive Editor: Jim Boyd
Editorial Assistant: Pamela Boland
Development Editor: Russ Hall
Operations Manager: Gina Kanouse
Senior Marketing Manager: Julie Phifer
Publicity Manager: Laura Czaja
Assistant Marketing Manager: Megan Colvin
Cover Designer: Chuti Prasertsith
Managing Editor: Kristy Hart
Project Editor: Betsy Harris
Copy Editors: Apostrophe Editing Services and Karen Annett
Proofreader: Kathy Ruiz
Indexer: Erika Millen
Senior Compositor: Gloria Schurick
Manufacturing Buyer: Dan Uhrig

This book is sold with the understanding that neither the authors nor the publisher are engaged in rendering legal, accounting, or other professional services or advice by publishing this book. Each individual situation is unique. Thus, if legal or financial advice or other expert assistance is required in a specific situation, the services of a competent professional should be sought to ensure that the situation has been evaluated carefully and appropriately. The authors and the publisher disclaim any liability, loss, or risk resulting directly or indirectly, from the use or application of any of the contents of this book.

FT Press offers excellent discounts on this book when ordered in quantity for bulk purchases or special sales. For more information, please contact U.S. Corporate and Government Sales, 1-800-382-3419, corpsales@pearsontechgroup.com. For sales outside the U.S., please contact International Sales at international@pearson.com.

Company and product names mentioned herein are the trademarks or registered trademarks of their respective owners.

First Printing August 2010

ISBN-10: 0-13-235810-7

ISBN-13: 978-0-13-235810-1

Pearson Education LTD.
Pearson Education Australia PTY, Limited.
Pearson Education Singapore, Pte. Ltd.
Pearson Education North Asia, Ltd.
Pearson Education Canada, Ltd.
Pearson Educatión de Mexico, S.A. de C.V.
Pearson Education—Japan
Pearson Education Malaysia, Pte. Ltd.

Library of Congress Cataloging-in-Publication Data

Dickson, Chip

The great deleveraging : economic growth and investing strategies for the future / Chip Dickson, Oded Shenkar.

p. cm.

ISBN 978-0-13-235810-1 (hbk. : alk. paper) 1. Investments. 2. Financial leverage. 3. Business cycles. 4. Economic forecasting. I. Shenkar, Oded. II. Title.

HG4521.D53 2011

332.6—dc22

2010018977

I dedicate this book to my parents for giving me life;
to my wife, Ellen,
for sharing her life; and to my children, Laura, Julia,
and Henry, always
Chip Dickson

To my late parents and to Miriam, Keshet,
Josh, and Riki;
my best investment.
Oded Shenkar

Contents

Acknowledgments

There are many people to thank, and that starts with my family because of the time spent working on and talking about this book. Their patience and attention were and are always appreciated. To many of my friends who listened to me discuss the book and read some of the drafts, your support is also appreciated. Specifically, I want to thank Greg Swenson, Greg Anderson, Warren Hatch, Monique Sinmao, Brett Kornfeld, Jack Malvey, Raheel Siddiqui Richard Gatward, and Dana Guido for their time.

—Chip Dickson

Thanks to my family, the Fisher College at Ohio State, and all the people at FT Press who have patiently worked with us through the ups and downs of the financial markets.

—Oded Shenkar

About the Authors

Chip Dickson is a cofounder, Director of Research, and Strategist of DISCERN, an equity research firm. This follows a Wall Street career of twenty years as an Equity Analyst, Strategist, and Associate Director of Research. The firms he worked at included Lehman Brothers and Salomon Smith Barney. His work received high rankings from Institutional Investor and Greenwich Associates. He earned his MBA and BSBA from Babson College and holds the Chartered Financial Analyst designation.

Oded Shenkar holds degrees in East-Asian (Chinese) Studies and Sociology from the Hebrew University of Jerusalem and a PhD from Columbia University. He is currently the Ford Motor Company Chair in Global Business Management and Professor of Management and Human Resources at the Fisher College of Business, The Ohio State University, where he heads the international business area and is also a member of the Centers for Chinese Studies and for Near East Studies. Professor Shenkar has been a Senior Fellow at the University of Cambridge and has taught at the Chinese University of Hong Kong, Hong Kong University of Science & Technology, Peking University, University of International Business and Economics (Beijing), and the International University of Japan, among many others.

Professor Shenkar has published close to a hundred articles in leading journals. His books include *The Chinese Century* (Wharton School Publishing), which has been translated into twelve languages, and *Copycats: how smart companies use imitation to gain a strategic edge* (Harvard Business Press). His work has been cited by *The Wall Street Journal*, *The New York Times*, *The Financial Times*, *The Los Angeles Times*, *USA Today*, *The Chicago Tribune*, *The Boston Globe*, *Business Week*, *The Economist*, and many others.

Introduction

This book addresses why the United States took on so much debt and, eventually, how the debt will be reduced—delevered—and the costs of that deleveraging. In between, it differentiates sources of real economic and financial market growth from those that hinder and undermine them. It also provides some perspective on asset class returns over the last nine decades and some insight into the foundation of past secular bear and bull markets. That perspective is meant to better frame some basic rules of the investment road and hopefully make for more effective future navigation in an increasingly shifting global economy and more diverse market environment. First, the book starts with a reminder of a time when the outlook seemed pretty bleak.

1980 was a difficult year around the world, and it was evident in the somber public mood. The governments of the United States and much of Europe were trying to reverse a decade-long tide of rising interest rates, high inflation, and poor economic growth. In the United States, the core inflation rate rose above 12.5%, the U.S. government paid about 17.5% for short-term money funded with 3-month T-Bills, the rate paid for a conventional 30-year mortgage reached 16%, and good corporate credits saw the prime rate rise above 20%. It was very expensive to take risks and few dared or could afford to borrow. All this happened at a time when the last of the baby boom generation was entering the workforce.

The rest of the world did not fare much better. Sub-Saharan Africa suffered from overwhelming poverty and growing political instability. The largely centrally planned economies of China and the Soviet Union remained unable to lift much of their population from abject poverty and the rest of Asia was not doing much better. Over half of the world's population lived under totalitarian rule while many democratically elected governments pursued a course enhancing the role of government relative to the private sector. The major exceptions were Japan, which was continuing its remarkable post-World War II rise, and the oil-rich countries, which remained the beneficiaries of a seemingly endless and vital resource in great demand—oil.

For the typical 1980 investor, the prospect of better economic times and surging financial markets seemed far-fetched. Any time the economy and the market rebounded, negative economic news would darken the horizon again. Virtually no one realized that this dismal year actually marked a dramatic inflection point. The leadership and structure of governments the world over was beginning to change, real economic growth was set to accelerate, a wave of technological innovation was about to take hold, and financial markets were ready to take off.

What had happened was that the same destructive forces of inflation and historically high interest rates that had wreaked economic havoc triggered a political backlash against the existing order of the time. The backlash started in the United Kingdom, where Margaret Thatcher and the Conservative Party came to power in 1979 and implemented reforms that eventually lowered the rate of inflation, reduced regulatory barriers, and set in motion an economic surge. The United States followed suit in 1980, electing Ronald Reagan. With Reagan and with Paul Volcker as the head of the Federal Reserve, trends started to reverse. After years of dealing with double-digit inflation and interest rates well over 10%, the stage was being set for the beginning of the Great Equity bull market that lasted in the United States until 2000.

Reducing inflation and lowering interest rates also meant that the cost of capital was reduced, which made investing more attractive. The risk-free rate fell as did the risk premium, which is another way of saying that growth expectations increased as investors' confidence grew. Lowering the cost of capital meant that the value of a dollar of profit rose. For the equity markets, it meant valuations rose. Concurrent with these changes were regulatory and technology developments, making investing more accessible and less costly to the individual investor. Investment products proliferated as did the number of financial markets around the world that were open to investors from other nations.

Five Major Events Driving Globalization

At about the same time, on the other side of the world, big changes were also brewing. In China, late 1978 saw the beginning of economic reforms that would eventually catapult China to its current position as the world's second-largest economy. After cautiously reopening the country for foreign investment, its paramount leader, Deng Xiaoping, declared that it was "glorious to get rich" and encouraged the Chinese to go into business and become entrepreneurs, first in small businesses and then on a grander scale. Since then, China's economy more than quintupled in size by sustaining an annual compound growth rate of over 12%. A $500 billion economy representing a mere 2% of the global economy in 1992 became an almost $3 trillion economy representing close to 6% of the world's economy in 2008. That growth greatly reduced the number of Chinese living in poverty: Between 1993 and 2005, the number of poor in China fell by about 70% (see Exhibit 1).

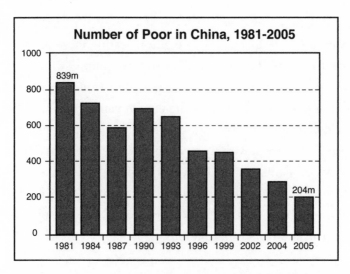

Number of Poor in China, 1981-2005

Exhibit 1   The Number of Very Poor in China Fell More Than 75% Between 1981 and 2005. (Source: Carpe Diem Blog)

The Great Openings

The Chinese reforms would be one of five major events creating the foundation for a major wave of globalization and, with it, the creation of financial wealth. The other four were the move toward free markets through the elections of Margaret Thatcher and Ronald Reagan, the fall of the Berlin Wall in 1989, the start of the World Wide Web in 1991, and the Free Trade initiative started under the first Bush administration and put into effect by the Clinton administration. Taken together, these events provided the foundation for a more open global economy, triggering a surge of innovation and productivity, a decline in geopolitical tensions, more open communication, and a surge in education. We call these "The Great Openings."

Over the next 25 years, that wave of technological and political change would alter many assumptions and some of the structures of daily life. Taken for granted today in most developed countries are the Internet, e-mail, cell phones, smartphones, PDAs, increased computer processing power, smaller devices, digital television, speech recognition, DVD players, music and video downloads, automated teller machines, 24/7 news, endless entertainment choices, blogs, GPS (Global Positioning System), and immediacy. Many of these technologies were introduced into developing markets much faster than previously was the case. As they grew, the economy and financial markets grew with them.

Between 1980 and 2007, the global economy grew more than 3.5 times. Global gross domestic product (GDP) reached almost $55 trillion; on a real basis, it grew more than 2.5 times (Exhibit 2). Per capita, GDP went from $2,771 in 1980 to $8,443 in 2007. The value of the world's stock markets increased from close to $675 per person to just under $9,500—up more than 14 times. The value of all financial assets increased from near $2,700 per person to an estimated $28,500. It was a period of significant global economic expansion and wealth creation.

Real Global Economic Growth–Actual and Expected

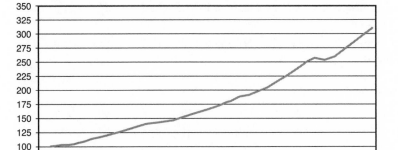

Exhibit 2   The Global Economy Index—Actual and Expected (Source: IMF)

Strong economic growth and attractive financial market performance coincided with population growth. It also coincided with other positive trends like lower poverty levels, rising life expectancy, and declining illiteracy. In 1981, almost 52% of the world's population lived on no more than $1.25 per day and almost 75% lived on less than $2.50 per day, as shown in Exhibit 3. By 2005, the number of people living on $1.25 per day fell to 25.2%, while the number of those living on $2.50 per day fell to 56.6%—a remarkable improvement. The global illiteracy rate fell from 30.3% in 1980 to 18.3% in 2005 according to UNESCO. In the United States, life expectancy rose from 73.7 years in 1980 to 77.8 years in 2005.

Exhibit 3   World Poverty Figures by Region, 1981–2005; Percent Living Below the Poverty Line (Source: Chen, Shaohua and Martin Ravallion, "The Developing World Is Poorer than We Thought, but no Less Successful in the Fight Against Poverty," *Quarterly Journal of Economics*, in press Fall 2010)

Region	$1.25/day				$2.50/day			
	1981	1990	1999	2005	1981	1990	1999	2005
East Asia & Pacific	77.7	54.7	35.5	16.8	95.4	87.3	71.7	50.7
Of which China	84.0	60.2	35.6	15.9	99.4	91.6	71.7	49.5
Eastern Europe & Central Asia	1.7	2.0	5.1	3.7	15.2	12.0	21.4	12.9
Latin America & Caribbean	11.5	9.8	10.8	8.4	29.2	26.0	28.0	22.1
Middle East & North Africa	7.9	4.3	4.2	3.6	39.0	31.2	30.8	28.4
South Asia	59.4	51.7	44.1	40.3	92.6	90.3	86.7	84.4
India	59.8	51.3	44.8	41.6	92.5	90.2	87.6	85.7
Sub-Saharan Africa	53.7	57.9	58.2	51.2	81.0	82.5	83.8	80.5
Total	51.8	41.6	33.7	25.2	74.6	70.4	65.9	56.6

Improvements in the quality of life occurred while the world's population expanded from 4.43 billion people in 1980 to more than 6.7 billion people in 2008. In 2005, in a global population of 6.5 billion, 1.2 billion people resided in developed countries and 5.3 billion lived in developing nations. The combination of population and economic growth brought with it a surge in the number of new businesses created. Those new businesses often came from new industries and product lines, such as personal computers, cell phones, semiconductors, the Internet, credit cards, mortgage banking, and health-care companies that made artificial joints—to name a few. New players also emerged: S&P companies like WalMart, Best Buy, Intel, Microsoft, Apple, Dell, Cisco, Amgen, Stryker, Visa, Master-Card, Yahoo!, and Google were not part of the S&P 500 Index in 1980.

The post-1980 period also saw an unprecedented wave of globalization, which was reflected first in the economic mix and only more recently in the investment mix. In 1992, the developed world's share of the global economy exceeded 75%. As recently as 2000, it remained close to that level, as shown in Exhibit 4. Since 2000, the developed world's share declined to 68% in 2007. Since 2001, the United States share of the global economy declined from about 32% to 23%, according to statistics from the World Bank. Since 1980, its peak level was almost a 34% share of global GDP in 1985. Japan's 2008 share of 8% global GDP represents a significant reduction in its share of global GDP since 2001 when it was 12.9% and from its peak of 18% in 1994.

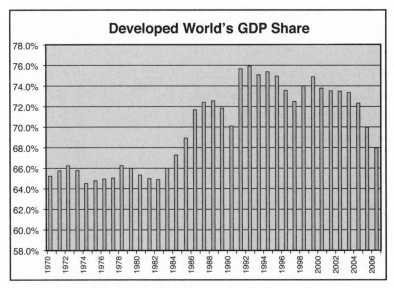

Exhibit 4 The Developed World's Shrinking Share of the Global Economy (Source: United Nations)

The developing world continued to gain share since 2001. For instance, based on the World Bank statistics, China saw its share of global GDP rise from 4.2% to 7.1% in 2008. The Russian Federation's share increased from 1.7% to 2.7% and reflects the tremendous increase in global demand for energy. Brazil's share of global GDP rose from 1.9% to 2.6%, and India's share rose from 0.5% to 2.0%. This was a period when low- and middle-income countries experienced faster economic growth and garnered a greater share of the global economy.

In line with the economic mix, the developed world controlled the dominant share of financial assets. As recently as 2001, the U.S. equity market represented over 50% of global equity market capitalization. By the end of 2007, however, the U.S. equity market represented about 30% of global equity with a market capitalization of over $60 trillion. Between 2002 and 2007, the size of the equity market almost tripled, and it increased more than six times between 1992 and 2007. An investor in the global equity market in 1980 saw their investment increase more than 20 times through 2007. With the global economy, the character and structure of the global financial markets also changed dramatically. The forces stimulating the growth of the financial markets started in the late 1970s as inflation and interest rates began to peak in much of the developed world. Also, the technologies driving the digitalization or the economy became more accessible, affordable, and impactful. This started the initial stage of financial asset growth relative to GDP in some of the world's developed countries.

The economic and financial success of the 1980–2007 era was constructed on some very durable foundations, but also on some false ones. There were weaknesses and structural decay only a few recognized. As is often the case, perception did not match reality. Since the end of 2007, the global equity markets lost more than 50% of their value from peak to trough, and much of the world's economy fell into recession. Future economic and financial prospects seem much less attractive two years ago even though the economic cycle turned and a modest recovery began.

Through it all, the world's population continued to grow. That growth is expected to continue through 2050, but at a slower rate. By 2050, the world's population is expected to exceed 9 billion, as shown in Exhibit 5.

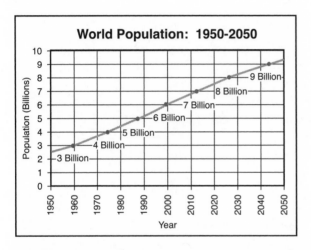

Exhibit 5   Global Population Expected to Exceed 9 Billion Before 2050 (Source: U.S. Census Bureau, International Data Base, June 2009 update)

The global population reached 6.76 billion in 2009, and by 2050, it is expected to reach 9.32 billion, an increase of 2.56 billion people or 38%. That increase is equal to the world's population in 1950. India is expected to pass China and become the most populous country. Its expected increase of 500 million people will be greater than the population of every country in the world except China. Combined, those countries are expected to house 33% of the world's population compared with 36% in 2009. The largest absolute growth from 2009 to 2050 is expected to come from the countries shown in Exhibit 6.

Exhibit 6   Top 25 Countries: Expected Population Increase Between 2009 and 2050 (Source: U.S. Census Bureau)

Country	2050 Estimated Population	Expected Change	Expected Percentage Change
India	1,656,553,632	499,655,866	43.2%
Ethiopia	278,283,137	193,045,799	226.5%
United States	439,010,253	131,798,130	42.9%
Congo (Kinshasa)	189,310,849	120,618,307	175.6%
Nigeria	264,262,405	115,033,315	77.1%
Pakistan	276,428,758	101,850,200	58.3%
Uganda	128,007,514	95,637,956	295.5%
China	1,424,161,948	85,548,980	6.4%
Bangladesh	233,587,279	77,536,396	49.7%
Philippines	171,964,187	73,987,584	75.5%
Indonesia	313,020,847	72,749,325	30.3%
Brazil	260,692,493	61,953,224	31.2%
Egypt	137,872,522	59,005,887	74.8%
Sudan	88,227,761	47,139,936	114.7%
Niger	55,304,449	39,998,197	261.3%
Mexico	147,907,650	36,695,861	33.0%
Madagascar	56,513,827	35,860,271	173.6%

Exhibit 6 Top 25 Countries: Expected Population Increase Between 2009 and 2050 (Source: U.S. Census Bureau)

Country	2050 Estimated Population	Expected Change	Expected Percentage Change
Burkina Faso	47,429,509	31,683,277	201.2%
Iraq	56,316,329	27,370,760	94.6%
Kenya	65,175,864	26,173,092	67.1%
Tanzania	66,843,312	25,794,780	62.8%
Afghanistan	53,354,109	24,958,393	87.9%
Turkey	100,955,188	24,149,664	31.4%
Yemen	45,780,651	22,922,413	100.3%
Vietnam	111,173,583	22,596,825	25.5%

The United States is expected to remain the third most populous country in the world with a population exceeding 400 million. Its population growth is expected to be greater than the global population growth in large part because of more open immigration. Growth is not expected everywhere and 15 countries are expected to experience a population contraction of more than 1 million, as shown in Exhibit 7.

**Exhibit 7   Fifteen Countries Expected to Experience the Largest
Population Decline by 2050 (Source: United Nations Population
Fund)**

Country	2050 Estimated Population	Expected Change	Expected Percentage Change
Japan	93,673,826	-33,404,853	-26.3%
Russia	109,187,353	-30,853,894	-22.0%
Ukraine	33,573,842	-12,126,553	-26.5%
Germany	73,607,121	-8,722,637	-10.6%
Italy	50,389,841	-7,736,371	-13.3%
Poland	32,084,570	-6,398,349	-16.6%
Korea, South	43,368,983	-5,139,989	-10.6%
Spain	35,564,293	-4,960,709	-12.2%
Romania	18,678,226	-3,537,195	-15.9%
Taiwan	20,161,286	-2,813,061	-12.2%
Bulgaria	4,651,477	-2,553,210	-35.4%
Belarus	7,738,613	-1,909,920	-19.8%
Czech Republic	8,540,221	-1,671,683	-16.4%
Hungary	8,374,619	-1,530,977	-15.5%
Serbia	5,869,146	-1,510,193	-20.5%

The global economy and financial markets should continue to be volatile and evolve, while the world's population continues to grow. There will be many challenges and there will be many opportunities.

To provide a better perspective, the book begins with a discussion of the "great leveraging," a flashback into the debt and risk accumulated in the United States, and is followed by a quick history of bull and bear markets, global economic growth, and the economic returns generated by different asset classes over time. We then detail the destruction of euphoria, including the telling story of Japan, and the way out of euphoria. Finally, we turn to market scenarios, signals, and the great deleveraging we are undergoing today, accompanied by the global economic outlook and its investment implications.

1

The Great Leveraging

All that growth, was it real?

At the end of the second quarter of 2009, over $50 trillion of debt was on the balance sheet of the United States—its citizens, state and local governments, businesses, farms, and other organizations. That is a remarkable increase from 2000, when total debt was about $25 trillion. In less than a decade, debt more than doubled, whereas the economy grew only by roughly 40%. The sectors with the fastest rate of debt growth during the period were government sponsored enterprises (GSEs) and financials. Exhibit 1-1 shows that government borrowing began to grow relatively faster starting in 2003. Household debt began to decline in 2009. The economy of the United States was using leverage to grow, improve returns, and get everything faster.

This is not a new phenomenon. Since 1952, the debt growth rate exceeded 8.5% per year, much higher than the 6.5% annual pace of economic growth. If debt growth equaled GDP growth over that period, total debt would be less than $20 trillion, and less than 150% of GDP. As debt grew faster, the U.S. economy became much more leveraged. At the end of the second quarter of 2009, total debt exceeded 375% of U.S. GDP. Back in 1999, debt was less than 250% of GDP, and in 1986, it was less than 200% of GDP. At its mid 2009 level, the debt-to-GDP ratio was at its highest point ever. The last major peak of debt to GDP occurred in 1932 and 1933 when debt approached 300% of GDP, as shown in Exhibit 1-2. From that point, the deleveraging process began and took 20 years to complete. When it ended, the debt-to-GDP ratio was less than 150%. During that period of deleveraging, the United States economy spent over seven years in a depression and almost ten years supporting wars.

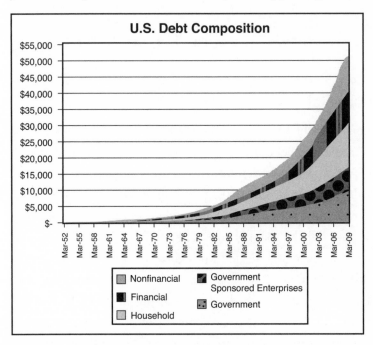

Exhibit 1-1   Dollar Composition of U.S. Debt (Source: Flow of Funds, authors)

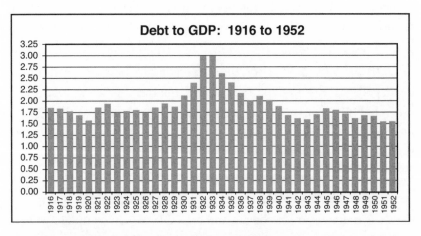

Exhibit 1-2   Before and After the Great Deleveraging of the Last Century (Source: Historical Statistics of the United States)

Since 1980, three of the four major economic sectors—households, financial corporations, nonfinancial corporations, and government—have dramatically increased their debt levels. Three of these sectors—households, financials, and government—continued to increase their debt load after 1990, whereas nonfinancial corporations did not use leverage as aggressively. Exhibit 1-3 provides a look at the composition of debt on a commonsize basis; that is, each sector's share of total debt. The share of debt controlled by the government declined pretty consistently until 2008. That decline reflects the maturing of the American economy and understates the government's real share because it does not include the unfunded entitlement obligations and it excludes the debt of the GSEs—which are now obligations of the federal government. If government debt and the debt obligations of GSEs were combined, the duration of the decline in share would be much shorter. It would have ended in the early 1970s, and, combined, its growth would have matched that of the private economy.

The pace of economic leveraging began to gain momentum in the early 1970s and accelerated sharply in the 1980s as the cost of debt began its decades-long decline. One of the major initial forces propelling debt levels higher was falling interest rates. As rates fell, a debtor's borrowing capacity increased. For instance, a borrower assuming a fixed-rate mortgage experienced more than a 40% increase in borrowing power when rates fell from 15% to 10%, an increase of over 60% when rates fell from 10% to 5%, and a greater than 35% increase if rates fell to 2.5% from 5%. If the borrower could afford to finance an $80,000 mortgage with their cash flow at 15%, a fall in rates to 2.5% would made that same cash flow capable of supporting a $256,000 mortgage loan. That is an increase in purchasing power of 300%. Exhibit 1-4 shows how borrowing capacity changes on a 30-year mortgage as interest rates change.

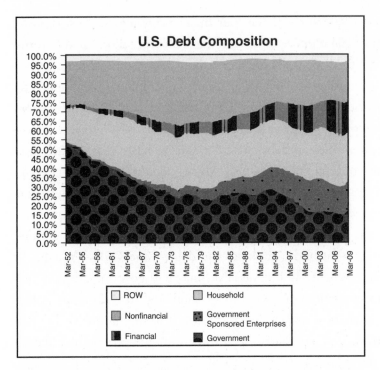

Exhibit 1-3   Commonsize View of U.S. Debt Composition (Source: Flow of Funds, authors)

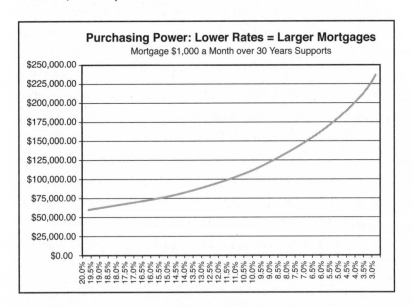

Exhibit 1-4   Purchasing Power of a $1,000 Monthly Mortgage Payment

Lower interest rates were not the only factor causing debt levels to rise. Credit became easier to get and often required less documentation and less financial risk on the part of the borrower. Different credit structures were created and embraced, triggering extraordinary growth for some. Also, government policies provided some encouragement for increased levels of mortgage lending at more lenient standards to higher risk parts of the population. The result at the end of the second quarter of 2009 was a peak level of leverage relative to GDP, as shown in Exhibit 1-5, and it was expected that such levels would go higher almost indefinitely.

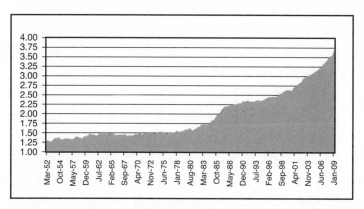

Exhibit 1-5   Debt to GDP (Source: Flow of Funds, authors)

Leverage enables purchases and investments to be made more quickly, in greater size, and often with less capital. It also creates more risk because it comes at a cost that must be covered by the returns on an investment or the income of the borrower. That cost is the interest payment. And there is also a claim on future cash flows in the form of debt repayment. The greater the amount of leverage assumed, the greater the risk taken. Greater risk also means that mistakes are magnified manifold with less room for error.

For individuals, too much leverage can lead to bankruptcy and the elimination of a lifetime of financial gains. It can also cause tremendous stress as individuals and families deal with the prospect of broken dreams, fewer opportunities, and a less-promising future. Much of that stress occurred during the housing bubble and the brutal bear stock market. Housing values declined over 25% from their peak and the stock market declined almost 60% from its peak. The result was the elimination of more than $10 trillion of household net worth, over 15%.

For a corporation, increasing levels of debt almost always trigger pressures to reduce expense levels absolutely or at least relative to revenues. These efforts often mean layoffs, benefit cuts, or both. If the corporation is a financial lender, too much leverage will usually reduce its risk propensity and, hence, lower its willingness to lend. Although the idea is risk reduction, good customers often also suffer and their difficulty obtaining funding means they are not able to operate as effectively and invest in new business opportunities. Eventually those prospective borrowers may suffer financial pain, and that is almost always felt by individuals, known as employees.

Governments are different. Greater leverage for state and local governments usually translates into higher taxes. According to the National Conference of State Legislatures, "All of the states except Vermont have the legal requirement of a balanced budget." With the exception of budget cuts that might be politically and socially difficult, taxes and financial engineering are the only ways to deal with the problem. The general lack of performance metrics measuring the performance of government programs and the absence of a balance sheet and income statement for the government often mask the sources of funds and the expenses they fund, which mitigates an effective challenge to government spending as opposed to raising taxes.

There is no restriction at the federal level: There is no balanced budget requirement. When the United States federal government runs a deficit, it borrows more money. In the last 60 years, it ran a budget deficit over 90% of the time, in 55 of the 60 years. Only in 1968 did the level of gross federal debt decline. Usually, the maturing federal debt is repaid with proceeds of newly issued debt, which is also used to fund the deficit.

The debt-to-GDP level shown in Exhibit 1-5 indicates the U.S. economy is now operating with the highest level of leverage ever. Debt-to-income, shown in Exhibit 1-6, leads to the same conclusion. The United States now has over $4.25 of debt for every dollar of income it generates. Into the mid-1990s, that relationship was closer to $2.75 of debt for every dollar of income. In less than 50 years, the debt-to-income ratio almost tripled. Not obvious from Exhibit 1-6 is the change in the composition of the national income. A rising share of it comes in the form of transfer payments. The sustainability of those transfer payments is dependent on the productivity of the private economy. The shift in share also means the level of debt to salaries and wages from the private industry rose even faster than the increase shown in Exhibit 1-6.

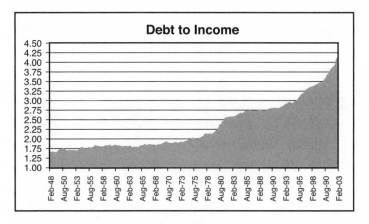

Exhibit 1-6 Total Debt to National Income of the United States Economy (Source: Flow of Funds, authors)

How could the situation get to this extreme? One answer is that not much attention is paid to a nation's financial statements. There is no regular focus on the amount of outstanding debt, national obligations, the national balance sheet, and national income. Financial reporting by state, local, and federal governments is opaque at best, with little transparency regarding the sources of revenues, their sustainability, and the nature of government expenditures. Spending and

unfunded commitments often go unquestioned and are rarely
included in debt counts as long as they do not require immediate
funding. These include unfunded government employee pension
funds, future Social Security benefits, Medicare, and Medicaid. Then
there are derivatives, which may create little-understood exposure
and place a potential claim on the country's assets and income. Like
unfunded mandates and obligations, there is no regular quantifica-
tion of aggregate magnitude and potential risk to derivatives. Disclo-
sure is limited and rarely provided in a timely manner.

To support a vibrant public sector, a country needs a robust private sector. The public sector will collapse on its own: Consider the
destruction and human misery created by totalitarian regimes. Private enterprises create jobs, while the government taxes those
employees and their companies to support its workforce, the public
infrastructure, and honor its role as a defender of the public. Ironi-
cally, the weaker the private sector becomes, the harder it becomes
for a government to do just that.

Play by the Rules!

Any game starts with a simple notion: Play by the rules. Not every-
body does—sometimes they get caught, and sometimes they don't.
Bernie Madoff finally got caught, but that was after he had managed to cheat investors out of billions of dollars. In baseball, the
use of steroids is considered cheating, and football has plenty of
rules that are broken during the course of the game, resulting in
penalties that sometimes change the course of the game.

Serena Williams, one of the great tennis players, won eleven grand
slam titles through 2009. In 2009, she won two of the three first
grand slam events, the Australian Open and Wimbledon. The
fourth, the U.S. Open, was a title she won twice. She made it to the
semifinal match and faced former 2005 U.S. Open Champion, Kim
Clisters. In a close match, Clisters won the first set 6-4. The second
set stayed on serve with Serena Williams serving down 5-6 and
down 15-30 in the game. That is when the match became different.

Serena went through her normal service motion and was called for a foot fault, putting the game score at 15-40. That meant she lost the point because of a rarely called penalty. Serena reacted badly to the call, cursed at the referee, and was penalized for her behavior. That penalty cost her another point, which cost her the game and the match.

Tennis, like other sports, is played by rules that define the game. Players and coaches do their best to take advantage of the rules. Every game has a rule maker—for the economy, the government sets the rules and enforces them. Those rules, the attempts to leverage and often circumvent them, as well as other forces, contributed to the leveraging of the national economy.

Sources and Forces of the Debt Expansion

Overview

The median five-year growth rate of debt since 1952 was 48.2% (Exhibit 1-7), which equals an annual growth rate of almost 8.2%. The era of the largest percentage growth started to appear in the early 1970s, suggesting that the seeds of rising debt growth were firmly planted in the 1960s. The era of rapid percentage growth carried on into the late 1980s, and during that period, growth rates

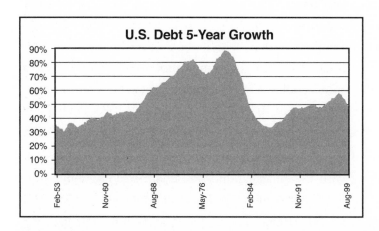

Exhibit 1-7   The Five-Year Growth Rate of Total Debt in the United States (Source: Flow of Funds, authors)

exceeded the median by as much as 40%, or not quite twice the median growth rate. The decade of the 1990s was a period of below-median growth, and "The Great Leveraging" did not commence until the late 1990s. For that period, the pace of growth was not as fast, but the magnitude of debt created was much greater and the level of leverage attained was much higher. The magnitude of debt created was much greater because the foundation from which it grew was much greater.

Starting in the late 1960s and ending in the early 1990s, the 5-year growth rate of debt was usually well above the median level for the 52-year period. The initial rise in debt above median growth rate was driven by government policies. Those policies included the Great Society, the War on Poverty, and the Vietnam War. What helped sustain the rising growth rate was a phenomenon those policies helped create: It is known as the Great Inflation. The shift in government policy that started in the 1960s resulted in more centralized economic decision making and an increased government role in resource allocation.

Ending inflation required historically high interest rates that pre-cipitated a deep recession, and with it, a substantial loss of tax rev-enues and much higher deficits. Those deficits were widened by the recession and exacerbated by government policies that did not cut government spending while tax rates were cut. The tax rate cuts spurred economic growth and helped create a more attractive invest-ment environment, but that benefit took time. In the meantime, higher deficits caused more government borrowing, which, in turn, caused government debt's share of total debt during that period to rise to 25% at the end of 1988. Between 1981 and 1988, federal gov-ernment revenues increased 55%, while expenditures increased 62%.

Government debt was not the only source of total debt rising; GSEs along with the financial and household sectors' demand for debt was much greater than the government's demand.

By the end of the 1990s, the pace of growth moderated; however, its impact was more meaningful because of its relative size, its sheer magnitude, and the level of leverage. Measured by total debt to GDP, the leverage at the end of the 1990s was more than two and a quarter times GDP. As the level of debt to GDP rises, it becomes a source of additional leverage; in effect a double leverage. This is because as the level increases, the impact of a constant difference between debt growth and GDP growth increases. So, when debt to GDP was 100%, a 5% difference in the growth rates would result in debt to GDP of 105%; at 200%, the difference results in 210%; and when debt to GDP starts at 300%, that disparity in growth rates results in debt to GDP next year of 315%. As a result, an already leveraged economy experienced the sharpest rise in debt to GDP starting in the 1990s. Economic growth did not keep pace with debt growth, as shown in Exhibit 1-8. The disparity in growth rates appears to have been sustained and, after 2002, that disparity rose.

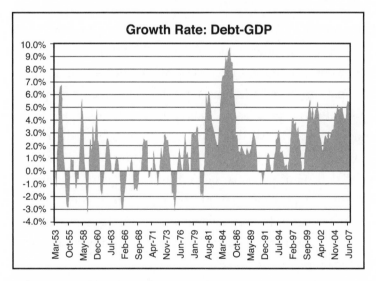

Exhibit 1-8   Difference Between Annual Rates of Debt Growth and GDP Growth (Source: Flow of Funds, authors)

New Normal

When debt to GDP dipped below 150% in the early 1950s, it was driven by strong government revenue growth created from strong economic growth resulting from a rapidly growing private sector. It also benefited from more modest growth levels of government spending after two wars and an aversion to debt that stemmed from the Great Depression. Since the late 1960s, the nation's leverage on GDP more than doubled. Some of that was natural—the "new normal." The forces behind the new normal debt expansion were many, including the shedding of the Depression mentality, which appears to have started in the early 1950s with the baby boom. Also contributing was the evolution of the economy beyond the industrial age into the information age. That brought with it the evolution of the Financial Services industry, which meant increasing availability and access to credit. There was also a tremendous shift in the financial behavior of individuals. These shifts and other contributing forces pushed the natural level of debt to GDP closer to 200%, in our opinion.

Other Forces

Still, most of the forces causing the country's debt to grow faster than GDP were not ones that contributed to the new normal. Instead, they contributed to more excessive amounts of debt. These other principal forces include housing policy, easy monetary policy, regulations, inflation, greed, and energy policy. All of those forces contributed to greater risk tolerance, which, in turn, led to more leverage. Changes in any of these forces could have helped reduce the level of debt and, perhaps, helped avoid the current financial crisis. Exhibit 1-9 provides our assessment of how these factors increased the debt-to-GDP ratio above 150%. For instance, the new normal took it up at least another 50% to 200%, and housing policy increased it another 35% to 235%.

Housing

The biggest factor driving the leveraging of the U.S. economy beyond its natural evolutionary path was housing and the government policies that supported it. In our estimate, at least, 50% of the incremental 225% of debt to GDP, or over 20% of the excess leverage, was caused by the housing policy. That is $7 trillion, which is the majority

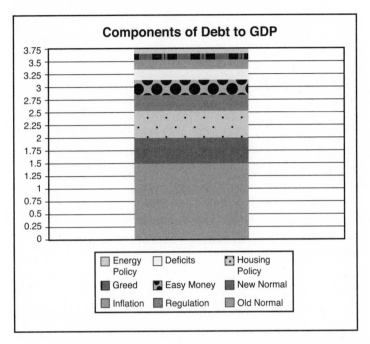

Exhibit 1-9 Estimated Contributors to Change in Debt to GDP from 1953 to Present (Source: authors' estimates)

of the debt extended to support the GSEs and their off-balance financing. Another metric is how fast housing grew relative to nominal GDP. Housing grew much faster: Had it grown in line with nominal GDP, the debt levels would have been $5 trillion lower.

Since the Great Depression, the U.S. federal government has taken steps to increase the level of home ownership and make housing more affordable. The leaders in government have long been advocates of home ownership, believing it would enhance social stability and engender pride in ownership and a "stakeholder society." This was a goal that both major parties subscribed to. Over time, the government has added the goal of making housing more available to those in below–median income households.

In 1938, the Roosevelt administration created the Federal National Mortgage Association to make sure that mortgage finance was available in an effort to increase home ownership and ensure

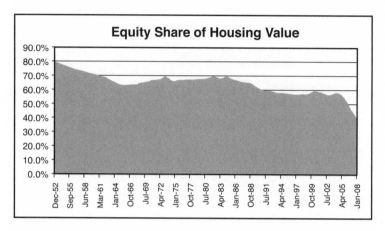

Exhibit 1-10   Household America: Equity Share of Housing Value (Source: Flow of Funds, authors)

housing affordability. In 1968, the association was split in two. One company was spun off as a public company to support the traditional mortgage industry. It was Fannie Mae and its borrowings had the implicit guarantee of the federal government. This was the first GSE; the other half would remain a division of the U.S. Department of Housing and Urban Development (HUD) and it was Ginnie Mae. It was "...formed as the Government National Mortgage Association, is a wholly owned government corporation within HUD administered by the Secretary of HUD and the President of Ginnie Mae. In 1970, Ginnie Mae developed and guaranteed the very first mortgage-backed security (MBS). Today, its primary function is to guarantee the timely payment of principal and interest on MBS that are backed by pools of mortgages issued by private mortgage institutions and insured by HUD's Federal Housing Administration (FHA) and the Office of Public and Indian Housing (PIH), the Department of Veterans Affairs' (VA) Home Loan Program for Veterans, and the U.S. Department of Agriculture's (USDA) Rural Development Housing and Community Facilities programs." In 1970, the Nixon administration decided Fannie Mae should have competition and Freddie Mac was created.[1]

The Great Depression was also a time of transition and support for the private financial industry supporting the housing industry. It started in the 1930s with the Building & Loan Industry, which subsequently changed its name to the Savings & Loan (S&L) Industry in the 1930s. It enjoyed the benefits of deposit insurance and federal regulation. It would sustain solid growth into the 1970s. The S&L business model was simple—gather longer-term deposits and extend mortgage loans. Borrowers were expected to complete detailed loan applications and typically made a down payment equal to 20% of a house's value. Over time, down payments declined as lenders became more lenient to the point of offering prospective homebuyers 100% financing. In 2006, 17% of mortgage loans required no down payment; in other words, they were made at 100% loan to value. In comparison, in 2001, only 1% of mortgage loans were 100% financed. The shift was not just driven by government policy; it was also caused by the drive for greater business volumes, higher revenues, and greater levels of profits. It was a focus on quantity and not quality.

Starting with the Carter administration, more emphasis was put on making mortgages available to low-income households and minority households. It is the reason the GSEs exist, and it was one of the Financial Services industry's fastest-growing businesses. The second biggest factor was the creation of off-balance sheet financing. By June 2008, over $5 trillion of home mortgage assets were either on the balance sheets of Fannie Mae or Freddie Mac, or securitized into the market with their guarantees. Either way, a great deal of debt was used to fund those assets and the ultimate obligor was the U.S. government. The combined total managed assets would more than double in less than eight years to $5.3 trillion (see Exhibit 1-11).

Monetary Policy

Since 1999, U.S. monetary policy has been used aggressively to limit the pain inflicted by the end-of-asset bubbles. It is a major change from the monetary policy of the early 1980s used to fight inflation. Then, the effective federal funds rate peaked at 22% for a

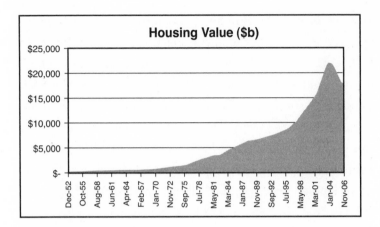

Exhibit 1-11   Household America: Housing Value (Source: Flow of Funds, authors)

few days. (This is not evident in Exhibit 1-12 because the time series is a weekly one.) Borrowing conditions were not only difficult, but the cost of borrowing bordered on prohibitive. Financial institutions found the costs hard to pass on in their pricing, and those borrowing costs severely constrained borrowing for investment and working capital purposes.

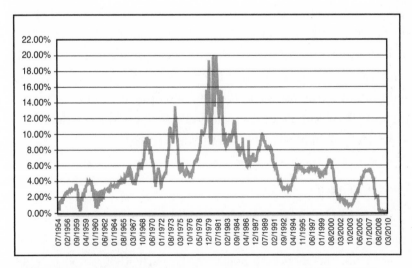

Exhibit 1-12   Effective Federal Funds Rate (Source: FRED—2009 research.stlouisfed.org)

The same conditions that existed in the Fed Funds market prevailed in the mortgage market as the 30-year conventional mortgage rate rose above 18% (see Exhibit 1-13). It took the better part of a decade to get the rate under 10%, and another decade to get the mortgage rate below 7.5%. Now, that rate is closer to 5% and that change means the same monthly payment can support a borrowing four times greater. The same level of cash flow supports more than three times as much mortgage in 2009 as it did in 1980.

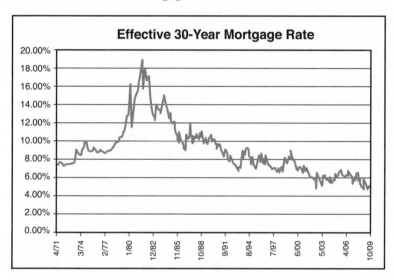

Exhibit 1-13   30-Year Conventional Mortgage Rate (Source: FRED—2009 research.stlouisfed.org)

The fall in interest rates and the historically low level of Fed Funds meant cheap credit. Actions by the Federal Reserve over the last 25 years suggest it is more inclined to apply monetary stimulus to stem market corrections and bear markets than it is to apply monetary restraint as asset prices rise. The low level of interest rates and aggressive actions by the Fed over the past decade contributed to an environment of very low risk aversion. That translated into very little sensitivity to differences in asset quality, duration, and so forth. It contributed to an environment that saw the level of national debt more than double in less than a decade. In our estimation, it was responsible for pushing debt to GDP up at least 30%, or over $4 trillion.

Regulation

Our estimate suggests that regulation is responsible for almost $5 trillion of the excess debt. That pushed debt to GDP up another 35%. Exhibit 1-14 shows just how much debt is used to finance off-balance sheet instruments. In aggregate, almost $10 trillion of debt is used to finance mortgage-backed securities guaranteed by the GSEs and other financial institutions, as well as debt used to finance asset-backed securities and funding corporations.

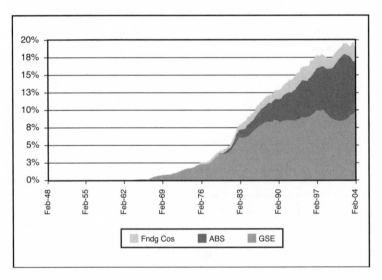

Exhibit 1-14   Off-Balance Sheet Debt to Total Debt (Source: Flow of Funds, authors)

This part of the Financial Services sector saw very little regulatory oversight. There was very little equity used to support these instruments. Their very creation meant the absolute level of leverage being assumed by members of the industry and ultimately the United States taxpayer was very significant and not understood. The combination of leverage, demand, and tolerance, if not outright support, for weaker lending standards created one of the principal sources of the financial crisis.

In aggregate, off-balance sheet debt reached $10 trillion on June 30, 2009, which compares to less than $1.4 trillion in 1990 and about $3 trillion in 1996. That suggests a sustained growth rate of 10% or more than twice nominal GDP growth and about three times real GDP growth for the period. In terms of leverage, very little equity was used to support off-balance sheet structures. High levels of leverage can help an investor realize attractive returns. The operating assumption behind the structures is that the funded assets would not experience a meaningful credit deterioration leading to write-down; however, in a period of unusually high losses, the equity cushion is quickly eliminated, causing the lenders to realize a loss.

In the case of Fannie Mae and Freddie Mac, U.S. taxpayers provided hundreds of billions of dollars to keep the companies operating after they generated losses well in excess of their capital. Not only did the common equity stockholders watch their investment vanish, but so did preferred shareholders. June 30, 2008, was the end of the second quarter for Fannie Mae and Freddie Mac, and it would be the last quarter the companies would report results as independent companies. The U.S. government took them over in September 2008 because of loan problems and funding difficulties. The second quarter reports provided evidence of their coming troubles: Their combined balance sheets were levered about 100 to 1 on tangible common equity. If their managed assets carried off-balance sheet and backed by their guarantees were added back, the leverage shot up to over 500 to 1. At that level of leverage, there is no room for error; a loss that equaled a return on equity of less than only -1% was still sufficient to wipe out the equity base. The losses were much greater. The age of illusion of greater and greater returns through rising levels of leverage ended.

Like the GSEs, the rest of the Financial Services sector saw the greatest demand for debt come from its off-balance sheet activities. These activities were also regulated. Where regulation was greatest, demand for debt was much more modest. Additionally, the activities of regulators were a major contributor to a growing number of companies

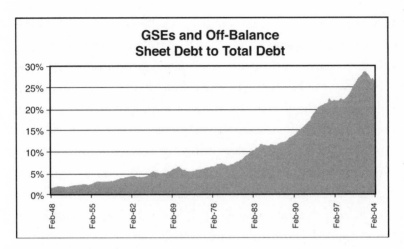

Exhibit 1-15   Debt of Government Sponsored Enterprises and Off-Balance Sheet Debt to Total Debt (Source: Flow of Funds, authors)

considered *Too Big to Fail*. At its peak, the debt used to fund the on- and off-balance sheet activities of the GSEs along with the off-balance sheet activities of the Financial Services sectors approached 28% of total debt outstanding and remained above 25% through the middle of 2009.

Exhibit 1-16 shows how the composition of the composition of the Financial Services sector changed. That change mirrored a change in the structure of the industry to one more focused on market activities. The industry participants become less dependent on using their balance sheets to support customer needs. At its peak, asset-backed security (ABS) funding represented over half of the sector's outstanding debt.

The Great Inflation

Starting in the mid-1960s, the U.S. government became a growing factor in the economic equation. The War on Poverty and the Vietnam War would increasingly compete for resources and financial assets. Initially, the result was increasing government deficits, higher levels of taxes, and rising price levels. To keep up with rising prices, many had

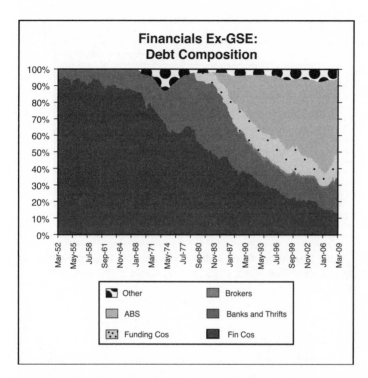

Exhibit 1-16   Debt Composition of the Financial Services Sector to Total Debt (Does Not Include GSEs) (Source: Flow of Funds, authors)

their wages indexed to inflation by a cost-of-living adjustment. The pressure of rising deficits led to a decision to end the system that pegged the dollar to gold and permit the dollar to float with other currencies. The result was the debasement of the dollar, rising prices, and artificially inflated levels of debt.

During the decade of the 1970s, inflation caused debt levels to at least double. Nominal annual GNP growth usually exceeded real GNP growth by almost 7% per year during the period (1970 through 1980). Much of the debt borrowed by households, businesses, and governments was done to keep up with rising prices. The burden caused by inflation was not immediately apparent, but the cost of breaking that inflation cycle shown in Exhibit 1-17 resulted in one of the worst recessions to date following World War II. It certainly was an indication of the magnitude of the burden caused by inflation.

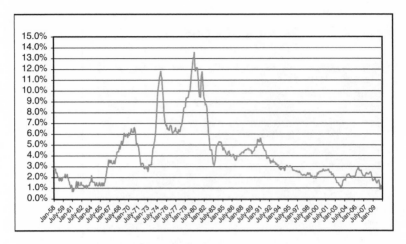

Exhibit 1-17   Core Consumer Price Index (Source: U.S. Department of Labor: Bureau of Labor Statistics; 2009 research.stlouisfed.org)

By the time inflation peaked in 1980, we estimate that over one third of the outstanding debt in the United States was the result of inflation in the prior period. We estimate the Great Inflation, the recession and resulting deficits caused by eliminating it, and the more moderate subsequent inflation were responsible for pushing debt to GDP up by 20%, or $2.75 trillion.

Debt was incurred to deal with the pressure of keeping up with rising prices. It is apparent how difficult that effort was, as shown in Exhibit 1-17. Core inflation would rise above 12.5% by the end of the decade, which meant the prices of goods except energy and food for a consumer were rising at a pace that would cause them to double in just less than six years. Even though many workers received cost-of-living adjustments (COLA), these were insufficient to meet their current financial needs and provide for the future. Not only would the amount of debt rise, so would the cost of borrowing. It was very high, and constrained financing for investment needs. Exhibit 1-18 shows how much higher debt growth was in the 1970s compared to the median level. That elevated growth rate appears to reflect the cost of funding a rapidly growing level of government spending over much of

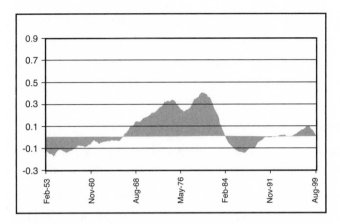

Exhibit 1-18   Relative Five-Year Growth Rate of U.S. Debt (Source: Flow of Funds, authors)

the period, the cost of recession caused by ending inflation, and the increased borrowing capacity of the private sector caused by falling interest rates.

Exhibit 1-19 shows just how much of nominal economic growth was tied to inflation. For most of the 1970s, over 70% of nominal GDP growth was inflation. Real GDP growth was often no more than 25% of nominal GDP growth. In 1980, inflation was responsible for almost 80% of nominal GDP growth. Before the Great Leveraging, the Great

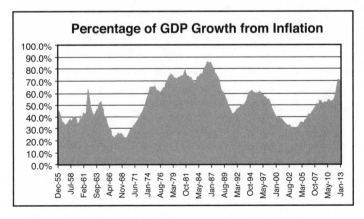

Exhibit 1-19   GDP Growth Tied to Inflation (Source: Flow of Funds, authors)

Inflation distorted the economy, creating unnecessary debt, requiring a deep recession as a cure, and causing the federal government's deficit to widen. Of course, it was government policy and Federal Reserve policy that created the environment that led to the Great Inflation.

The stress of inflation was also evident in the balance sheet of nonfinancial Corporate America. Industry did not generate sufficient returns to keep growing its capital base in line with inflation. In fact, the 1970s were a period of poor returns and rising losses for many parts of Corporate America. The combination of rising inflation and poor returns led to rising levels of debt and leverage. As inflation declined, the financial condition of nonfinancial corporate America, as measured by liabilities to net worth, improved. Starting in 1980, the ratio fell from almost 275% to almost 150%. Unlike other parts of the economy, the balance sheet of nonfinancial corporate America became less leveraged (see Exhibit 1-20).

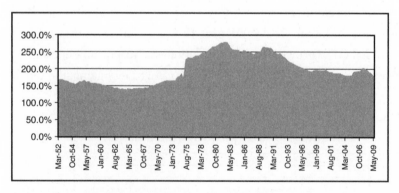

Exhibit 1-20   Nonfinancial Companies; Liabilities to Net Worth (Source: Flow of Funds, authors)

Government Deficits

Since 1952, U.S. government aggregate net deficits are expected to approach $7 trillion by the end of fiscal year 2009, as shown in Exhibit 1-21. At the end of fiscal year 2008, the aggregate deficit number was closer to $5 trillion. The deficits contributed to the

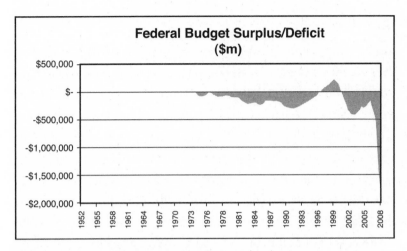

Exhibit 1-21   U.S. Federal Government—Annual Surplus/Deficit (Source: http://www.whitehouse.gov/omb/budget/Historicals)

buildup of debt and by our estimation, contributed over $2.75 trillion of the excess debt pushing debt to GDP up at least another 20%.

The deficits are expected to remain high. The 2009 deficit dwarfs the others and exceeded 50% of government revenues in 2009. Since the end of World War II, the deficit never exceeded 30% of revenues.

Greed

Human greed is clearly a contributor to the excess debt created. We estimate it caused debt to GDP to rise another 10%, or over $1.4 trillion. In search of higher returns and greater compensation, many financial company management teams chose to use more leverage without considering, or fully understanding, attended risks. Many companies with investment banking activities decided to actively pursue a greater level of proprietary trading activities funded with borrowed funds. These actions and activities were allowed: There were no regulations prohibiting them. There was also no sense of restraint or proportion on the part of many management teams. Too many in leadership roles ignored the examples they were setting.

Energy Policy

Despite experiencing two energy crises in the 1970s, the leaders of U.S. government never created a coherent energy policy. Then and now, the United States is dependent on importing foreign oil to meet its energy needs. The cost of that dependency is growing, increasing the country's trade deficit as well as the size of its external debt. We estimate it was responsible for over $1.4 trillion of increased debt. Since 1971, the total value of oil imports exceeded $3 trillion. Starting in 2000, the net oil import bill first exceeded $100 billion, as shown in Exhibit 1-22. It has remained over that level since 2000 and the aggregate cost of net oil imports is close to $2 trillion for that period. Any actions to change the energy policy would have yielded some progress in reducing the level of net imports as well as the debt created to finance them.

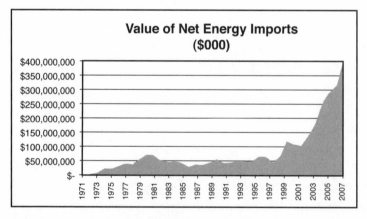

Exhibit 1-22   Value of Energy Imports (Source: Energy Information Administration—U.S. Department of Energy)

These are the major contributors to the rise in debt levels since the last deleveraging ended in 1953. Not included in the calculations are off-balance sheet debt, other obligations, and risk exposure that dwarf the national debt. They include derivatives and the government's unfunded mandates like pension plans, Social Security, and Medicare. Including these items would push leverage levels much higher.

Sources and Endnotes

Ginnie Mae description—http://www.ginniemae.gov/ReportToCongress

[1] Ginnie Mae 2008 Annual Report.

2

Growth Realities

Is it real or is it an illusion?

The many advances and periodic setbacks since 1980 are reminders that economies and markets have cycles. They are also reminders that not all of the sources of growth underlying the expansion were real or sustainable. The Great Leveraging helped create a false sense of prosperity and wealth on what was otherwise meaningful progress and a solid foundation for future growth. Eventually, the incremental benefit of each additional dollar of debt became insignificant and then destructive. The excessive amounts of debt used to support poor policies and greed were laid out in Chapter 1, "The Great Leveraging." This chapter focuses on some of the sources and realities of a good, solid, fundamental growth, both economic and for markets. We call them "growth realities."

Leverage is not a source of organic growth. It can be an integral part of the investment process and funding. However, taken in the extreme, leverage can be a source of destruction taking not just from the present, but also from the future. Some of these "growth realities" are highlighted in this chapter. These are factors to consider when assessing the return potential of an investment or the potential growth of a country. They are:

1. *Economic and market cycles are a fact of life*—Expect ups and downs. Often steps taken to smooth out the cycles only made the aftermath more extreme.

2. **The private sector is critical**—Just as people need many of
   the basic services provided by government for a better life, so
   the public sectors depend on a robust private sector to provide
   the revenues necessary to afford those basic services.

3. **Dispersion and diversity, not concentration**—Concentrating
   decisions, assets, and education lead to a concentration of wealth
   and power. It also creates a much higher level of risk and dependency and seems to always result in destruction. More often than
   not, bigger is not better.

Cycles

Economies and markets have cycles. Some cyclical periods are
more volatile than others. Relative to each other, economic cycles do
not always move in tandem with market cycles—equity or fixed
income. There are ups and downs to an economy and to investments.
Expecting constant growth is a bad assumption. The pursuit of constant growth usually results in a dependence on unsustainable and
artificial growth sources.

The National Bureau of Economic Research is responsible for
identifying the economic cycles for the United States. It traces economic cycles since June 1854. Since then, there have been 32 complete cycles with the 33rd likely completed. They are summarized in
Exhibit 2-1. The average expansion lasted 38 months and the average
contraction lasted 17 months. Between 1854 and 1919, the lengths of
the expansions and contractions were about the same at 27 and 22
months, respectively. Between 1919 and 1945, the economy became
less agrarian and more manufacturing oriented. During that period,
the average length of the expansions increased over 25% to 35
months, while the length of the contractions declined to 18 months.
Since 1945, the average length of expansions continued to rise, while

the average length of contractions fell again. The average length of an expansion rose to 57 months, an increase of over 60%, while the average length of a contraction fell to 10 months, a decline of over 40%.

Exhibit 2-1   National Bureau of Economic Research: Economic Business Cycle Summary (Source: National Bureau of Economic Research)

Business Cycle Reference Dates		Duration in Months			
Peak	Trough	Contraction	Expansion	Cycle	
Quarterly dates are in parentheses	Peak to Trough	Previous Trough to This Peak	Trough from Previous Trough	Peak from Previous Peak	
	December 1854 (IV)	—	—	—	—
June 1857 (II)	December 1858 (IV)	18	30	48	—
October 1860 (III)	June 1861 (III)	8	22	30	40
April 1865 (I)	December 1867 (I)	32	46	78	54
June 1869 (II)	December 1870 (IV)	18	18	36	50
October 1873 (III)	March 1879 (I)	65	34	99	52
March 1882 (I)	May 1885 (II)	38	36	74	101
March 1887 (II)	April 1888 (I)	13	22	35	60
July 1890 (III)	May 1891 (II)	10	27	37	40
January 1893 (I)	June 1894 (II)	17	20	37	30
December 1895 (IV)	June 1897 (II)	18	18	36	35

Exhibit 2-1   National Bureau of Economic Research: Economic Business Cycle Summary (Source: National Bureau of Economic Research)

Business Cycle Reference Dates		Duration in Months			
Peak	Trough	Contraction	Expansion		Cycle
Quarterly dates are in parentheses		Peak to Trough	Previous Trough to This Peak	Trough from Previous Trough	Peak from Previous Peak
June 1899 (III)	December 1900 (IV)	18	24	42	42
September 1902 (IV)	August 1904 (III)	23	21	44	39
May 1907 (II)	June 1908 (II)	13	33	46	56
January 1910 (I)	January 1912 (IV)	24	19	43	32
January 1913 (I)	December 1914 (IV)	23	12	35	36
August 1918 (III)	March 1919 (I)	7	44	51	67
January 1920 (I)	July 1921 (III)	18	10	28	17
May 1923 (II)	July 1924 (III)	14	22	36	40
October 1926 (III)	November 1927 (IV)	13	27	40	41
August 1929 (III)	March 1933 (I)	43	21	64	34
May 1937 (II)	June 1938 (II)	13	50	63	93
February 1945 (I)	October 1945 (IV)	8	80	88	93
November 1948 (IV)	October 1949 (IV)	11	37	48	45

Exhibit 2-1 National Bureau of Economic Research: Economic Business Cycle Summary (Source: National Bureau of Economic Research)

Business Cycle Reference Dates		Duration in Months			
Peak	Trough	Contraction	Expansion		Cycle
Quarterly dates are in parentheses		Peak to Trough	Previous Trough to This Peak	Trough from Previous Trough	Peak from Previous Peak
July 1953 (II)	May 1954 (II)	10	45	55	56
August 1957 (III)	April 1958 (II)	8	39	47	49
April 1960 (II)	February 1961 (I)	10	24	34	32
December 1969 (IV)	November 1970 (IV)	11	106	117	116
November 1973 (IV)	March 1975 (I)	16	36	52	47
January 1980 (I)	July 1980 (III)	6	58	64	74
July 1981 (III)	November 1982 (IV)	16	12	28	18
July 1990 (III)	March 1991 (I)	8	92	100	108
March 2001 (I)	November 2001 (IV)	8	120	128	128
December 2007 (IV)			73		81

Exhibit 2-1   National Bureau of Economic Research: Economic Business Cycle Summary (Source: National Bureau of Economic Research)

Business Cycle Reference Dates		Duration in Months		
Peak	Trough	Contraction	Expansion	Cycle
Quarterly dates are in parentheses	Peak to Trough	Previous Trough to This Peak	Trough from Previous Trough	Peak from Previous Peak
Average, all cycles:				
1854–2001 (32 cycles)	17	38	55	56˙
1854–1919 (16 cycles)	22	27	48	49˙˙
1919–1945 (6 cycles)	18	35	53	53
1945–2001 (10 cycles)	10	57	67	67

˙31 cycles ˙˙15 cycles

Following the end of World War II, the U.S. economy experienced three expansions of more than seven years and one lasting ten years. The shift away from an industrial-based economy to an information-based, service-oriented economy seemed to bring much less volatility. From February 1945 to December 2007, the U.S. economy spent 761 months in expansion and 112 months in contraction. Since December 2007, the economy has been in contraction, the longest of the post–World War II period. In that period, the global economy experienced one global recession, starting at the end of 2007. In other words, despite economic problems in certain countries, the global economy grew in most years.

The U.S. equity markets were more volatile. According to Global Financial Data, the U.S. equity markets were in a bull cycle 66% of the last century, which means the equity market was in a bear cycle 34% of the time. Globally, the world equity markets between 1929 and 2002 were in a bull cycle 73% of the time and in a bear cycle 27% of the time. Like other equity markets, the worst market for the global equity market was during the Great Depression when the global index of Global Financial Data fell 71% between August 1929 and June 1932. The longest and strongest bull market took place from the ashes of World War II. It started in 1944 and lasted until June 1962. In that period, the global index rose 716%.

Equity markets are considered a leading indicator; they reflect expectations about the economic future. In March 2009, the stock markets in the United States bottomed after falling over 50% from the cyclical peak. The equity markets then began to rise. What the markets' rise signaled was an end to the concerns of systemic failure tied to the bankruptcy of Lehman Brothers and the federal government takeover of AIG, Fannie Mae, Freddie Mac, and General Motors, among others.

The cycles of economies and markets reflect many natural ebbs and flows. They are also a result of excesses that can no longer be supported or sustained. In cases of extreme excess, the recovery is usually weaker. Still, most contractions represented the natural rhythm of a growing economy adjusting to cyclical flows that eventually allowed it to move higher. The volatility of those cycles lessened as the economy transitioned from an agrarian to an industrial economy, and now to a service-based information economy. The global recession that started at the end of 2007 is really the first services recession with a job loss of more than 2.5% over the course of a year. It is the first time there has been a year-over-year loss of service jobs of more than 0.5% since 1960, as shown in Exhibit 2-2.

Aside from the cyclical recessions, there are the more protracted and severe contractions tied to asset excesses (bubbles) and the worst of those are financed with debt. In the past century, there have been two major global contractions—the Great Depression and the one starting at the end of 2007, which Kenneth Rogoff and Carmen Reinhart call "The Second Great Contraction." They included deep stock market corrections, but were made more severe by the contraction of the financial system tied to excessive leverage, elevated real estate prices, and subsequent bank failures. The most extreme examples are what followed the stock market crash of 1929, the Great Inflation of the 1970s, the Japanese real estate and market crash that started in 1990, and the 2008 global housing bubble.

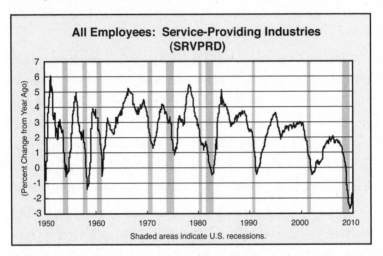

Exhibit 2-2   Year-over-Year Growth Rate of Service Sector Employees (Source: U.S. Department of Labor: Bureau of Labor Statistics; 2010 research.stlouisfed.org)

Most economies rebound even after a major correction. However, the magnitude of the subsequent recovery is always an uncertainty, and equity markets will usually rebound in anticipation of the economic recovery. That anticipation is tied to the expectation of much stronger earnings caused by the resumption of revenue growth from a private sector that usually lowers its cost base during the correction. The private sector is then poised for earnings growth to exceed revenue growth because of the operating leverage created by the surviving companies during the downturn.

Government policies serve as a major factor in determining the magnitude and duration of that recovery and nature of a market rebound. They can contribute to the tendency of the economy to grow from the bottom of a contraction, or those policies can be viewed as onerous and act as an economic constraint.

A Strong Private Sector Is a Must

The importance of government policy is underscored by its principal source of funding. For the U.S. federal government and most governments, the principal source of funding is the private sector. About 80% of the workforce in the United States is employed by the private sector and over 80% of workers' wages come from companies in the private sector. Because personal income taxes and social insurance taxes represent over 80% of federal government tax revenue, it is clear the private sector is the primary source of tax revenue supporting government activities. And that is before corporate taxes, which represent over 15% of federal government revenues. According to the Bureau of Economic Advisors, over 85% of economic value added is created by the private sector and by households.

A viable and responsive public sector requires and depends on a profitable and growing private sector. China and India are recent examples of the economic benefit of unleashing the power of the private sector. Those countries are experiencing robust economic growth that is greatly enhancing the capacity of the public sector to meet the needs of its citizens.

When the private sector cycle turns down and declines, the public sector must have established the foundation necessary to hold the public trust to bridge periods of economic decline. However, the private sector must ultimately regain its footing and grow again for the public sector to sustain its viability.

To fund a growing level of public programs, including education, security, defense, welfare, entitlements, and other programs, the collections of tax revenues from the private sector must rise. If the growth of tax revenues is insufficient to cover the cost of government programs, then the government must usually borrow—it must go into debt. That debt is a claim on the assets of the nation's aggregate balance sheet and cash flow. The balance sheet is the total of the nation's assets, which are funded by debt and equity. The greater the amount of debt used to fund those assets, the greater the leverage of the nation, and the more risk being assumed on the part of the general population.

The alternatives to borrowing more are increasing taxes, increasing other levies, or cutting government spending. Higher taxes and rising levels of debt cannot continue forever. They reach a point of diminishing returns and eventually destroy the revenue streams on which the revenues are dependent. Cutting spending levels, or at least lowering the rate of growth, are more realistic and more durable. That is easy to say, but hard to accomplish. Spending levels of the U.S. federal government have not fallen since 1954 and as shown in Chapter 1, the cumulative deficits of the U.S. federal government exceed $9 trillion. State and local government spending levels have risen every year since the end of World War II (Exhibit 2-3).

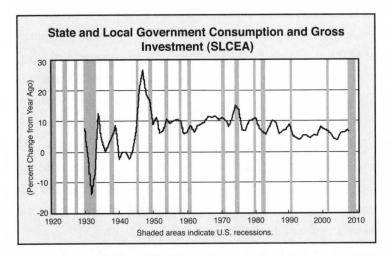

Exhibit 2-3   State and Local Government Spending—Annual Growth Rate (Source: U.S. Dept. of Commerce: Bureau of Economic Analysis; 2010 research.stlouisfed.org)

Over the past century, there are really no good examples of a robust and growing public (government) sector that existed without the support of a growing private sector from one of the world's major economies. Few examples of small, government-controlled economies without a robust private sector are countries that depend on revenues tied to the export of natural resources, principally oil. The increase in the demand for that oil was a result of growing private demand. In those situations, the economic mix is highly concentrated and does not appear to be sustainable for a large global economy. Indeed, except for a very few resource-rich countries, the absence of a robust private sector means those countries with a growing public sector are eventually burdened with onerous deficits and future commitments. As pressures grow to support the commitments, governments often follow the well-worn path of decline. They debase their currency and ignite inflation. Some even default on their debts.

For a private company to maintain its existence, it must sustain a profit and positive cash flow. An inability to do that means bankruptcy, and more recently for some, government control. Thus, management and employees of a private company focus on improving returns, which means innovating and becoming more productive. They must do that because their customers will become accustomed to the current product and expect it to be even better in the future. Standing still is not an option—others will innovate or try to gain an advantage. That innovation and productivity often leads to new products and services, while lowering the costs of existing ones. It also leads to new and more jobs.

As the collective profit of corporations rise, government tax revenues increase. The following charts show that Federal Government receipts are closely tied to national income and the level of taxes from corporate net profits. Recent data shows national income falling more than at any period during the last half century and, not surprisingly, government receipts experienced their greatest fall. One reason for the recent volatility in government receipts is the increased contribution from market-related income in the form of capital gains and income from the exercise of options. In 2000, we estimate revenues from such items contributed more than 15% of federal government revenues from personal income taxes. However, with the subsequent market decline and change in accounting to require the option expense to be included in corporate income statements, we estimate the contribution fell by more than half before rising again. In the past, national income grew more slowly during recessions, and receipts usually declined. The most recent recession caused an absolute decline in receipts and income. It is a reflection of the more severe nature of the decline, which was the end of a debt-driven real estate supercycle.

With the exception of the artificial inflation growth of the late 1960s and 1970s, government receipts' growth was most robust during periods of economic expansion and following tax cuts, as shown in Exhibit 2-4. Three notable tax cuts to highlight were the early 1960s cut by President Kennedy, the early 1980s tax cut by President Reagan, and the early 2000s tax cut by President Bush. All three were faced with a period of declining tax revenues, and all three triggered a multiyear period of sustained tax revenue growth. The stimulus provided by a tax cut is understandable. The message to a taxpayer from the government is that a greater percentage of pretax income is in the taxpayer's control. That provides a taxpayer with greater confidence in their ability to meet future needs. It is also a message to many businesses that their consumers should have more money to spend and given the prospect of increased revenues, the risk-reward of investing in their businesses just improved.

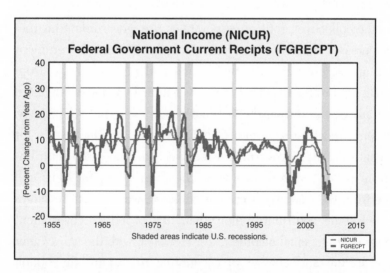

Exhibit 2-4   Annual Growth Rates of National Income and Federal Government Current Receipts (2010 research.stlouisfed.org)

So, government policy should encourage the growth of the private sector and strive to provide an economic environment conducive to investing and not speculating. For tax revenues to continue growing, corporate management teams must feel they are in a position to increase their payrolls. That means a combination of more employees and higher compensation levels. This will happen if managements believe there are opportunities to grow their business and generate an attractive return. If, on the other hand, profit margins are contracting or there is concern about pressure on profit margins, managements will be more likely to take actions to reduce their workforce. Business owners expect to generate a superior return for taking a risk that investing in a business will entail. The risk-taking activity is critical to the process of innovation and improving productivity. The volatility of corporate results is evident in Exhibit 2-5.

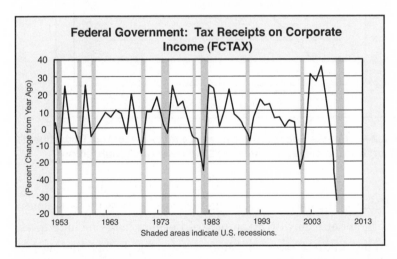

Exhibit 2-5   Corporate Tax Revenues—Annual Growth Rate (Source: U.S. Department of Commerce: Bureau of Economic Analysis; 2010 research. stlouisfed.org)

Government activities, on the other hand, are not expected to be profitable. Nor is a return measured on its activities. Many of the public sector activities are considered necessary and for the public good. Unfortunately, there are few good metrics with which to assess either the government's fiscal condition or the performance of many of its parts. Furthermore, the balance of a government's activities and its claims on its citizens is neither easy to measure nor easy to understand. Its activities lack transparency and its employees are not held to the same standards applied to most private sector employees. Still, to support those activities and employees, a growing private sector is needed. The recent financial crisis left private sector employment back at levels of the late 1990s, as shown in Exhibit 2-6.

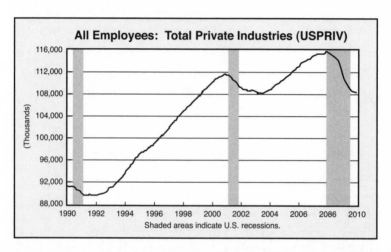

Exhibit 2-6   Private Sector Employment Level (Source: U.S. Department of Labor: Bureau of Labor Statistics; 2010 research.stlouisfed.org)

Higher and rising costs of doing business depress the willingness of management to invest. Examples of business costs include taxes, regulations, interest rates, and uncertainty. The higher the level of taxes, the higher the price companies must charge to realize a targeted return to warrant an investment. To the extent that companies lack pricing power, the burden of realizing the return will fall on the employees in the form of a reduction in compensation, workforce reduction, or both. Either way, raising the level of taxes reduces the economic potential of a business enterprise.

Concentration, Dispersion, and Diversification

Concentration of decision making and resources creates unnecessary risks and tensions in a society and in an organization. The greater the concentration of resources and decision making, the greater the likelihood there will be a catastrophic risk to an organization or country. From the standpoint of decision making for any large organization, a high level of concentration assumes an unrealistic level of expertise, which can limit valuable input. From the standpoint of resources, too much dependence on a single resource, asset, investment, or other factor exposes an entity to a greater chance of catastrophic risk.

Consider the environment that was exposed by Hurricane Katrina. Hurricane Katrina portrayed an ugly picture of the United States. It showed the country's leadership and system unable to take care of some of its then most vulnerable citizens. Even worse, that leadership seemed to be ignoring the weakest. People were screaming for help and not until the picture portrayed on television was so awful, did leadership appear to react. President Harry Truman kept a sign on his desk in the Oval Office that read "The Buck Stops Here." For President Bush, whatever the failings at other levels of government, the blame for what happened and the public frustration stopped with him.

The lesson from Hurricane Katrina reinforces points already made in this chapter, the most important being that a concentration of authority carries with it great risk. However, authority is not often held to account commensurate with the responsibility and control it is given. In Douglas Brinkley's book *The Great Deluge*, there was an account of how officials used money meant for the levees to build a playground where sand boils materialized. "...Over the years, Congress habitually diverted funding from flood-protection projects to economically promising ones... The result was community confusion regarding the levee protection around New Orleans. The Corps of

Engineers asserted that the system could withstand a fast-moving Category 3 hurricane. That was the assurance when Beth LeBlanc of Lakeview, a savvy, attractive middle-aged woman, saw water rising in her yard alongside the 17th Street Canal on Bellaire Drive in late November 2004. It soon became a pond, 75 feet wide and 10 feet long. The mystery water was taking over her well-manicured lawn and turning it into Swamp Hollow. An agitated LeBlanc appropriately reported the front-yard flood to the Sewerage and Water Board, which sent several investigators."

Here is what happened next: "One of them (investigators) concluded water was coming from the canal. 'They sent repair crews out,' LeBlanc said. They tore up sidewalks and driveways. 'Things got better, but it never got dry.' That ought to have shocked Sewerage and Water Board officials into fast-track action, but instead reports on the seepage disclosed by LeBlanc—and many others concerning the same vicinity—were filed away and forgotten. Out of sight, as the adage goes, out of mind."

"The Orleans Levee District was a state-chartered organization with two hundred employees and a peculiarly independent board of directors. For example, in the months just before Katrina, while a $427,000 repair to a crucial floodgate languished in inexcusable bureaucratic delay, the board went ahead with happier pursuits, building parks, overseeing docks that it had constructed, and investing in on-water gambling, leasing Bally's *Belle of New Orleans* casino boat on Lake Pontchartrain in Gentilly." Sand boils are a sign a levee is failing. The city officials were probably not aware of the levee problems, and they were likely more focused on doing something symbolic instead of something not obvious, but substantial. Too often, political actions are long on form and short on substance because of the pursuit of votes and the resulting power from holding office. The result of the long-term neglect of the New Orleans levee system was the destruction of many lives and homes. It was not a matter of if it would happen, just when. The government's poor response made the tragedy worse. Like other tragedies, there were many instances of wonderful individual efforts, people doing the right thing, and people doing what they felt was their responsibility.

There is also another stark contrast from Hurricane Katrina. That is, the poor response of the many levels of government with the quick response of the colleges and universities around the country. New Orleans is home to many colleges and universities, including Tulane, Loyola, University of New Orleans, and Xavier. Except for the incoming freshman class, evacuating New Orleans was not a new experience for most students. In two of three previous years, they evacuated three times. Many of those students left New Orleans as Katrina approached, leaving many personal items behind and fully expecting to return and get on with their fall semester. That did not happen. Instead, they would have to make other plans and there were no official agencies to help them. Find help, they did! Despite the absence of a formal structure, the vast majority of students were absorbed into the higher education system. They completed most, if not all of their fall semester, and then returned to New Orleans for their spring semester.

The larger, more rigid structures with responsibility at many levels to maintain the infrastructure around New Orleans failed and then responded poorly in the aftermath of the hurricane. The absence of structures to assess the progress in maintaining and rebuilding the levee system, or for that matter most other infrastructure, left the region unnecessarily vulnerable. The responsibility did not seem to be taken seriously. It was not a result of malice, but it was a reflection of a system that often did not respond to situations unless there was an emergency or a need for votes. The government structure built in a relationship of dependency for the most vulnerable, and almost any other initiative to help people in that group only intensified that relationship. When Hurricane Katrina hit, government at all levels did not live up to expectations. Its most dependent constituency was let down.

On the other hand, students expect to attend college and get an education. The level of education achieved is largely dependent on their effort. They have a responsibility to participate, or risk failing. The people running the universities and colleges know they must provide a quality education, or the demand for their institution will fall and funding will be tougher to attract. For whatever reason, the leaders of most universities and colleges outside of New Orleans and affected institutions in Mississippi felt a responsibility to accept some of the displaced students.

Tony Lorino is one of those who was prepared. A long-time member of Tulane University's administration and now Senior Vice President and Chief Financial Officer, he had been through many hurricanes in New Orleans. He was there in 1965 when Hurricane Betsy hit. New Orleans flooded then too, but not nearly as much as it did because of Hurricane Katrina. Still that experience was one of the forces behind Tulane creating evacuation plans for hurricanes, including getting students without a means of transport to a facility at Jackson State University in Mississippi, where, even through Katrina, the administration knew the students were safe. Because of his experience, Tony knew hurricanes affected New Orleans differently from other places because "water runs in; it does not go anywhere; it just sits there."

He also noted that the structure to embrace displaced students was created at the time of Katrina. News coverage helped. Some of the help seems extraordinary. For instance, Baylor University took on Tulane's entire medical school, including its faculty, and members of Tulane's administration reached out to many college- and university-related organizations. Of course, things did not immediately return to normal. For Tulane, there was a meaningful drop in the size of the next freshman class—it was about 900 compared to what was a normal size of 1,580. The following year's freshman class was 1,300, and four years later, the undergraduate enrollment was close to where it was before Hurricane Katrina. Tulane's recovery, as that of other colleges and universities, benefited from a strong and flexible network of support, not a rigid one.

That rigidity is reflected in a more concentrated level of decision making. The more concentrated the level of decision making, the greater the magnitude of failure in this case. The government was ill prepared and did not respond well, whereas the more dispersed and diverse higher education system was able to respond effectively.

For economies to generate solid, sustained growth, diversity of economic resources and greater levels of participation are a must. The more economic decision making is concentrated, the greater the risks tied to an error in judgment, and the greater the benefits of those decisions will be disbursed to a narrower part of the population.

Another way of framing the issue is considering the saying "Bigger is better!" Bigger is often not better. The larger an entity gets, the less responsive it will likely become and the harder it will find it to adapt. Also, the larger a company gets, the harder it becomes for it to generate organic growth. Growth becomes more dependent on acquisitions, rationalization, and financial engineering, all of which involve greater risk and are less sustainable than good organic growth, which requires constant innovation and customer focus.

The last point is another problem with large businesses and bureaucracies: They become more focused on internal issues. They become less responsive and eventually provide less value. Many financial service firms reached a size in the past decade that meant there were few business situations that offered meaningful growth opportunities. One that did was the mortgage business.

In this chapter, we reviewed a few growth realities that touch on most economies, markets, and investment opportunities. There will be cycles, or ups and downs. Those cycles are periodically exaggerated by bad policy choices and artificial sources of growth, particularly the abundant use of leverage. Those policy choices will be much less effective and potentially destructive if they restrict the growth potential of the private sector. Ideally, there should be greater dispersion and diversity of economic activity and decision making. The start of the three major bull markets in the United States all began as decision making and economic participation began an extended period of becoming more diverse and more dispersed. The great leveraging caused greater concentration. That will become more evident in subsequent chapters.

3

Nine Decades of Real Asset Class Returns

Nothing stays the same forever!

After World War I, the U.S. stock market took on a more important role in everyday life. It also helped define a decade—"The Roaring Twenties"—and it played a principal role in what was the greatest economic crisis of the last century—"The Great Depression." Equities provided the best returns in the 1920s, but there were investment alternatives. Like equities, the markets for those alternative investments expanded and gained depth as the nation shifted from an agrarian economy to an industrial one. During the transition, the ability and opportunity to invest grew.

This chapter looks at the returns of eight different asset classes by decade starting in 1920. The asset classes covered include equities, liquidity, fixed income, and commodities. Equities include three indexes meant to measure total returns in the United States (S&P 500, developed world ex-USA, and emerging markets). Fixed income and liquidity include four total return indexes. For fixed income, they are corporate bonds, T-Bonds, municipals; and for liquidity, the index used is the one measuring the total return of T-Bills. Commodities are the eighth asset class. Their returns were determined using the Commodity Research Bureau (CRB) Index. Gold is not included because the price was fixed until the early 1970s, and it was often not possible for an individual to purchase gold as an investment.

Like economic performance over that period, investment performance varied a great deal. Clearly, economic outlooks and conditions were reflected in the returns. No asset class always outperformed, and there were periods when all asset classes were only able to deliver very modest real positive returns, at best. More often, the returns of one or two asset classes offered very attractive returns, and far exceeded the returns of the other asset classes.

The investment business evolved a great deal since 1920. Back then, there were no computers to help process the trades and record the information. The principal source of information was the newspaper, and the investor base was smaller and few markets were well developed.

Nowadays, the investor class is much larger, many more investment products are available, and there is much greater access to products and information. Whole new businesses have been built and started to support this growing business. The school of financial theory, which was very young in 1920, continues to evolve and adapt. Many theories, like efficient markets and the capital asset pricing model (CAPM), have been challenged as part of the natural process of intellectual vetting and because reality has not always supported theory. For instance, the investment strategy "buy and hold" is increasingly being challenged after more than a decade of poor returns from the U.S. equity markets.

However, one thing has not changed and that is market movements continue to surprise and evoke many explanations. This brief history of the past nine decades of returns shows how much market returns varied over the period, and some of the common themes accompanying the returns during those decades.

Nine Decades of Real Returns for Eight Asset Classes

Since 1920, there were four decades when compound annual returns from the equity indexes of the developed world were at least 15% per year. They were the 1920s, 1950s, 1980s, and 1990s. Of the remaining five decades, there were three decades when no asset class generated real compound annual returns of 10% or better, and the equity indexes of the developed world returned no more than 5% per year. Those decades were the 1930s, 1940s, and 1960s.

Remaining are the 1970s and 2000s, which were periods defined by floating exchange rates, tremendous economic and political change and dislocation, and financial shocks. In those periods, the asset classes providing the best returns were commodities and emerging market equities. Gold, which was increasingly more accessible as an investment, also performed well. The rest of the asset classes generated real annual returns of no more than 3%. There is some correlation between emerging market equities and the CRB Index because many emerging markets are populated by economies deriving a disproportionate percentage of their gross domestic product (GDP) from the exploration, development, and distribution of their natural resources. Of the nine decades, the worst real returns delivered by U.S. equities were the most recent—the 2000s. Adjusted for inflation, the annual rate of return was –4.5%, as shown in Exhibit 3-1. The Developed World ex-USA index sustained a negative real annual total return of 3.6%, while the Emerging Market equity index generated a compound real annual return of 6.0% for the decade.

In the last four decades, the emerging market equity asset class provided the most consistent attractive positive returns. For the five prior decades starting in 1920, the S&P 500 Index provided the most consistent attractive returns. That five-decade period does include the 1930s and during that period, nominal returns were about 2% less than real returns because of the deflation gripping the U.S. economy for most of the decade. Excluding the 1930s, the common traits of the United States through the end of the 1960s and emerging markets since 1970 are their relatively superior economic growth rate, apparent increase in economic stability, increasing level of democratization, and declining inflation rates. Like the United States through the 1960s, emerging market equities also benefited from a growing demand for raw materials and growing globalization.

The results of the nine periods are summarized in Exhibit 3-1.

Exhibit 3-1   Asset Class Annual Report per Decade (Source: Global Financial Data)

	1920s	1930s	1940s	1950s	1960s	1970s	1980s	1990s	2000s
CRB Index	0.0%	1.5%	1.7%	0.5%	1.8%	10.2%	0.7%	–1.3%	0.6%
Corporate Bonds	7.8%	7.2%	–0.3%	–0.7%	1.2%	0.5%	9.4%	5.7%	4.3%
T-Bills	4.7%	2.4%	–5.2%	-0.2%	1.5%	–0.9%	4.0%	2.0%	–0.6%
S&P 500	*15.4%*	2.3%	*2.8%*	16.9%	5.1%	–2.1%	12.3%	*15.2%*	–4.5%
T-Bonds	6.1%	5.7%	–3.4%	–1.6%	–0.2%	–1.6%	7.6%	5.1%	4.6%
Munis	5.4%	*7.9%*	–3.8%	–3.1%	–3.0%	–3.0%	2.0%	4.9%	3.6%
Gold	0.8%	7.4%	–4.1%	–3.6%	–2.6%	*25.0%*	–8.3%	–7.0%	*11.5%*
World ex-USA Equity	NA	4.5%	–10.7%	*18.4%*	2.6%	2.1%	*17.3%*	4.2%	–3.0%
Emerging Market Equity	NA	5.4%	–1.9%	4.1%	*5.6%*	10.4%	12.1%	8.0%	6.0%

As a broad asset class, equity exposure provided superior returns in seven of the nine decades, with the S&P 500 being the top performer in three of the decades. Those three decades were the 1920s, the 1940s, and the 1990s. Of the three, only two delivered the kind of robust returns that have come to be expected of equities—the 1920s and the 1990s. Those returns were realized on a foundation of relatively low valuation and occurred during periods of robust economic growth, technological advance, low to moderate inflation, disinflation, and relatively benign regulatory environment. While still delivering real compound annual returns of more than 10% in the 1950s and 1980s, the S&P 500's performance was eclipsed by other global stock markets of developed countries—"World ex-USA Equity" in the table. Nonequity asset classes provided the best returns during the 1930s and the 1970s.

Within each decade, there were periods of tremendous investment returns, periods of severe investment loss, and times of not much change. These periods like the decades were parts of the structural bull and bear markets.

1920s and Before

The major economic investment themes of the decade included:

1. Shift to a peacetime economy
2. Global political dislocations caused by the peace process
3. The emergence of new technologies and products
4. Low investor expectations at the beginning of the decade
5. The "industrialization" of the developed countries
6. Falling risk premiums
7. Hyperinflation in Germany
8. Increased urbanization
9. Structural equity bull market
10. Risk investments worked best (risk means riskier asset classes)

During the 1920s, U.S. equities delivered the most attractive returns (Exhibit 3-2). For the decade, the annualized return of 15.4% meant investors would have more than quadrupled their money. Like the beginning of other periods of strong equity returns, the public mindset at the beginning of the 1920s was one of low expectations. The effects of World War I lingered while the U.S. economy experienced its

highest level of inflation in the young century, and that was followed
by a relatively short economic depression.

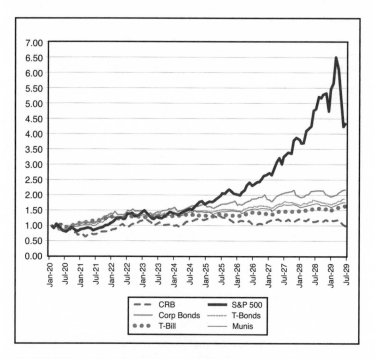

**Exhibit 3-2   U.S. Real Asset Class Returns of the 1920s (Source: Global
Financial Data)**

Note: Data for equities outside the United States were not available for
the 1920s. It is the only period for which we were unable to make the
comparison.

Those low expectations did not anticipate the surge of consumerism about to begin, nor the benefits tied to the expansion of
productive capacity during World War I. That consumerism was
brought about by several relatively new technologies—the radio and
the automobile. Also, the desire to get beyond the pain, suffering, and
stress of a wartime environment would greatly magnify the potential
of the economic surge. The economic potential was magnified

because the United States was able to rebound after World War I faster because it did not suffer the physical destruction or the human toll experienced in Europe.

Across the Atlantic, Europe would continue to struggle with the pain suffered during the war. Much rebuilding was required, and a substantial percentage of a generation of young men was lost. The European Allies of World War I typically lost more than 2% of their population to war deaths, while an even greater number were wounded. France lost over 13% of its male population between 15 and 49 years of age. For the Central Powers, the human toll was even greater as all lost at least 3% of their population, and more than 5% was wounded. According to the book *To Hear Only Thunder Again*, "Germany lost roughly 35% of its men born between 1892 and 1895."[1]

Contrast that destruction with what occurred in the United States where the war necessitated the creation of a great deal of productive infrastructure, as shown in Exhibit 3-3. That infrastructure was created to support the war effort. Military spending rose almost 18 times, and over 10% of the workforce was drafted. Productive capacity in the United States of steel ingots and total production more than doubled between January 1915 and March 1917, the equity market was about flat on a nominal basis and down in real terms (Exhibit 3-4). From the time the United States entered the war until the armistice, the United States stock market lost about one third of its value in real terms. That decline would continue for the next two years, as concerns about the effects of inflation and economic depression would weigh on it.

Commodities as highlighted by the CRB Index generated the lowest returns in the 1920s. This reflects the low inflation environment of the period and a demand that was less stressed because of the peacetime environment. All other asset classes did well with riskier financial assets performing best.

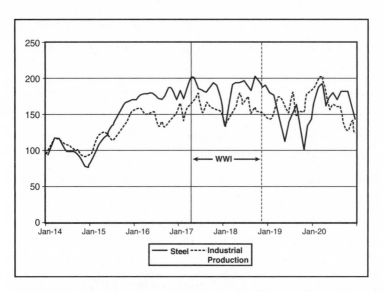

Exhibit 3-3   Steel Ingots and Total Industrial Production, 1914 to 1920 (1909=100) (Source: Hugh Rockoff, Rutgers University)

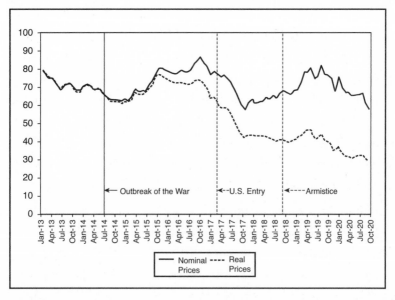

Exhibit 3-4   The U.S. Stock Market, 1913 to 1920 (Source: Hugh Rockoff, Rutgers University)

The second-best performing asset class was corporate bonds, which generated attractive real returns of more than 7% per year in the 1920s. The 1920s was a period of record corporate bond issuance, risk premiums fell, and leverage grew as financing terms grew looser. Like other extended periods of attractive investment returns, excesses began to occur as investor risk tolerance grew. The period also preceded one of large corporate bond losses and a tremendous reduction of liquidity in the financial markets.

1930s

The major economic and investment themes of the decade included:

1. Global economic depression
2. Rapid increase in global protectionism followed by a modest decline
3. Substantial decline in private investment
4. Rising tax rates
5. National governments centralized economic decision making
6. Rising risk premiums
7. Low interest rates
8. Over 20% of global economy is still agrarian
9. Massive military buildup
10. Dollar devaluation
11. Structural bear market
12. Era of risk aversion

The Great Depression and the global political turmoil preceding the buildup to World War II defined the decade of the 1930s. The gross domestic product of the United States was no higher at the end of the decade than it was at the beginning. It would fall by almost 40% in the first three years of the decade. Unemployment would soar to above 25% in early 1933 and then fall to 11% in 1937, only to rise back to 20% in 1938 before the buildup to World War II began in earnest.

Of the nine decades, the 1930s was the only period of deflation. Price levels were lower at the end of the decade than at its beginning. As a result, this is the only period when real returns were greater than nominal returns.

For U.S. equity investors, the early part of the 1930s was a catastrophe, resulting in a real loss on investment of 70%—and closer to 90% if that investment was made at the market's peak in September 1929 (Exhibit 3-5). During that period, investor sentiment got progressively worse. The market bottomed in 1932 and then began to rise as concerns about the potential collapse of the banking system began to fade, unemployment levels began to fall, actions such as U.S. dollar devaluation were taken to stimulate the economy, and a change in administrations seemed inevitable. All of this helped investor sentiment to improve.

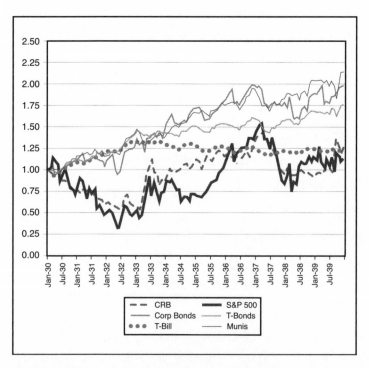

Exhibit 3-5   U.S. Real Asset Class Returns of the 1930s (Source: Global Financial Data)

As bad as the equity market was in the 1930s, the decade would include two of the best return years in stock market history. Those years were 1933 and 1935 and in terms of yearly stock market returns, they rank #1 and #4, respectively. That is according to the book *It Was a Very Good Year* by Martin S. Fridson.[2] He looked at annual stock market returns for most of the twentieth century—the book was published in 1998, and his findings still apply in 2009. Since 1900, only three years delivered an annual return over 50%, and in only ten years were returns in excess of 36.5% realized.

During 1933 the stock market rebound represented a continuation of a market rally that began in June 1932 from the stock market's bottom—its low point. That best market year was sufficient to reverse less than 17% of the losses sustained from the market peak in 1929 to its bottom. It is a stark reminder of one aspect of investment math, that a larger percentage gain is required to offset a corresponding loss and the greater the loss, the relatively more significant the gain required. For instance, a 50% rise in the market is only sufficient to compensate for a 33% market decline. The stock market gains of 1933 were part of a bull market rally that would last 56 months and end in February 1937. Like most rallies, investors began to sense that the bottom was reached and economic fortunes, while awful, would begin to improve.

The following graphs provide differing pictures of the unemployment rate for the United States. They show how rapidly the economy deteriorated and improved in the early 1930s. Exhibit 3-6 is from the National Bureau of Economic Research's data archives and provides the monthly unemployment rate starting in 1929 and ending in 1942. The unemployment rate went from under 1% in September 1929 to 25% in early 1932, less than three years later. That period coincided with the most severe U.S. stock market decline. It then fell to just above 10% in 1937 before shooting back up to close to 20% in less than a year as the Roosevelt administration took actions to close the federal government deficit that included increases in the tax rate and a tighter monetary policy.

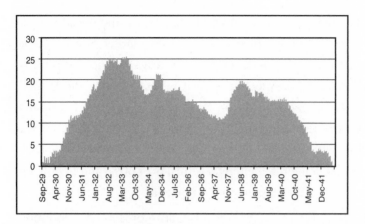

Exhibit 3-6   U.S. Unemployment Rate, 1929 to 1941 (Source: National Bureau of Economic Research)

Exhibit 3-7 comes from the Fourth Edition of *Historical Statistics Back to Colonial Times*. Its authors include the workers in the Federal Emergency Relief Program as employed, which makes a meaningful difference and substantially reduces the level of the unemployment rate. In the Third Edition, the nonfarm unemployment rate remained over 20% for the entire decade. Whatever the real rate of unemployment in the 1930s, the economy operated well below capacity and a substantial portion of the population was not gainfully employed in jobs that offered a future, nor would those jobs add to the government's revenue base, which must ultimately be achieved to sustain a viable public sector.

The Great Depression brought with it not only a change in political leadership, but a dramatic increase in the level of government involvement in the economy. Herbert Hoover attempted to stimulate the economy with higher levels of government spending, but they were not sufficient to offset the economic destruction caused by the protectionist legislation—Smoot Hawley, the collapse of the banking system, a declining money supply, deteriorating global economies, lack of trust in private enterprise, and growing lack of confidence in the government.

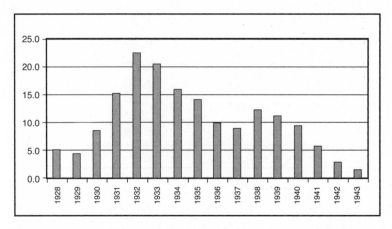

Exhibit 3-7   U.S. Unemployment Rate, 1928 to 1943—a Different Perspective (Source: Fourth Edition of *Historical Statistics Back to Colonial Times*)

With the change in administrations came an even greater level of government involvement in the economy, but also an improvement in the level of public trust. Still, the lack of clear direction in economic policy and the new administration's apparent hostility to private enterprise depressed the level of private investment. Income tax rates rose. The highest marginal rate rose to 79% in 1936; and a marginal tax rate of 99.5% on incomes of more than $100,000 was actively considered and supported by President Roosevelt. So, it is not surprising that the relatively undeveloped municipal securities market provided the best return for the decade. Its superior performance benefited from the tax status of municipal securities, rising income tax rates, concerns about additional increases in personal tax rates, and very low interest rates.

The few other global equity markets that were open offered modestly better returns than the U.S. equity market (Exhibit 3-8) principally because they did not experience the magnitude of the stock market crash experienced in the United States. Also, many countries recovered from the Great Depression before the United States and that appears to be reflected in the superior performance of their markets, too. The first country to fully recover from the Great Depression was Sweden.[3] By 1935, its economy would be greater than the previous 1929 peak and growth would continue. Its government's success is attributed to following Keynesian solutions.

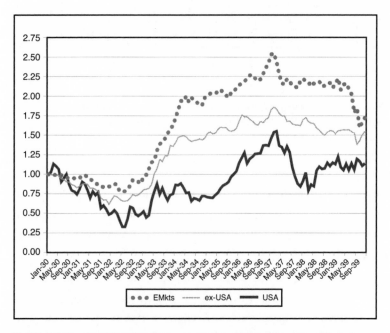

Exhibit 3-8   Real Equity Returns of the 1930s (Source: Global Financial Data)

Emerging market equities outperformed those of developed countries because they were less exposed to the preparation for World War II and the Great Depression. Still, as the probability of another world war became more apparent, the performance of all equity markets suffered. For the 1930s, the asset class generating the best return was municipal securities. Risk aversion was a critical element to a successful investment strategy in the 1930s.

1940s

The major economic and investment themes of the decade included:

1. World War II
2. The dislocations caused by WWII
3. Recovery from the war
4. Global schism following WWII
5. The emergence of the industrial age in the developed countries
6. Low-risk premiums
7. Low inflation
8. Low and controlled interest rates
9. Industrial age drives migration toward the Midwest
10. Bear market bottom
11. Interest rates controls produce negative real returns

The bear market continued into the 1940s. The U.S. Asset Real Returns chart for the 1940s (Exhibit 3-9) shows how in the early part of World War II, only one asset class provided positive returns and that was the CRB Index, which measures the performance of a basket of commodities. The U.S. stock market declined to mid-1942 when the fate of the war was in doubt. As confidence in an Allied victory grew, the stock market soared and almost tripled returns by mid-1946 with the steepest rise coming after Japan surrendered. Of course, very few people were thinking about investing during World War II or just after the war.

The investor optimism following the war's end eventually faded, and concerns about another economic depression, inflation—the future—set in. Inflationary concerns were reflected by the CRB Index, which shot up after the war as efforts to rebuild much of the developed world's infrastructure began in earnest.

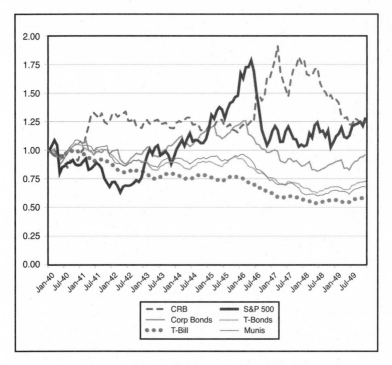

Exhibit 3-9   U.S. Real Asset Class Returns of the 1940s (Source: Global Financial Data)

Fixed-income instruments did not offer attractive returns as the U.S. government continued its policy of fixing short- and long-term rates on government instruments. T-Bills were priced to yield 0.375% and T-Bonds were priced to yield 2.50%. In an environment where investors were growing increasingly concerned about inflation, these yields grew less attractive. At the end of the decade, concerns about inflation abated as the United States entered a recession and the performance of the fixed-income asset classes improved.

The destruction of World War II left the United States as the dominant global economy. This was reflected in the superior performance of its equity market. During World War II, many of the world's equity markets were closed. Not surprisingly, after the war, the equity markets in the developed countries outside the United

States suffered the most as the end of the war also signaled the end of a way of life for some (Exhibit 3-10). As a result, in 1945 the ex-USA equity market plummeted almost 50%. The destruction to the economic foundation of many developed economies outside the United States caused the equity index to fall more than another 40% by the end of the decade.

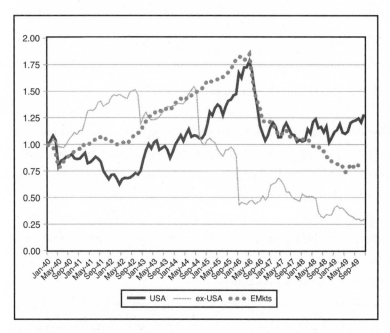

Exhibit 3-10   Real Equity Returns of the 1940s (Source: Global Financial Data)

1950s

The major economic and investment themes of the decade included:

1. The shift to a peacetime economy
2. The Cold War
3. Beginning of the space age

4. The interstate highway system and the suburbanization of the United States

5. Reindustrialization and a rise in free trade

6. Low-risk premiums

7. Low interest rates

8. Low inflation

9. The beginning of the baby boom

10. Television

11. Government's economic role shrinks

12. Beginning of the structural bull market

The 1950s brought with it the end of four decades that included two world wars and a Great Depression. It also represented the beginning of a much bigger role for private enterprise, the baby boom in the United States, a new technology called television, the space age, a new democratic beginning for much of Western Europe and Japan, the splitting of Korea with the end of the Korean War, and the emergence of communism as a major global force controlling over half of the world's population.

For investors, equities were the asset class of choice in the 1950s (Exhibit 3-11). In fact, the 1950s were the best decade for equities. The valuation of markets at the beginning of the decade was very low, investor expectations were very modest, and very few people could anticipate the changes that were about to occur in the free world. It was the best decade for the S&P 500, but only good enough to rank the S&P 500 second among the nine asset classes. The best returns were generated by World ex-USA. Those markets surged between 1953 and 1955, and then surged again in 1958 to the end of the decade (Exhibit 3-12).

Exhibit 3-11   U.S. Real Asset Class Returns of the 1950s (Source: Global Financial Data)

The strong performance of those equity markets benefited from a move to peacetime economy and the rebuilding effort taking place in many of the countries after World War II. By the end of the war, the economies of much of Western Europe experienced a level of destruction that again set their economies back decades. Japan's economy was essentially destroyed and in 1950, its GDP was less than 5% of that of the United States. By 1980, the Japanese economy grew to equal 40% of the U.S. economy. For many of these developed countries, the growth outlook was enhanced by the military protection provided by the United States. It lessened the defense burden many of those governments would otherwise have felt compelled to provide.

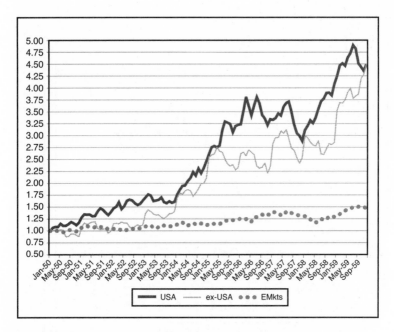

Exhibit 3-12   Real Equity Returns of the 1950s (Source: Global Financial Data)

In 1950, the Japanese economy began to grow at a pace that would make it almost tenfold larger by 1980. In the first ten years, the size of the Japanese economy more than doubled, as did per capita GDP. In Western Europe, the German economy would more than double, the Italian economy would grow more than 80%, and the French economy would grow more than 50%; the United Kingdom's economy, however, grew by less than 30%. The economic growth, combined with a starting point of low expectations and valuations, ultimately provided for some of the best asset class returns of any decade.

Investment returns provided by the other asset classes were negative for the period with the exception of the CRB Index. This was caused by the gradual pickup of inflationary pressures and rise in interest rates from artificially low levels. The value of existing fixed-income instruments declines in a rising rate environment because the value of its expected cash flow stream is less than a new fixed-income issue with a higher interest coupon. Risk aversion was penalized.

1960s

The major economic and investment themes of the decade included:

1. Social and political turmoil
2. The emergence of the Great Society
3. The Vietnam War
4. The baby boom generation begins to mature
5. The Cold War continues
6. Interest rates begin to rise
7. Inflationary pressures build
8. The Go-Go Years
9. Risk premiums begin to rise
10. Rosy expectations at the beginning
11. Stage for the next bear market set

Unlike the previous three decades, the start of the 1960s was a more optimistic time; expectations were higher, much higher. The S&P 500 P/E was closer to 17.0x at the beginning of 1960 compared with less than 7.5x at the beginning of 1950 (Exhibit 3-13). That P/E level would rise initially, but over the course of the 1960s, that valuation level would prove to be difficult to sustain. The performance of the S&P 500 reflected some of that early optimism.

During the 1960s, the baby boom generation went to school and, by the end of the decade, started graduating from college. The Cold War cast a shadow, but the source of another military conflict was not apparent at the beginning of the decade. That would change quickly with the Bay of Pigs and the Cuban Missile Crisis, the installation of the Berlin Wall, and the escalation of force in Vietnam. Social turmoil intensified with the Civil Rights Movement and the assassinations of President Kennedy, his brother Robert Kennedy, Martin Luther King, and Malcolm X. The aura of increased possibility seemed to bring with it a sense of increasing awareness of what was not being achieved and a growing impatience with the pace of change. We call this phenomenon of increasing prosperity leading to growing aware- ness of real and perceived disparities, "prosperity's illusion." That is, the illusion that the conditions and disparities are new and greater than before and easily addressed. Part of what creates the illusion is the assumption the current prosperity is real and sustainable.

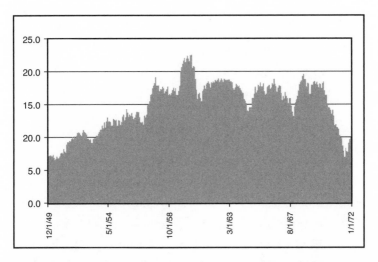

Exhibit 3-13   Trailing P/E of the S&P 500—1949 to 1975 (Source: Global Financial Data)

Nonequity asset classes performed poorly in the 1960s and began to generate real negative returns as the period known as "The Great Inflation" began (Exhibit 3-14). It precipitated the beginning of the second structural bear market in the United States and triggered a period of rising interest rates that would last well over a decade. For people dependent on fixed incomes, it would be a period of ever-increasing financial pressures as the value of their financial assets was debased by inflation and eventually a weaker currency. In the United States, that inflation was driven by the escalating cost of the Vietnam War, the cost of the War on Poverty, and other government programs. T-Bonds and municipal bond investing were most sensitive to the rise in interest rates, with municipal securities generating real negative returns of over 40% from the middle of the decade to its close.

Exhibit 3-14   Real U.S. Asset Class Returns of the 1960s (Source: Global Financial Data)

Equity markets outside the United States offered even less-attractive returns for most of the decade (Exhibit 3-15). After a very strong performance in the 1950s, western European equity markets

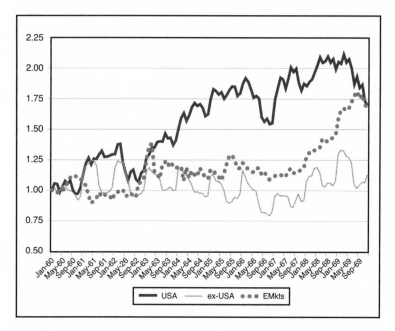

Exhibit 3-15   Real Equity Returns of the 1960s (Source: Global Financial Data)

slipped sideways in the 1960s as inflationary pressures built and the role of government increased. Japan's GDP continued to grow at a real rate of 10.5% per year in the 1960s. For the Japanese population, that growth translated into 9.3% per capita GDP every year, almost tripling in a single decade. During the 1960s, Japan's per capita GDP went from 1.43 times global per capita GDP to 2.59 times. The cost of living in Japan was relatively inexpensive, and the buildup of the industrial infrastructure was still taking place. The population was relatively young and the cost of social programs modest. The foundation for continued growth was still in place. Part of that foundation was the market's valuation and relative to GDP, the Japanese market remained attractively valued during the decade of the 1960s and through much of the 1970s, as shown in Exhibit 3-16.

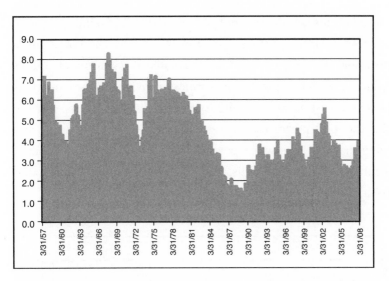

Exhibit 3-16   Japan GDP to Topix—1957 to 2008 (Source: Global Financial Data)

1970s

The major economic and investment themes of the decade included:

1. Political turmoil—Watergate
2. Global currency market turmoil caused by the end of Bretton Woods
3. Two energy crises
4. Inflation and rising interest rates
5. Equity valuations fall
6. The door to China starts to open
7. Level of government intervention continues to rise
8. Rising risk premiums
9. Rising levels of pessimism
10. The baby boom generation enters the workforce
11. Rising pressures for trade protection
12. Structural bear market

United States investors were hard pressed to find a financial asset
class that generated a positive return in the 1970s. The Great Inflation occupied the entire decade. It overmatched government actions
to subdue it and that depressed investment activity and the valuations
prospective investors were willing to pay for financial assets. For the
decade, the best-performing asset classes were commodities and
emerging markets. The worst-performing asset classes were municipal securities, T-Bonds, T-Bills, and the S&P 500. Corporate bond
real returns were about 0.5% annually (Exhibit 3-17).

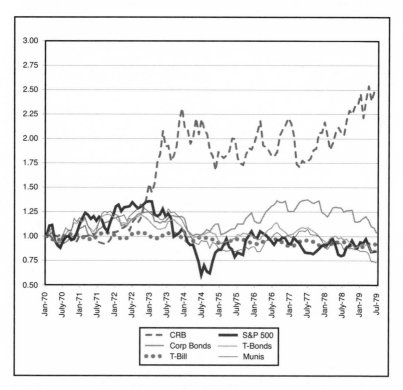

**Exhibit 3-17   U.S. Real Asset Class Returns of the 1970s (Source: Global
Financial Data)**

During the 1970s, there were two energy crises, Watergate, the end of Breton Woods and the move to a "fiat money" system, the end of Vietnam, and two recessions. There was also a structure many countries had in place that tried to preserve purchasing power by automatically increasing wages based on a given level of prices. Those adjustments were called cost-of-living adjustments or "COLA" for short. The mentality supporting this kind of structure also supported more government involvement in the economy, and during the decade, various forms of government programs and social welfare grew relative to the real economy. The effect would slow and often eliminate real economic growth.

The shift away from financial assets reflected the end of a global currency system tied to gold in favor of a floating-rate system. The dollar remained the global reserve currency because of the relative size of the U.S. economy to the global economy, but because of the political instability reflected by Watergate, Vietnam, and the energy crises, the dollar declined in value relative to other currencies. Emerging markets benefited more than the markets of other developed countries because of their greater economic dependence on natural resources, greater growth potential, and less sensitivity to the shift toward more government control of the economy (Exhibit 3-18). That trend of greater government involvement in economic decision making rose in many developed countries.

The economic markets of many of the world's most populous countries remained closed to outside investors in the 1970s, and local financial markets did not exist. In 1975, the combined population of China and the former USSR approached 1.2 billion people, or almost 30% of the world's population. India's population represented 15% of the world's population in 1975 and its Sensex index did not open until 1986.

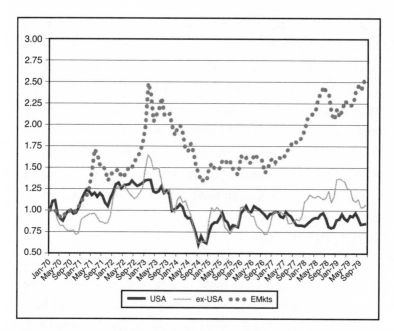

Exhibit 3-18   Real Equity Returns of the 1970s (Source: Global Financial Data)

In total, the markets of countries representing over half the world's population of more than 4.4 billion in 1980 were not open. They were closed because of their political system, their lack of economic development, or both. Whatever the reason, the opportunity for outside investors to help their countries expand did not exist and their economic growth and economic growth potential was, at best, repressed as a result.

1980s

The major economic and investment themes of the decade included:

1. Inflation ends and disinflation begins
2. Interest begins to fall from peak levels

3. The information age begins in earnest

4. Communist governments begin to lose share of the world's population

5. The Berlin Wall falls

6. Tax rates are lowered

7. Investor expectations and consumer expectations rise—quality is expected

8. Falling risk premiums and rising equity valuations

9. The S&L Crisis

10. The baby boom family formation is at its peak

11. Japan's stock market peaks at the end of 1989

12. The bull market

Although highlighted in the Introduction, it is worth repeating here—the early 1980s represented the end of the Great Inflation. The period that followed would be one of the great bull markets for stocks ever—and also maybe the greatest bull market for bonds ever. T-Bills, municipal securities, and the CRB Index were the weaker-performing asset classes, reflecting a deflationary period, a decline in interest rates, and a decline in tax rates (Exhibit 3-19).

Domestically, the S&P 500 was the best-performing asset class. Like the other bull markets, this one started with very low expectations and what appeared to be a high degree of investor skepticism. The trailing P/E for the S&P 500 fell below 6.7x in the first quarter of 1980, less than half the median P/E for the last 100 years. That reflected concerns about continued inflation and high rates of interest. That concern would change with the elections of Margaret Thatcher in the United Kingdom and Ronald Reagan in the United States. Both believed in a more limited role for government and both understood the economic peril presented by inflation. In less than two years in office, the concern about inflation was addressed at some economic expense. Still, the U.S. economy generated real GDP growth of over 2.5% pretty consistently for the rest of the decade after the economy recovered from the recession in 1982.

Exhibit 3-19   U.S. Real Asset Class Returns of the 1980s (Source: Global Financial Data)

Since dealing with inflation, the global economy has been in a period of disinflation and sometimes, modest deflation. The decline in interest rates and lowering of inflationary pressures reduced the pricing power of commodities and depressed the prices of some. Oil prices peaked in the early 1980s and on a real basis lost more than 50% of their value over the next decade.

As good as the market was for U.S. equities, it was better for the equities of other developed countries (Exhibit 3-20). The shift to disinflationary pressure and lessening of the role of government of most developed countries, combined with the eventual stock market bubble in Japan, made World ex-USA the best-returning asset class.

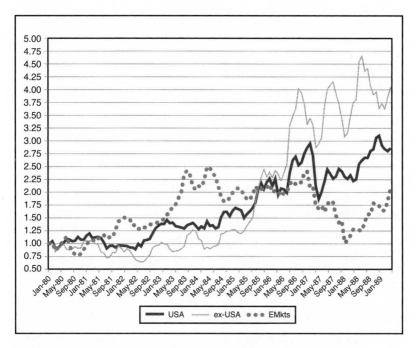

Exhibit 3-20   Real Equity Returns of the 1980s (Source: Global Financial Data)

Emerging market equities produced attractive results through the end of 1983 because of their perceived growth opportunities. That perception would change because of declining commodity prices, serial government defaults, and bouts with hyperinflation in many countries. From its peak level near the end of 1983 through September 1988, the Emerging Markets Index fell almost 60%. It highlighted and reinforced the more volatile nature of Emerging Market equity investing and set the stage for a rebound. By the end of the decade, the Index doubled from its bottom.

1990s

The major economic and investment themes of the decade included:

1. The S&L Crisis is resolved
2. Equity market valuations go from attractive to expensive
3. Desert Storm, the peace dividend, and more open trade
4. Interest rates continue to trend down
5. Disinflationary pressures continue
6. The World Wide Web is launched and e-mail takes hold
7. Entrepreneurial activities in China begin to soar
8. The "tech bubble" forms
9. Investor interest in the stock market rises to peak levels
10. Expectations rise and optimism soars during the decade
11. Y2K
12. Long-Term Capital Management fails and Russia goes bankrupt, while the likes of Enron and WorldCom appear to prosper
13. Bull market

In 1990, the United States was dealing with the S&L Crisis. More banks would fail during that period than in any other since the FDIC was formed. That crisis would contribute to a recession that would ultimately end just before the 1992 presidential election. However, it would not be apparent the recession ended for years after the election. So, much like 1920 and 1980, 1990 was a year of modest expectations anchored by the economic stress of that era. What followed 1990 was a period of strong economic growth, but not as strong as that experienced in the 1980s after the recession. Contributing to the growth were technological advancement, a more benign government regulatory environment, and what was believed to be a "peace dividend." Like the 1920s, the U.S. equity market's total returns in the

1990s quadrupled over the course of the decade (Exhibit 3-21). And like the 1920s, the 1990s started with low expectations and ended in an equity market bubble. This one would be called the tech bubble.

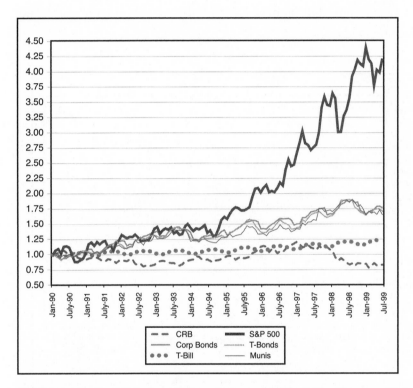

Exhibit 3-21   Real U.S. Asset Class Returns of the 1990s (Source: Global Financial Data)

More than most other decades, the best returns were to be found in the United States and usually in longer-duration asset classes. T-Bills produced negative returns as short-term yields rose during the second half of the decade. Commodity prices continued to fall because global economic growth and investment slowed outside the United States. Japan entered a structural bear market at the beginning of the decade and as of the time of this writing remains mired in it. For corporate bonds, T-Bonds, and municipal securities, returns were attractive because long rates declined during the decade, credit risk premiums declined, and marginal tax rates rose.

The 1990s also represented the beginning of a more global economy, the Internet, and an acceleration of the declining role of communism. That shift helped the returns of the emerging markets (Exhibit 3-22).

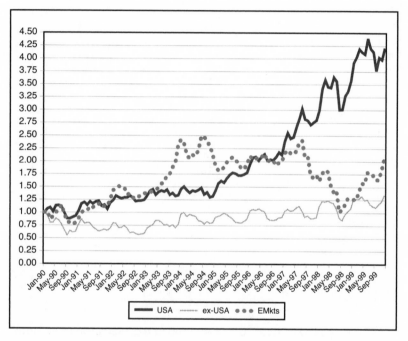

Exhibit 3-22   Real Equity Returns of the 1990s (Source: Global Financial Data)

The 2000s

The major investment themes of the decade included:

1. The tech bubble bursts

2. The coming shift in the world's economic order becomes apparent as China goes from the seventh largest economy in 2000 to the third largest in 2008

3. Corporate governance problems—Enron, WorldCom, Tyco, Adelphia, and so on

4. The Great Leveraging accelerates

5. Record low interest rates

6. Concerns about deflation

7. The shadow banking system and the housing bubble

8. Risk premiums fall once equity markets bottom and evidence little investor sensitivity to risk until the housing bubble bursts

9. Lehman Brothers fails

10. The Iraq War—War on Terror

11. Energy prices soar

12. Japan is in its second lost decade

13. Global liquidity crisis, not risk aversion trigger market collapse

14. U.S. bear market—global bull market

Like the 1930s, risk aversion was a rewarding investment strategy in the decade of the 2000s. The two major financial events for the decade were the bursting of the tech bubble in March 2000 and the financial crisis called the housing bubble that began in 2007 and culminated with the bankruptcy of Lehman Brothers. Despite very low interest rates most of the decade, the S&P 500 generated real negative returns (Exhibit 3-23). From its 2000 peak to the bottom in 2000, the S&P 500 lost more than half of its value and the NASDAQ lost more than 70% of its value. The S&P 500 came close to fully recovering in early 2007 before losing more than half of its value again by March 2009. The NASDAQ never got close to its 2000 market high.

The confluence of the bursting of the housing bubble, the formation and bursting of a commodities bubble, the financial crisis, and the emergence of China and India as economic leaders helped create a change in the investment calculus. Concerns about the economic ramifications of the market crash and then the aftermath of the housing bubble led to a very accommodating Fed policy and short-term interest rates that were often below the level of inflation as measured by the consumer price index (CPI). That led to negative real returns from the T-Bill. Commodities were very volatile and spiked just as the financial crisis began to gain traction and then collapsed during the financial crisis followed by a rally.

Exhibit 3-23   Real U.S. Asset Class Returns of the 2000s (Source: Global Financial Data)

The remaining asset class, fixed income, delivered strong returns in a difficult environment. Municipal securities edged out corporate bonds for the top-performing asset class, and both were closely followed by T-Bonds. Higher-quality corporate credits and less-risky government related credits were much less exposed to housing-related problems and also benefited from low long-term interest rates.

Other equity markets of developed countries fared only a bit better, and still delivered negative returns. The World ex-USA bounce from the 2002 bottom was more significant, but so was its decline caused by the financial crisis. The Emerging Markets participated in the Tech crash and quintupled from the bottom. The risk aversion triggered by the financial crisis caused a decline of more than 60% in the Emerging Market Index. Once liquidity was restored, Emerging Markets rebounded and retraced about half of the loss tied to the financial crisis. For the decade, the Emerging Market equity index outperformed the other two by more than 150% (Exhibit 3-24).

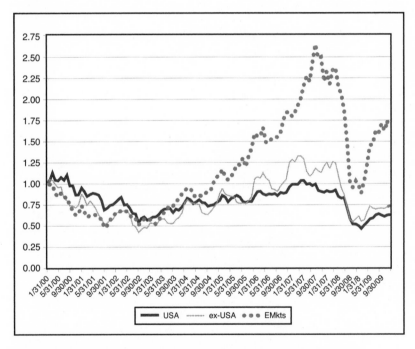

Exhibit 3-24   Real Equity Returns of the 2000s (Source: Global Financial Data)

Endnotes

1 Van Ells, M.D. (2001). *To Hear Only Thunder Again*, Lexington Books.

2 Fridson, M.S. (1998). *It Was a Very Good Year*, John Wiley & Sons, Inc.

3 http://www.huppi.com/kangaroo/Timeline.htm#Back-Sweden

4

Global Economic Growth

The wealth of which nations?

Economies have cycles, too! Those cycles have been more frequent than the structural phases of the equity markets. Including the Great Depression, there have been 14 recessions or economic recessions since 1929. Since 1980, the duration of economic expansion in the United States grew, whereas the incidence of economic contractions declined. Still, the deep global recession of 2008 and the struggles of Japan to generate economic growth after two decades of stagnation are reminders that economic cycles exist and that difficult times can persist for a long time. The magnitude and duration of any period of decline is related to the prior period's level of excess and the coincident and subsequent government policy responses. Beyond those cycles are secular shifts that continue to alter a nation's economic mix and the global economy.

Over the last century, much of the world participated in an economic structural shift from an agrarian to an industrial economy. The resources required to drive the shift to the Industrial Revolution became increasingly concentrated, and in 1913, four countries—the United States, Britain, France, and Germany—controlled two-thirds of the world's manufacturing capacity. These were countries that pursued and embraced the forces creating the Industrial Revolution and adopted the new sources of energy required to support it.

In the past four decades, the global economy began its second structural shift to a service-based information economy. In the process, the world population continues to shift from rural areas to urban areas, is even more dependent on carbon-based products for growing energy demands, and is enjoying greater freedom of movement and elaborate communications and an ever-increasing level of connectedness. These forces mean more concentrated population centers. By 2050, about 70% of the world's population is expected to live in urban areas compared to just over 50% by 2010, and about 30% in 1950. So, the world's urban population is expected to almost double in the next 40 years, as shown in Exhibit 4-1.

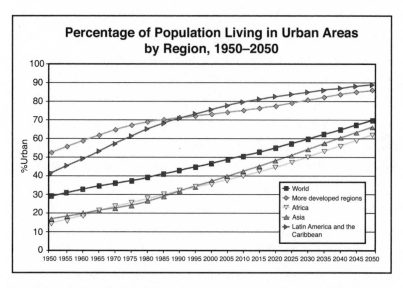

Exhibit 4-1   Worldwide Urban Population Trend (Source: UN World Urbanization Prospects, 2007)

These trends, and their benefits, vary widely across countries and regions. Although their effect varies a great deal from country to country, these long secular economic shifts enable consumer acquisition of new technologies to occur more rapidly. In the United States, telephone, automobile, stove, and electricity were new technologies in 1920. At that point, consumers could not purchase a radio, refrigerator, or clothes washer. The time for most of the products to be adopted by at least one-half of the consumers was about two decades, and electricity took more than 30 years to be available to 70% of the households in America. The adoption rate of new products by consumers is much faster now.

Since the Industrial Revolution began, GDP per capita increased more than nine times through 2000 and more than ten times through 2005. That growth, although unevenly distributed, provided the foundation necessary for the global economy to enter this second structural shift. It should also be contrasted with the growth of the period that preceded it, which was modest at best and left the vast majority of the world's population in poverty and much more vulnerable. Compared to the almost tenfold increase in per capita GDP since the beginning of the Industrial Revolution, the 800-plus-year period up to 1820 created global per capita GDP growth of less than 50% for the entire period. Life in the Agrarian Age was labor-intensive; progress was limited to little mobility and fueled by plants and trees. The level of exploration rose after 1500, and the pace of growth accelerated.

The United States Emerges as the Leading Global Economy

At the dawn of the nineteenth century, the United States was a young democracy that did not rank in the top five global economies. It would surprise the world by overtaking England and other established economic powers to become the world's leading economy in that century. At the dawn of the twentieth century, the United States was already firmly established as the world's leading economy, a position it would solidify and continue to hold more than 100 years later.

At one point a country with apparently similar prospects, Argentina took a different path. On a per capita to GDP basis, Argentina's economy was equal to that of the United States in 1820 and then proceeded to fall behind. However, between 1900 and 1913, Argentina experienced a surge in GDP per capita and achieved a level greater than that sustained by Western European nations before World War I. Argentina's per capita income was $3,797 compared to $3,482 for Western Europe and $5,307 for the United States. Over the next eight decades, Argentina's level of per capita income would barely double, Western Europe's level would more than triple, whereas the United States would experience a quadrupling of its per capita to GDP level. For the Argentine population, the country's evolution would follow a much less economically robust and beneficial path.

According to the book *False Economy*, Argentina's leaders were much less open to change. "On the face of it, the economies of the two countries also looked similar: agrarian nations pushing the frontiers of their settlement westward into a wilderness of temperate grasslands. In both nations the frontier rancher—the gaucho and the cowboy—was elevated into a national symbol of courage, independence, and endurance. But closer up, there were big disparities in the way the frontiers were settled. America chose a path that parceled out new land to individuals and families; Argentina delivered it into the hands of a small elite."

The Argentine Government was much more focused on maintaining the status quo. Its determination to maintain a status quo and not embrace the winds of change is one of the characteristics of economies that eventually lag others. The United States embraced the change and grew. The more recent experience of the City of Detroit seems to echo these themes: It was one of the fastest growing cities in the first half of the twentieth century because it embraced the change brought by the Industrial Revolution in the form of the automobile. Its great success would become its downfall as it tried to hold on to the past and an unsupportable economic lifestyle, while resisting the new forces of change.

Demographic and Other Shifts

Other larger economic powers of the time also did not fare that well. In 1900, the five largest economies were, in order, United States, China, United Kingdom, Germany, and India. Around 1900, China, a much older economy and the world's largest economy until 1875, was struggling to remain the world's second largest economy. It held the rank of second largest economy in 1925 and fell to third largest in 1950. By 1975, its economy did not rank among the top five even though it had the world's largest population. The potential for a long descent was evident in 1900 when it was in the midst of a precipitous decline caused by pressure from Western powers and the destructive forces of internal strife. Shortly after 1911, its dynastic rule would collapse and fall. After the United States, England, and China came two other major powers: Germany, on and off the largest European economy, and India, which, like China, had seen better days. Also like China, India would begin to reemerge as a global power at the beginning of the twenty-first century.

Then, like now, economies in the process of becoming more open fared much better than ones that were closed and centralized. Of course, then most of the global economy was agrarian. Those economies that grew fastest became more democratic and more inclusive and embraced the new technology of the time, which was industrialization. By 2008, China was the world's third largest economy and well on the way to becoming the second largest economy (Exhibit 4-2). Brazil, which was just 4% the size of the United States' economy in 1970, grew to equal more than 10% by 2008. The Russian Federation rebounded from the distractions and destructions of old entities following the dissolution of the Soviet Union.

In the United States, the fastest growing states in the first half of the twentieth century were the ones embracing the industrialization wave, and they were in what today is known as the Rust Belt. Industrialization was the second of four major U.S. demographic waves. The first was the settling of the Northeast, and the second was industrialization, which brought with it a tremendous migration to the new sources of jobs. Those sources were located principally in the Midwest, which would be known as the Rust Belt as the factories aged and many of the companies died, or just lost their competitive edge. What followed industrialization was the move of many people westward. They moved west in search of a better life and job opportunities. That mostly meant moving to California, which ultimately became the most populous state in the union. In 1900, California's population was smaller than that of Iowa. The result of the population migration west would be the creation of the second largest city in the United States, Los Angeles; and five of the 15 largest cities.

Exhibit 4-2   Size of the World's Major Economies Since 1970 (Source: United Nations)

Country	1970	1980	1990	2000	2008
United States	$1,025	$2,769	$5,757	$9,765	$14,097
Japan	$203	$1,055	$3,018	$4,667	$4,911
China	$92	$307	$404	$1,193	$4,327
Germany	$209	$920	$1,714	$1,900	$3,649
France	$147	$691	$1,244	$1,328	$2,857
United Kingdom	$126	$545	$1,007	$1,478	$2,666
Italy	$109	$460	$1,133	$1,097	$2,303
Russian Federation	NA	NA	$570	$260	$1,677
Spain	$40	$226	$521	$581	$1,604
Brazil	$42	$228	$479	$645	$1,595
Canada	$86	$269	$583	$725	$1,502
India	$61	$185	$327	$468	$1,254
Mexico	$43	$228	$288	$637	$1,082
Australia	$43	$166	$311	$400	$1,017
South Korea	$9	$67	$275	$533	$929
WORLD	$3,283	$11,855	$23,733	$31,768	$60,428

GDP/breakdown at current prices in U.S. dollars (all countries-$b)

The fourth population shift was the southward migration to Texas and what the website New Geography calls the New South. Like the westward movement, the population shift to the South appeared driven in part by a lower cost of living, a more competitive business environment, the rapidly growing retiree segment of the population and the search by many of warmer weather. The increasing availability of air conditioning and lower taxes were other factors supporting the migration.

Per Capita Growth

During much of its reign of more than a century as the world's largest economy, the United States was not only the largest economy in absolute terms, but it also produced more economic output per capita. Although in 1900 it still trailed the United Kingdom in per capita GDP, by 1950 it was number one by a large margin from the UK, which has fallen into third place behind another former colony, Canada. The United States and Canada benefited more from demographic growth and improved productivity, two basic keys of economic growth. They also benefited from avoiding the physical destruction of world wars, while the United Kingdom and many other major economies were devastated by World War II. For the United States and Canada, World War II brought tremendous investment in the industrial infrastructure and little physical destruction.

China, which was not one of the central parties in either world war, still experienced the worst per capita GDP performance for the first half of the twentieth century, reflecting the destruction caused by an insular command and control structure that forced most of its population to pursue a subsistent life style with inadequate tools. According to the Angus Maddison statistics, China's level of per capita income fell more than 10% between 1900 and 1950, while it more than doubled in the United States and Canada. That period for China should rank as one of the world's Dark Ages because it left the China of 1950 with a lower living standard on a per capita basis than the China of 1500 when per capita GDP was $500.

With European powers devastated in the aftermath of World War I and again after World War II, the United States solidified its lead as the world's dominant economy. According to Prof. Angus Maddison, the United States generated 27 percent of the global economy, greater than Western Europe and approximately 50 percent more than the entire continent of Asia.

Through the Marshall Plan, the United States carried on its shoulders much of the burden of reviving the West European economies while lending a hand to the rebuilding of the Japanese economy and later reconstructing and developing the economies of Taiwan and South Korea. Over time, West European powers such as France and Germany rebuilt their economic power. Some, most notably the UK, would not regain their pre-war standing. Still, the shift from a wartime economy to a much more modern industrial peacetime economy combined with the incremental move toward a common market breathed new life in West European economies. As a combined economic entity, it would come to equal, and on some measures surpass, the economy of the United States. The fall of the Soviet Union at the end of the century would free Central and Eastern European nations, triggering the eventual expansion of the European Union while creating a low-cost, competitive base in Europe's backyard. The European Union would come to rival the economy of the United States in absolute size, whereas its per capita GDP remains just behind that of the United States.

Across the Pacific, and with considerable help and guidance from America, Japan rebuilt its economy, shifting in three decades from the manufacturing of toys and simple electronics to become a global player in the automotive, steel, shipping, and electronics, among other industries. By the end of the 1960s (and before the energy cri-sis of 1973, which is commonly cited as the main trigger for the expansion), Japanese automobile exports to the United States were expanding rapidly while American cars were held back by walls of Japanese tariff and nontariff barriers. Initially confined to entry level Toyotas and Datsuns (Nissan's initial brand name in the United States), simple TV sets made by Matsushita Electric (manufacturer of Panasonic and National brands) and similar products, Japanese pro-ducers climbed up the value chain to become associated with quality and value for money before entering the market for premium prod-ucts such as the Acura, Lexus, and Infiniti automobiles decades later. In a generation, the customer image of Japanese manufacturers was transformed from being a provider of low-quality products to being a producer of some of the highest-quality products in the world. Those producers included Sony and the Lexus division of Toyota.

The transition from economic devastation to an economy of basic manufacturing to high-quality manufacturing stimulated an eco-nomic boom that pushed Japan to become the second largest econ-omy in the world. By the end of the 1980s, that success also helped create an image for Japan as being one of the most successful economies with a sustainable formula for success. That image would be short lived as economic growth decelerated and ultimately declined from the market peak of 1989. Since that peak, the Japanese economy has generated almost no new net job growth in the follow-ing two decades. Its economic boom and subsequent slowdown is evi-dent in Exhibit 4-3 that shows the 5-year compound annual growth rate of Japan's economy starting in 1962. For a period of 15 years, the economy sustained an annual GDP growth of more than 15% in a low-inflation environment—a remarkable record. By the 1990s, that level of growth was usually less than 1% annually.

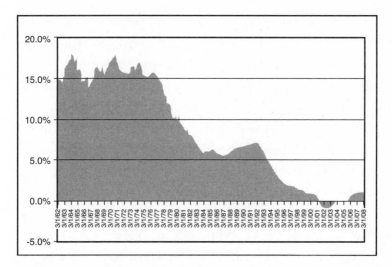

Exhibit 4-3   5-Year Compound Growth Rate (CAGR) of Japan's GDP (Source: Global Financial Data)

Elsewhere in the Pacific were lurking the "four tigers" or, as they were alternatively called, the "four little dragons" of South Korea, Taiwan, Hong Kong, and Singapore. The little dragons' companies took a page from Japan, entering the lower segments of the market and pressuring their Japanese competitors to accelerate their move up-market. The little dragons also tended to copy Japan's model of a "guided" economy that channeled resources to strategic and promising areas as identified by the government, showering them with incentives and shielding them from foreign competition while often using weak currencies to retain a competitive advantage in export markets. At the same time, domestic markets remained mostly closed to the United States and, to a lesser extent, European manufacturers even as Asian exports were beginning to flood U.S. and European markets, resulting in substantial merchandise trade deficits. All the four dragons had at that time quasi-authoritarian regimes that replicated the tightly controlled model of "Japan, Inc."

Three of the dragons, Taiwan, Hong Kong, and Singapore, were predominantly Chinese societies. Taiwan initially laid claim to the Chinese Mainland as the Republic of China; although the Mainland continued to see it, as it does today, as a renegade province. Led by the authoritarian rule of Chiang Kai-shek and later his son, the Taiwanese economy consisted of a combination of a number of large, state-owned or state-sponsored firms and a great multitude of small business. Hong Kong, then a British colony, leveraged its position as the gateway to the Chinese mainland to become a middleman and stepping point for trade in the area. The territory established a thriving manufacturing sector, becoming, despite its small size, a key player in labor-intensive industries such as textiles and toys. In toys, for instance, Hong Kong has gradually grown from modest origins in the 1960s to become the leading world exporter by the 1990s. Also a one time British colony, Singapore has been independent since 1959.[1] (Although during 1963–1965, it was in a federation with Malaysia.) The city state, a titular democracy with an effective one-party rule, established a thriving manufacturing industry and lured multinational players offering a stable and supportive government, skilled workforce, and an independent judiciary in the British tradition, like that of Hong Kong.

South Korea, the only non-Chinese country among the four dragons nevertheless shared some culture and institutions with its counterparts. Devastated by long Japanese occupation from which it emerged at the end of the World War II, Korea was destroyed again by the Korean War in the early 1950s, which tore the country apart. Like the other tigers, South Korea enjoyed considerable American support that has helped it grow its economy, then consisting of light manufacturing relying on cheap but relatively skilled labor. All the tigers, however, have had greater dreams that were driven as much by necessity as by ambition, namely to climb up the value chain and compete on brand and quality rather than cost.

When the little dragons were labeled as such, many people thought of Japan as the big dragon. After all, the little dragons imitated many features of the Japanese economy, that is, government guidance and support for "pillar industries" and active support of large industrial champions. (Hong Kong was an exception.) The

Japanese economy was making great strides moving up the value chain, and Japanese companies were beginning to challenge their U.S. and European competitors on their own turf. Still, the big dragon lurking behind was different. It was the People's Republic of China and beyond it, the then dream of Greater China.

At the end of 1978, the Chinese reformers who won a power struggle after the death of Mao Zedong embarked on a long journey to repeal his zealous and often disastrous economic policies, engineering a series of reforms that were to unleash the country's enormous potential and strong entrepreneurial spirit. In less than a generation, China has been transformed from an economic basket case to one of the world's dominant economic powers.

In 1980, shortly after the launch of the reforms, the Chinese economy represented 2.6 percent of the global economy. By 2008, its share has almost tripled to 7.2 percent. The prospect of China overtaking the United States to become the world's largest economy progressed from being outlandish to being considered a high probability. According to a Goldman Sachs's forecast, this watershed event that would have ended a century and one-half of global economic leadership by the United States is scheduled to happen around 2040, whereas other forecasts target a much earlier date; for example, Prof. Angus Maddison predicts around 2030, and co-author Prof. Oded Shenkar predicts that this will happen no later than 2024.

At the dawn of the twenty-first century, India too began to shed elements of its socialist economy, promptly registering growth rates among the highest in the world. Initially pulled by a number of globally competitive software firms, India has started to expand into other sectors such as pharmaceuticals and has begun to reform its justifiably maligned bureaucracy. Like China, India could also rely on a vast Diaspora of well-educated and experienced people who saw the emerging opportunity and contributed their skills and capital to the reform effort. Like China, it would also rely on foreign players to bring in the know-how and experience while seeing the advance of

Indian conglomerates starting to venture into foreign markets. India however would pursue a different path, embarking on its reform efforts roughly two decades later than China and suffering such problems as weak infrastructure that the Chinese have had time to at least partially address. A democracy, India has also suffered from frequent paralysis, the result of political bickering and coalition politics, though this has also benefited its economic base, for instance, in the provision of a solid and relatively independent judiciary.

Taken together, the rise of China and India was a watershed event that would change the parameters of the international economy. Cleary, one wonders not only how those two powers will progress, but also what would be the impact on the other players in the world economy and how will a new global economy look and behave in the years to come. In their early initial growth stage, China and India ranked in the top ten growth economies among the world's largest economies for the 28-year period ending 2008. Although the United States managed to sustain GDP growth about equal to that of the global composite, the countries in the top ten growth economies were emerging from a period of centralized control (such as China and Poland) and benefited from the growing demand for natural resources, or a combination of both (see Exhibit 4-4). Of the 25 largest countries excluding the Russian Federation, the countries unable to sustain economic growth in line with the global rate tended to have more rigid work laws, costly social programs, and high levels of taxes.

Generating the fastest GDP growth does not necessarily translate into generating the best investment returns. However, it does make it easier for companies to grow. A better understanding of the nature and scope of an economic cycle is as important as an understanding of the drivers of investment returns tied to that economic growth and cycle. One positive characteristic is the importance of a more open economy, which is inextricably tied to a country's political system. China is still a communist system, but one that is increasingly open to change and dialogue. Contrast that with Venezuela, which supposedly holds free elections, but where the government plays a growing role in economic decision making and corporate ownership. In China, the fortunes of the citizens are improving even during a global recession, while the conditions continue to deteriorate in Venezuela.

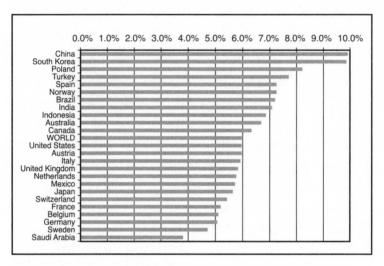

Exhibit 4-4   Comparative GDP CAGRs for Period 1980 to 2008 (Source: United Nations)

The growth of China and India created external pressures and triggered a tremendous surge in commodity prices and demand for related industrial products. Mexico, Saudi Arabia, Mexico, Indonesia, and Norway all benefitted from that surge as the value of their natural resources more than doubled in a 5-year period. Finding some of tomorrow's best investment opportunities will be a result of understanding and anticipating how the global economy evolves, which countries lead that growth, and which experience the greatest structural shifts. Exhibit 4-5 shows how important a successful economic and political context is to a country's population. It compares GDP per capita of the United States and Japan to some other East Asian countries. By 1900, there was a clear gap between the United States and Japan relative to China, Indonesia, and India. That gap got wider over the course of that century. It appears the gap is in the process of narrowing, which is somewhat evident in Exhibit 4-5. According to United Nations data, Japan's per capita GDP is still below levels reached in the early 1990s. Since 2001, China's per capita GDP more than tripled, achieving a compound annual growth rate of almost 18%. China has been investing in its infrastructure and population, while expanding the amount of decision points in its economy. Japan is using its savings to fund it borrowings and economic decision making remains fairly concentrated. Subsequent chapters determine how and if that trend will continue.

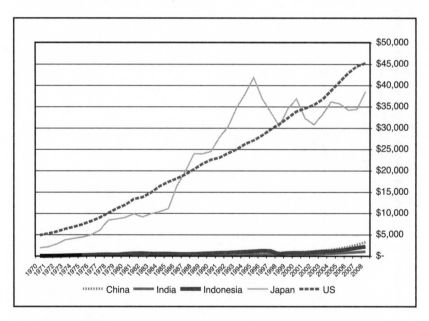

Exhibit 4-5   Per Capita Income Since 1970 in U.S. Dollars (Source: United Nations)

Exhibit 4-6 serves as a reminder that recessions are tied to many factors. It highlights the prominent factors behind recessions and depressions in the United States dating back to 1929. The most severe are caused by financial excesses, especially too much debt.

Exhibit 4-6 Recessions in United States (Source: *A Short History of the Global Economy Since 1800* by Alam, M. Shahid., 2003 and *False Economy* by Alan Beattie, Riverhead Books, 2009, pp 10–11 for Argentina and comparative data)

Name	Dates	Duration (Months)	Time Since Previous Recession (Months)	Peak Unemployment	GDP Decline (Peak to Trough)	Characteristics
Great Depression	Aug 1929–Mar 1933	3 years 7 months	1 year 9 months	35.3% (1933)	–26.7%	Stock markets crashed worldwide. A banking collapse took place in the United States. Extensive new tariffs and other factors contributed to an extremely deep depression. Although sometimes dated to last until World War II, the U.S. economy was growing again by 1933, and technically the United States was not in recession from 1933 to 1937.
Recession of 1937	May 1937–June 1938	1 year 1 month	4 years 2 months	26.4% (1938)	–3.4%	The Recession of 1937 is only considered minor when compared to the Great Depression but is otherwise among the worst recessions of the twentieth century. Three explanations are offered for the recession: Tight fiscal policy from an attempt to balance the budget after the expansion of the New Deal caused recession; tight monetary policy from the Federal Reserve caused the recession, or declining profits for businesses led to a reduction in investment.

Exhibit 4-6 Recessions in United States (Source: *A Short History of the Global Economy Since 1800* by Alam, M. Shahid, 2003 and *False Economy* by Alan Beattie, Riverhead Books, 2009, pp 10–11 for Argentina and comparative data)

Name	Dates	Duration (Months)	Time Since Previous Recession (Months)	Peak Unemployment	GDP Decline (Peak to Trough)	Characteristics
Recession of 1945	Feb–Oct 1945	8 months	6 years 8 months	5.2% (1946)	−12.7%	The decline in government spending at the end of World War II led to an enormous drop in gross domestic product making this technically a recession. This was the result of demobilization and the shift from a wartime to peacetime economy. The post-war years were unusual in a number of ways (unemployment was never high), and this era might be considered a "sui generis [unique] end-of-the-war recession".
Recession of 1949	Nov 1948 – Oct 1949	11 months	3 years 1 month	7.9% (Oct 1949)	−1.7%	The 1948 recession was a brief economic downturn; forecasters at the time expected much worse, perhaps influenced by the poor economy in their recent lifetime. The recession began shortly after President Truman's Fair Deal economic reforms. The recession also followed a period of monetary tightening.

Exhibit 4-6   Recessions in United States (Source: *A Short History of the Global Economy Since 1800* by Alam, M. Shahid., 2003 and *False Economy* by Alan Beattie, Riverhead Books, 2009, pp 10–11 for Argentina and comparative data)

Name	Dates	Duration (Months)	Time Since Previous Recession (Months)	Peak Unemployment	GDP Decline (Peak to Trough)	Characteristics
Recession of 1953	July 1953 –May 1954	10 months	3 years 9 months	6.1% (Sep 1954)	–2.6%	After a post-Korean War inflationary period, more funds were transferred to national security. In 1951, the Federal Reserve reasserted its independence from the U.S. Treasury, and in 1952 the Federal Reserve changed monetary policy to be more restrictive because of fears of further inflation or of a bubble forming.
Recession of 1958	Aug 1957–April 1958	8 months	3 years 3 months	7.5% (July 1958)	–3.1%	Monetary policy was tightened during the 2 years preceding 1957, followed by an easing of policy at the end of 1957. The budget balance resulted in a change in budget surplus of 0.8% of GDP in 1957 to a budget deficit of 0.6% of GDP in 1958, and then to 2.6% of GDP in 1959.
Recession of 1960–61	Apr 1960–Feb 1961	10 months	2 years	7.1% (May 1961)	–1.6%	Another primarily monetary recession occurred after the Federal Reserve began raising interest rates in 1959. The government switched from deficit (or 2.6% in 1959) to surplus (of 0.1% in 1960). When the economy emerged from this short recession, it began the second longest period of growth in NBER history.

Exhibit 4-6 Recessions in United States (Source: *A Short History of the Global Economy Since 1800* by Alam, M. Shahid., 2003 and *False Economy* by Alan Beattie, Riverhead Books, 2009, pp 10–11 for Argentina and comparative data)

Name	Dates	Duration (Months)	Time Since Previous Recession (Months)	Peak Unemployment	GDP Decline (Peak to Trough)	Characteristics
Recession of 1969–70	Dec 1969–Nov 1970	11 months	8 years 10 months	6.1% (Dec 1970)	–0.6%	The relatively mild 1969 recession followed a lengthy expansion. At the end of the expansion inflation was rising, possibly a result of increased deficits. This relatively mild recession coincided with an attempt to start closing the budget deficits of the Vietnam War (fiscal tightening) and the Federal Reserve raising interest rates (monetary tightening).
1973–75 recession	Nov 1973–Mar 1975	1 year 4 months	3 years	9.0% (May 1975)	–3.2%	A quadrupling of oil prices by OPEC coupled with high government spending because of the Vietnam War led to stagflation in the United States. The period was also marked by the 1973 oil crisis and the 1973–1974 stock market crash. The period is remarkable for rising unemployment coinciding with rising inflation.

Exhibit 4-6   Recessions in United States (Source: *A Short History of the Global Economy Since 1800* by Alam, M. Shahid., 2003 and *False Economy* by Alan Beattie, Riverhead Books, 2009, pp 10–11 for Argentina and comparative data)

Name	Dates	Duration (Months)	Time Since Previous Recession (Months)	Peak Unemployment	GDP Decline (Peak to Trough)	Characteristics
1980 recession	Jan–July 1980	6 months	4 years 10 months	7.8% (July 1980)	–2.2%	The NBER considers a short recession to have occurred in 1980, followed by a short period of growth and then a deep recession. Unemployment remained relatively elevated in between recessions. The recession began as the Federal Reserve, under Paul Volcker, raised interest rates dramatically to fight the inflation of the 1970s. The early '80s are sometimes referred to as a "double-dip" or "W-shaped" recession.
Early 1980s recession	July 1981–Nov 1982	1 year 4 months	1 year	10.8% (Nov 1982)	–2.7%	The Iranian Revolution sharply increased the price of oil worldwide in 1979, causing the 1979 energy crisis. This was caused by the new regime in power in Iran, which exported oil at inconsistent intervals and at a lower volume, forcing prices up. Tight monetary policy in the United States to control inflation led to another recession. The changes were made largely because of inflation carried over from the previous decade because of the 1973 oil crisis and the 1979 energy crisis.

Exhibit 4-6   Recessions in United States (Source: *A Short History of the Global Economy Since 1800* by Alam, M. Shahid., 2003 and *False Economy* by Alan Beattie, Riverhead Books, 2009, pp 10–11 for Argentina and comparative data)

Name	Dates	Duration (Months)	Time Since Previous Recession (Months)	Peak Unemployment	GDP Decline (Peak to Trough)	Characteristics
Early 1990s recession	July 1990–Mar 1991	8 months	7 years 8 months	7.8% (June 1992)	–1.4%	After the lengthy peacetime expansion of the 1980s, inflation began to increase, and the Federal Reserve responded by raising interest rates from 1986 to 1989. This weakened but did not stop growth, but some combination of the subsequent 1990 oil price shock, the debt accumulation of the 1980s, new banking regulations following the S&L Crisis, and growing consumer pessimism combined with the weakened economy to produce a brief recession.
Early 2000s recession	Mar–Nov 2001	8 months	10 years	6.3% (June 2003)	–0.3%	The 1990s were the longest period of growth in American history. The collapse of the speculative dot-com bubble, a fall in business outlays and investments, and the September 11th attacks, brought the decade of growth to an end. Despite these major shocks, the recession was brief and shallow. Without the September 11th attacks, the economy might have avoided a recession altogether.

Exhibit 4-6   Recessions in United States (Source: *A Short History of the Global Economy Since 1800* by Alam, M. Shahid., 2003 and *False Economy* by Alan Beattie, Riverhead Books, 2009, pp 10–11 for Argentina and comparative data)

Name	Dates	Duration (Months)	Time Since Previous Recession (Months)	Peak Unemployment	GDP Decline (Peak to Trough)	Characteristics
Late 2000s recession	Dec 2007–?	TBD	6 years 1 month	10.2% (Oct 2009)	–3.9%	The subprime mortgage crisis led to the collapse of the U.S. housing bubble. Falling housing-related assets contributed to a global financial crisis, even as oil and food prices soared. The crisis led to the failure or collapse of many of the United States' largest financial institutions: Bear Stearns, Fannie Mae, Freddie Mac, Lehman Brothers, and AIG and a crisis in the automobile industry. The government responded with an unprecedented $700 billion bank bailout and $787 billion fiscal stimulus package. By July 2009, a growing number of economists believed that the recession might have ended. This view was bolstered with the initial estimate of a 3.5% rise in the GDP (Q3 09). As is often the case at the end of a recession, unemployment is still rising. The National Bureau of Economic Research will not make this official determination for some time.

Endnotes

[1] Singapore became a self-governing state in 1959. Following a 1962 Merger Referendum, it joined Malaya together with Sabah and Sarawak to form the Federation of Malaysia on September 16, 1963, but was expelled two years later. Singapore became an independent state on August 9, 1965.

5

Bull and Bear Markets

Bears and Bulls make money; Pigs get slaughtered.
Wall Street Wisdom

Risks posed by the leveraging discussed in Chapter 1, "The Great Leveraging," were not often reflected in the financial markets. The duration of leverage cycles appears to be at least as great as that of a structural bull and bear equity market period. Although they are not always in sync, the shift from a period of leveraging to deleveraging impacts the outlook for equities and other financial assets.

This chapter focuses on establishing a better understanding of the characteristics of structural bull and bear markets. Equity markets move in cycles formed by the random movement of daily activity. Those cycles almost always last more than one year and frequently more than two years. The phase when the markets trend up and provide investors with positive returns is called a bull market, and the phase when the markets trend down and usually generate negative returns for investors is called a bear market.

Determining the cycle of the market is important. Accurately assessing the environment means a greater likelihood of establishing an effective investment strategy and achieving attractive returns. It also means there is a greater likelihood of avoiding large losses. In bear markets, investor expectations often turn out to be unrealistic and entail greater than desired risk. During a bear market, gains prove much more illusive, and the resulting losses are difficult to replace. Investment math proves this point and underscores the importance of identifying the market cycle—any loss requires a percentage gain of greater magnitude just to get back to even. For instance, a 20% loss in one period requires a gain of 25% in the next period just to get back to even, and that does not even include the time value of money.

So, is it a bull market or a bear market? The answer to that question is a critical part of the equation in developing an investment strategy and the appropriate asset allocation because it defines the markets' environment and the near-to-intermediate term outlook. If the market assessment is correct, then the investment strategy is much more effective and more profitable. This chapter focuses on equity markets.

The phrase bull market or bear market is most often applied to equity markets. For equities, a bull market means equity prices are trending higher, and a bear market means prices are trending lower. For fixed income markets, a bull market phase is when interest rates are trending lower. Rising interest rates mean that the value of fixed income bonds already issued is declining as newly issued bonds yield more. Commodity bull markets, like equity bull markets are apparent when prices are trending higher and are considered bear markets when prices are trending lower. A currency is in a bull market when it is appreciating against other currencies, and it is in a bear market when it is depreciating against other currencies. This chapter focuses on equity markets.

Characteristics of an Equity Bull Market

For equities, most bull markets start after valuation levels have been depressed by prior bear market, whereas bull markets end with higher valuation levels. That means that investors are usually much more skeptical about the outlook at the beginning of a bull market than they are at the end. Looking at a standard method of valuing equities, we can say that a combination of the following happens during the course of the bull market:

1. The assumed risk premium declines.

2. Growth expectations rise.

3. The risk-free rate falls.

Some bull markets are part of a longer structural bull market, and that is the case with some discussed in this chapter. Structural bull markets usually start after prolonged periods of negative, or at least, indifferent market performance and in tandem with strong economic recoveries. Those economic recoveries are often accompanied by an introduction of new technologies, and the combination helps build investor confidence in the durability of the economic recovery and bull market. An equity bull market also often coincides with periods when a country's currency is stable or strengthening, and it frequently follows periods of more stressful global turmoil. One dangerous lesson investors usually learn in a bull market is to treat any dip in the market as a buying opportunity. The longer the duration of the bull market, the more entrenched that behavior becomes and leaves most much less well prepared for a coming bear market.

Characteristics of an Equity Bear Market

Just as bull markets start at lower valuation levels reflecting a more skeptical investor psychology, bear markets usually start as valuations peak and investor psychology turns almost euphoric. Investors become confident and show little fear, and their ranks swell as more people seek to participate in the "winning" game. This trend leads many seasoned market observers to monitor retail investor behavior. The more active retail investors become, the more likely the market is close to a peak. Looking at that same valuation equation, here is what happens in a bear market:

1. The assumed risk premium rises; investors become more risk averse.

2. Growth expectations decline; investors become more cautious and skeptical.

3. The risk free rate becomes less relevant to the equation.

There are often environmental changes facilitating the euphoria. One such change involves leverage. Investors are more willing to use leverage for investment purposes as a bull market ages, and institutions are more willing to supply the leverage as the recent history shows little loss experience on the part of the more aggressive suppliers of leverage and often much greater near-term profitability. The longer a bull market rages, the more readily available resources become to allow participation in the market. So, one characteristic causing a bear market to be deep and protracted is the snap back caused by an unwinding of leverage. Another environmental change involves the regulatory climate: Often bear markets are preceded by, or coincide with, deleterious regulatory decisions, and, in turn, they are the harbinger of periods of extreme economic difficulty such as recessions and rising inflation. Finally, there is political turmoil, and it usually deepens and prolongs a bear market, but it is rarely the catalyst for one.

Overview: We define bear and bull markets for equities in two ways. The first uses prices and gives a sense of the shorter cycle historic rhythms of the markets. The longer secular look is based on valuation, inflation, and other factors. Since 1901, Global Financial Data's information suggests the S&P 500 and its predecessors were in a bull market 66% of the time and in a bear market 34% of the time. This definition uses cyclical price peaks and troughs.

Crestmont Research takes a longer view and looks at bull and bear markets on a structural basis. It suggests there were four complete bear and bull markets since 1901 in the United States. In aggregate, the market was in a bull phase more often than a bear phase at 54 years to 46 years. Right now, the Dow is in its fifth bear market. The determining factors used by Crestmont are valuation peaks and troughs based on the S&P 500 P/E, along with inflation trends and other analysis. For the shorter cycles of Global Financial Data, the determining factors were price peaks and troughs. We used that data set because we believe it fairly identifies the various cycles of many of the global equity markets. The combination of the two data sets provides a useful backdrop from which to better understand the forces leading to the beginning and end of bull and bear markets.

The good news is that a bull market tends to last longer than a bear market. The bad news is the typical (median) price-driven bear market eliminated 75% of the gains realized by the prior bull market. Of the S&P 500's 22 bear markets since 1901, six eliminated more than 100% of the gains of the prior bull market, and the mildest two bear markets eliminated less than 20% of the prior bull market's gains. Those bull markets averaged less than 6 years, whereas the average bear market lasted just under 3 1/4 years. The median bull market gained 77%, whereas the median bear market lost 35%. Relative to a bull market, the impact of the same percentage change in a bear market is greater: the median loss of 35% requires a gain of 54% to break even. Again, this is the investment math and a critical reason to be sensitive to the market's phase.

The Great Bull Markets

The Roaring Twenties: 1921–1929

Following World War I, a bout with inflation, and a quick depression, *Modern Times* visited the United States. New technologies changed the way we live. Automobiles and radios were new to the market and market valuations were low. Starting with 1921, markets would post gains in 7 of the next 8 years. The S&P 500 Index would start with a valuation of five times earnings and peak around 28 times earnings, and prices would rise 490%. Crestmont Research places the end of this bull in 1928 because the inflation trend turns the wrong way (up) in 1929, whereas the market peaked in September 1929.

For Europe, the period was generally good for equity markets; just not as robust as the one experienced in the United States. The meaningful reduction in global turmoil following World War I was clearly beneficial. In a bull market lasting over 7 years, the MSCI price index rose 158%. Of the major European markets, France was the most robust, rising 427%.

The Big Bounce: 1932–1937

The period from 1932 to 1937 was less of a great bull market and more of a bounce. It is included here as a reminder that even gloomy periods offer investment opportunities, and that avoiding losses should be one of the primary objectives of any investor. In July 1932, the Dow bottomed at 41.42, and that would be the low for the period following the establishment of the Federal Reserve System. From there, it would more than double in the next year and rise 118%. It would drop back 23% over the next 3 months and then start rising again. Over the next 3 1/2 years it would rise 132% and reach 194.4. So, over the course of 4 years and 9 months, the Dow rose 370% yet still only reached about half the peak level attained during *The Roaring Twenties*. Coincidentally, this bounce started about the same time the U.S. last great deleveraging resulted in a decline in debt to GDP.

The Fabulous Fifties: Europe: 1949–1961, United States: 1949–1956

This post–World War II market started with a stronger footing than the one following World War I. Some markets commenced their bull leg in 1946, whereas others waited until 1949. Oddly, the UK's performance would be the most volatile. Japan's market would rise up, but in a more volatile fashion as well.

For the broad European market, the bull started in November 1949 and ended in May 1961. During that period, the MSCI European price index rose 463%, providing a compound annual price increase of 14.3%. The rebuilding of more productive economies and the benefits of the Marshall Plan were all ingredients contributing to the strong performance.

For the United States, it was the first of the three major bull market cycles to occur after World War II. It started in 1946 and it was the longest in duration, lasting almost 7 years. During that period, the S&P Composite Index rose 267%, and the market's P/E rose from 10 to 18. During June 1949, the Dow Jones Industrial Index reached a low valuation of 6.8 times earnings and yielded 7.5%. This bull started the same year the Korean War started. It would grow stronger after that war ended and 7 of its 8 years would be up markets. During the cycle, inflation stayed around 1%, and the economy was generally strong, as shown in Exhibit 5-1. Domestic auto output has more than doubled and corporate profitability grew by more than 10% annually.

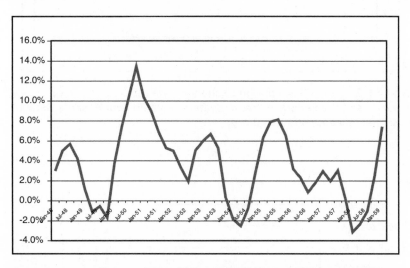

Exhibit 5-1   Real Gross National Product: 1949–1959 (Source: U.S. Department of Commerce: Bureau of Economic Analysis; 2008 Federal Reserve Bank of St. Louis: research.stlouisfed.org)

The Rising Sun—Japan's Great Bull Market: 1974–1989

The great Japanese bull market started in 1974 and lasted until the end of 1989; a period of just more than 15 years. During the period, the Nikkei price index rose over ten times, for a compounded annual price increase of 58%. One catalyst pushing the market higher was a strengthening currency (Exhibit 5-2) and a strong economy (Exhibit 5-3).

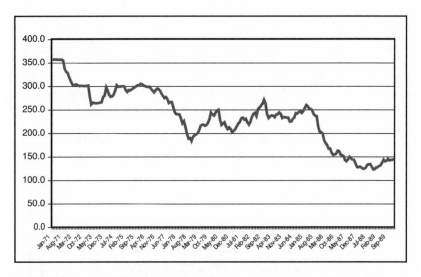

Exhibit 5-2   Japan/U.S. Foreign Exchange Rate (Source: Board of Governors of the Federal Reserve System; 2008 Federal Reserve Bank of St. Louis: research.stlouisfed.org)

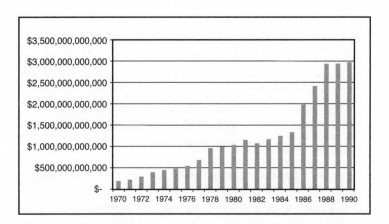

Exhibit 5-3   Japan's GDP ($): 1970–1990 (Source: World Bank)

Many factors drove the Japanese market higher, but initially the forces were just good, strong fundamentals. The Japanese economy was not as severely affected by the inflation of the 1970s as other developed economies. Indeed, its currency began a process of gaining strength against the dollar in 1974. At that time, its weaker currency was a competitive advantage for a country dependent on exports. That advantage helped the Japanese economy double in size between 1975 and 1980, and double again by 1986.

Between 1975 and 1986, the Nikkei 225 rose 250% (Exhibit 5-4). In 1986, the beginnings of an equity market and real estate market euphoria were evident. Fundamental metrics eventually became irrelevant. Over the next 3 years, the Nikkei 225 would almost triple. Commercial real estate values would increase almost 250%, and residential real estate prices would almost double (Exhibit 5-5). The pace of the increase was not sustainable, and as it turned out, the valuations could not be supported. Like other great bull markets, the Japanese one started from a foundation of solid and improving fundamentals that eventually morphed into a euphoria that set the stage for one of the longest bear markets.

Exhibit 5-4   Nikkei 225: 1970–2007

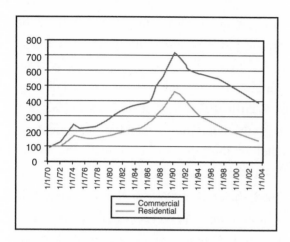

Exhibit 5-5   Japanese Real Estate Price Indexes: 1970–2004

A New Beginning and the End of the Malaise: 1982–1987

This was not the longest nor the greatest of the post World War II bull market cycles in the United States, but it is probably the best known. It came at the end of The Great Inflation and coincided with the bursting of the energy bubbles, and it would be a period that would precede the fall of communism. When it started, investor psychology remained extremely skeptical following a 16-year period that saw valuations trend lower. The S&P 500 was trading at 7.0 times earnings, and the S&P 500 traded under 8.0 times earnings. On a forward basis, the S&P 500 traded at less than 6.5 times earnings at times in 1982, as shown in Exhibit 5-6.

The beginning of the bull market was supported by a strengthening dollar (Exhibit 5-7), which had lost a great deal of value during the decade of the 1970s.

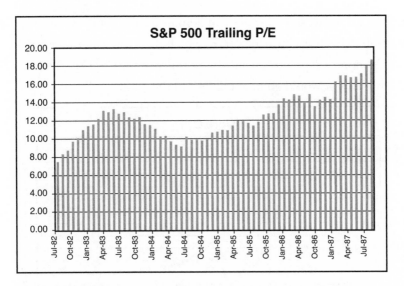

Exhibit 5-6   S&P 500 Trailing P/E: 1982–1987 (Source: Global Financial Data)

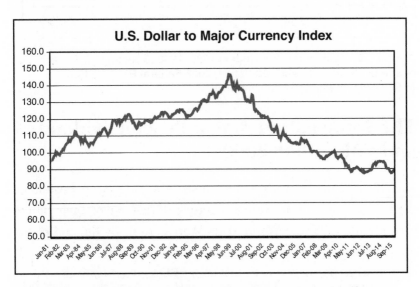

Exhibit 5-7   Trade Weighted Dollar Index—Major Currencies (Source: Board of Governors of the Federal Reserve System; 2008 Federal Reserve Bank of St. Louis: research.stlouisfed.org)

Helping support a stronger dollar and stronger market was an end to the inflationary pressures plaguing the country through the 1970s and into the early 1980s (Exhibit 5-8). Those pressures would continue to abate into the next millennium. The bull market was interrupted by the Crash of 1987, which saw the largest one day drop (in nominal points) of all time, and the S&L Crisis. Despite these hurdles, it would go much higher in the 1990s.

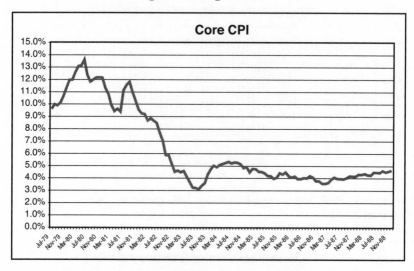

Exhibit 5-8   Consumer Price Index: 1980–1988 (Source: U.S. Department of Labor: Bureau of Labor Statistics; 2008 Federal Reserve Bank of St. Louis: research.stlouisfed.org)

The Information Age, a Peace Dividend, and Y2K: 1990–2000

This bull market cycle lasted almost a decade. At its beginning, the Internet and CNBC were just getting started and on their path to ubiquity. In 1995, the World Wide Web started. By the end of the decade, e-mail was a common form of communication, and cell phones were on their way to becoming PDAs. Geopolitically, things seemed stable after Desert Storm. Energy prices would fall 50% before bottoming, and job growth was robust.

From start to finish, the market rose almost 400% with a sharp correction in 1998. That correction was tied to financial problems including the implosion of Long Term Capital Management, which followed a series of events including the acquisition of Salomon

Brothers by Travelers, a currency crisis that depressed Asian economies and markets, and the default of the Russian financial system. Like in other bull markets, rising valuations were a common characteristic, and at its end, valuations were higher than ever before—42 times trailing earnings for the S&P 500 and 200 times estimated earnings for the NASDAQ. The latter would double in the course of a year on its way to the peak. It would come down almost as fast, as shown in Exhibit 5-9.

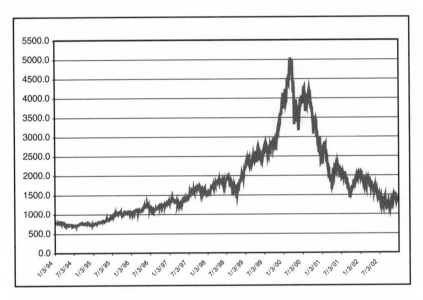

Exhibit 5-9   NASDAQ Index: 1994–2002 (Source: Global Financial Data)

In 1999, economic activity was robust and exaggerated by the event called Y2K, which caused a tremendous amount of capital spending to be accelerated, leaving an unanticipated economic hole in the following years. It also forced the Fed to inject $50 billion of additional funds into the banking system. From an investment perspective, it was not just that valuations were too high or that the strong economic activity was unsustainable; there was also a great deal of corporate malfeasance in the form of overstated financial results. Indeed, some accounting standards also enabled financial statements to be presented in their most favorable light.

The Big Bear Markets

Almost Total Destruction: Germany: May 1918–October 1922

Germany experienced perhaps the most destructive bear market of the past century. Its stock market lost more than 98% of its value. The decline came as World War I ended and coincided with a period of hyperinflation and complete debasement of the currency. Monetary policy was loose. At the end of 1918, a dollar was worth 4 to 5 marks. On November 23, 1923, the exchange rate reached 4 trillion marks for a dollar. Bank interest rates reached 900%. Before that point, the equity market lost almost all its value, just as the German currency had already lost most of its value. The period was marked by a period of loose monetary policy and political unrest.

The Big Bear—The Great Depression: 1929–1932

The worst of all bear markets in the United States started in September 1929. After peaking at 381.17 on September 3, the Dow Jones Industrial Index bottomed on July 8, 1932, when the index price was 41.22 for a loss of more than 89% of its value (Exhibit 5-10). The Dow would not pass its previous peak until November 23, 1954, when it closed at 382.74—more than 30 years later.

The causes of the market crash and the ensuing bear market were many and included the euphoria that masked a weakening economy and pushed valuations to record highs at the time, reaching 28 times earnings. By the time the Dow bottomed in 1932, investors were willing to pay only 8 times earnings, a major revision. Other causes for the crash included bad regulatory decisions, which exacerbated an already fragile situation triggered by the Crash. Specifically, tight money policies and protectionist legislation made things much worse. The banking system came under extreme duress during and following the Crash, and thousands of banks ultimately failed (Exhibit 5-11) leading to a bank holiday after the market bottomed and eventually the formation of the Federal Deposit Insurance Corporation (FDIC). The global economy was also weak, and the beginnings of the political turmoil that led to World War II were becoming evident. The pressure put on the economy was deflation, and the first countries to take measures to reinflate their currencies were the first to experience economic recoveries. The United States economy did not retrace its 1929 peak until 1940 when the demands of the pending war provided the necessary economic stimulus (Exhibit 5-12). For most of the decade of the 1930s, government expenditures were usually more than twice the size of revenues, but nowhere hear the current level of spending to GDP.

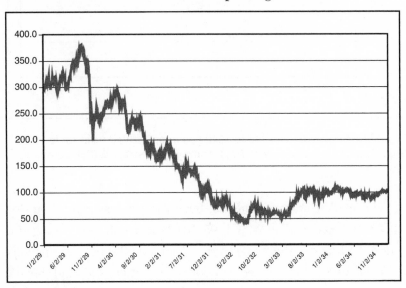

Exhibit 5-10   Dow Jones Industrial Index: 1929–1933 (Source: Global Financial Data)

Exhibit 5-11   Number of Banks and Bank Suspensions: 1929–1934 (Source: *Historical Statistics of the United States: Colonial Times to 1970*, p. 912, Table V 20–30)

Year	Number as of 12-31	Suspensions
1929	24,633	659
1930	22,773	1,350
1931	19,970	2,293
1932	18,397	1,453
1933	15,015	4,000
1934	16,096	57

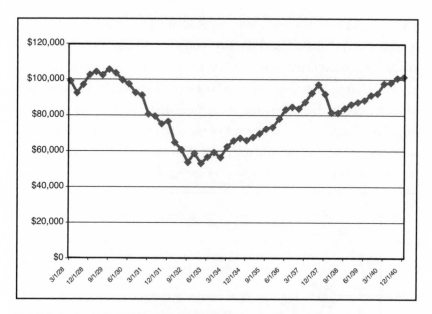

Exhibit 5-12   U.S. GNP: 1928 to 1940 (Source: Derived from Table 16.1, *Business Cycle Indicators, Vol. II,* **Geoffrey H. Moore, ed. [Princeton, 1961], p. 133)**

The market crash was global, but relatively less painful outside the United States. The MSCI World Return fell 71% during this period. In Europe, the market price declined 62% between January 1929 and June 1932. France was down 75%, Italy 65%, and the UK 52%. The German market was already experiencing volatile times, and this particular bear market started earlier—in May 1927, and like the others, bottomed in 1932. The timing of the Canadian bear market almost mirrored that of the United States and the Canadian market fell 80%. Australia's bear market started in February 1929 and ended in August 1931 after a decline of 46%.

The Second Bear of the 1930s: 1937–1938

Unlike the other major bear markets following the formation of the Federal Reserve System, this one was not tied to the end of a period of euphoria but instead was more the beginning of a period of growing disappointment. The foundation for the bear market was set by expectations of continued economic growth, lofty market valuation, and the growing prospects of a global conflict. In March 1937, the Dow Jones Industrial Average valuation reached 19.3 times trailing earnings. As the Dow drifted lower over the next 5 years, its decline would be principally driven by a downward revaluation of the Dow to 12.0 times earnings (Exhibit 5-13).

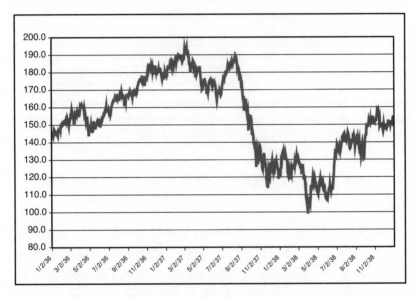

Exhibit 5-13   Dow Jones Industrial Index: 1936–1938 (Source: Global Financial Data)

The economy began to decline again in 1938, as shown in Exhibit 5-14. Unemployment rose to high levels and would peak at 19%. Concerns began to grow that the New Deal programs were insufficient to trigger an economic recovery. The onset of World War II provided the catalyst and the jobs. The policy mistakes included raising taxes and tighter monetary policy. In less than 13 months, the Dow declined 49% and then surged 61% over the next 7 months. From that point, the Dow would fall 41% over the next 3 1/2 years before setting a lower low of 92.92 on April 28, 1942.

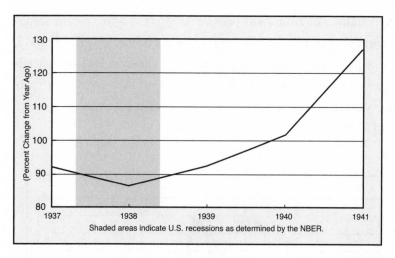

Exhibit 5-14   U.S. Gross National Product: 1937–1941 (Source: U.S. Department of Commerce: Bureau of Economic Analysis; 2008 Federal Reserve Bank of St. Louis: research.stlouisfed.org)

The World War II Effect: Various Periods Starting in the 1940s

The physical destruction of World War II could not be captured in the equity markets, but there was some reflection of it. During and after the war, the Japanese market fell 35% from October 1942 to August 1946. France's market declined 46% between August 1944 and July 1945. Italy's market plunged 53% between December 1944 and March 1946. The German market fell the most—down 80% between February 1946 and August 1948. The UK market fell 29% between January 1947 and November 1949.

The Nifty Fifty: 1973–1974

The forces driving the market lower included the narrowness of the market advance. It was considered a two-tier market, and it was the era of the Nifty Fifty. Large cap growth stocks generated strong earnings growth, and investors valued them in a way that suggested they expected that growth to continue. Like most high P/E stocks, a day of reckoning came and their valuations plummeted. At the precipice, there was little concern about the downside as valuations were high by any standard, as shown in Exhibit 5-15.

Exhibit 5-15   Morgan Guaranty P/E Ratios and Annualized Returns

	1972 P/E	Annualized Return	
Polaroid	90.7	–14.68	
McDonald's	85.7	10.50	
MGIC Investment	83.3	–6.84	(1.41)
Walt Disney	81.6	8.97	
Baxter Travenol	78.5	10.10	
Intl Flavors & Fragrances	75.8	5.66	
Avon Products	65.4	6.04	
Emery Air Freight	62.1	–1.37	(-0.16)
Johnson & Johnson	61.9	13.35	
Digital Equipment	60.0	0.93	(7.14)
Kresge (now Kmart)	54.3	–1.07	
Simplicity Pattern	53.1	–1.47	(-1.32)
AMP	51.8	11.17	(11.92)
Black & Decker	50.5	2.45	
Schering	50.4	13.19	
American Hospital Supply	50.0	12.36	(5.16)
Schlumberger	49.5	10.37	
Burroughs	48.8	–1.64	
Xerox	48.8	0.89	
Eastman Kodak	48.2	1.72	
Coca-Cola	47.6	13.15	
Texas Instruments	46.3	11.27	
Eli Lilly	46.0	13.14	
Merck	45.9	14.27	
Upjohn	41.1	9.95	(10.98)
Chesebrough Ponds	41.0	10.96	(6.55)
Minnesota Mining (3M)	40.8	9.78	
American Express	39.0	10.30	

Exhibit 5-15   Morgan Guaranty P/E Ratios and Annualized Returns

	1972 P/E	Annualized Return	
American Home Products	38.9	13.13	
Schlitz Brewing	38.7	6.68	(–0.67)
Halliburton	38.3	3.19	
IBM	37.4	9.68	
Lubrizol	36.9	7.62	
J.C. Penny	34.1	4.83	
Squibb	33.9	14.21	(10.26)
Procter & Gamble	32.0	11.94	
Anheuser-Busch	31.9	13.55	
Sears Roebuck	30.8	6.94	
Heublein	30.1	14.66	(4.20)
PepsiCo	29.3	15.55	
Pfizer	29.0	16.99	
Bristol-Myers	27.6	15.35	
General Electric	26.1	15.57	
Revlon	26.1	12.40	(6.05)
Phillip Morris	25.9	17.68	
Gillette	25.9	14.12	
Louisiana Land & Exploration	25.6	4.91	(8.54)
Dow Chemical	25.5	10.80	
First National City	22.4	13.36	(12.11)
ITT	16.3	9.99	
S&P 500	19.2	12.01	

The preceding tables depicting "The Nifty Fifty" come from an article by Jeff Fesenmaier and Gary Smith of Pomona College called "The Nifty-Fifty Re-Revisited" (http://www.economics.pomona.edu/GarySmith/Nifty50/Nifty50.html). They note the stocks with two performance brackets were ones involved in mergers or buyouts. Their first performance number assumes proceeds from the sale then invested in the surviving firm and the second price (parenthetical) assumes the funds were reinvested in the remaining Nifty Fifty.

In 1974, IBM would fall to 12 times earnings, and McDonalds would hit 12 times earnings. The Dow Jones Industrial Index would bottom at 5.8 times earnings.

During the market decline, the economic conditions steadily deteriorated, as shown in Exhibits 5-16 through 5-19. Inflation started to rise and would eventually peak at 12% in 1975, establishing the high for the century. The Fed kept hiking the Fed Funds rate in an effort to halt the inflationary pressures. Preceding the decline in economic conditions was the decision to end the Bretton Woods Agreement and take the dollar off of the gold standard. That started a period of prolonged dollar devaluation resulting in a decline of almost 25% of its value. Finally, this bear market coincided with an energy crisis, which brought with it long lines at gas stations, shortages, and resource allocation. It would foreshadow a constant challenge facing the United States for years to come.

It was also a period of tremendous political upheaval. The Watergate hearings gained tremendous momentum in July 1973, when the existence of White House tapes was disclosed by John Dean.

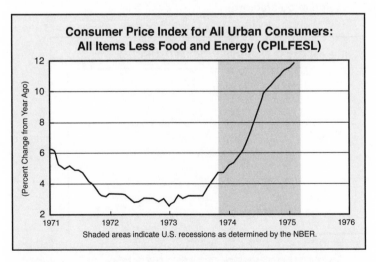

Exhibit 5-16   Consumer Price Index: 1971–1976 (Source: U.S. Department of Labor: Bureau of Labor Statistics; 2008 Federal Reserve Bank of St. Louis: research.stlouisfed.org)

President Nixon resigned but only after many members of his administration had been forced out. The Vietnam War was coming to a close and the Yom Kippur War evidenced growing tensions in the Middle East.

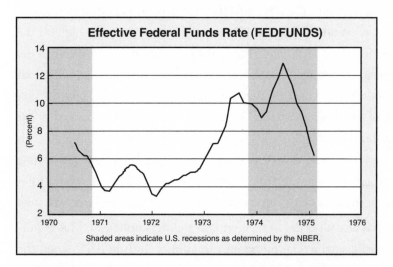

Exhibit 5-17   Effective Federal Funds Rate: 1970–1976 (Source: Board of Governors of the Federal Reserve System; 2008 Federal Reserve Bank of St. Louis: research.stlouisfed.org)

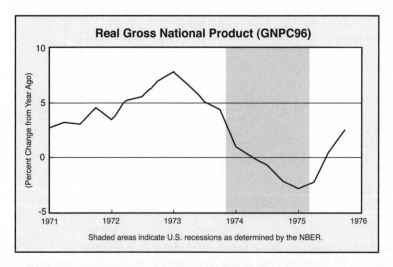

Exhibit 5-18   Real Gross National Product: 1971–1976 (Source: U.S. Department of Commerce: Bureau of Economic Analysis; 2008 Federal Reserve Bank of St. Louis: research.stlouisfed.org)

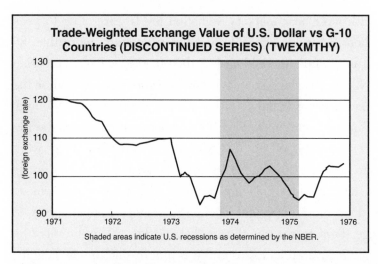

Exhibit 5-19   Trade-Weighted Dollar Index: 1971–1976 (Source: Board of Governors of the Federal Reserve System; 2008 Federal Reserve Bank of St. Louis: research.stlouisfed.org)

The Lost Decade for Japan: December 1989 to Present

The Japanese Bear market was initially known to many as the "lost decade", but the more appropriate phrase is the "two lost decades." From the peak of the bull market at the end of 1989, Japan's bear market stretched to 2010. It was the longest of all the bear markets during the last half century, and it brought with it a price decline of 80% between the peak and the bottom in March 2009. As of this writing, the Japanese market seems to be in an endless bear market. The continued pressure makes the concept of an Echo Bubble more relevant because the subsequent rebounds were always false starts. Those subsequent rallies often pull investors back into the market as their duration grows, whereas the following subsequent declines were not always of the same absolute magnitude of the previous decline, but their impact on investor confidence was just as great leaving a weaker foundation for the next rally.

As with most bear markets, valuation levels were close to peak levels when it started. The Nikkei index was trading more than 80 times earnings and was yielding less than 0.50%. A bigger problem for the Nikkei was the role of the government—"The day after the October crash, representatives of Japan's largest brokerages, Nomura, Daiwa, Yamaichi, and Nikko Securities, collectively known as the Big Four—were summoned to the Ministry of Finance. They were ordered to make a market in NTT shares and keep the Nikkei average at about the 21,000 level. Complying with this request, the brokers offered their most important clients guarantees against losses to encourage them to reenter the market. Within a few months, the Nikkei had recovered its losses and was progressing to new heights. In private, Ministry of Finance officials boasted that manipulating the stock market was simpler than controlling the foreign exchanges" (page 303 in *Devil Take the Hindmost* by Edward Chancellor, Plume Books, 2000). The problem was the government was unable to sustain the role. Unfortunately, investors expected no change, and when the Japanese government stopped supporting the market, investor interest and faith in the market were greatly diminished.

The Tech Bubble: 2000–2002

The end of the millennium brought with it a new age— the Information Age—and an accompanying euphoria that drove valuations to record levels. The Dow traded at 42.0 times earnings, and the S&P 500 reached almost 30.0 times earnings and more than 25.0 times estimated earnings. Misunderstood at the time, capital expenditures tied to Y2K represented a massive shift in corporate spending that would push economic activity forward at the expense of future activity, while creating unnecessarily large franchises to support the temporary surge in activity. Supporting the appearance of strong economic activity was corporate malfeasance and lax accounting standards.

The names of Enron, Worldcom, Adelphia, Global Crossing, and Tyco would be added to the Rogue's Gallery corporations from eras of excess. Accounting rules appeared to facilitate the excesses. Corporations issued options without accounting for them in their income statements. Pension accounting allowed for aggressive assumptions and prohibited conservative funding practices. A look at many footnotes in the annual reports of companies populating the S&P 500 showed they assumed their pension fund assets would generate returns of more than 9% annually. As a group, it appeared their pension funds were overfunded by more than $250 billion (+25%) in 1999. The 2000 Bear Market put their collective pension funds in an underfunded position, and with some moral suasion from officials of the U.S. Federal Government, their pension accounting assumptions became more conservative. Finally, the 1990s saw a surge of consolidation. Much of it was done using a method of accounting for business combinations that was discontinued around the time the bear market got started. The method was called pooling-of-interests and allowed mergers to be accounted for in a way that permitted corporations not to record the premium paid.

Summary: Exhibit 5-20 is a checklist that can help an investor determine if the equity market is more likely to be a bear market or a bull market. Not included in the table is the level of leverage. At the beginning of any structural bull market, debt levels are relatively low, while structural bear markets often start with a high level of debt that ultimately reaches a tipping point. That tipping point can be created by the absolute amount of debt, which becomes too great to support, or an unsupportable high rate of interest rates.

Exhibit 5-20   Bear and Bull Market Checklist

Factors	Bull Market	Bear Market
Valuation	Low	High
Valuation trend	Up	Down
Inflation	Stable to down	Stable to up
Domestic currency	Stable to stronger	Stable to weaker
Geopolitical risk	Stable to improving	High to extreme
Regulatory environment	Stable to loosening	Intrusive

6

Global Growth Drivers

In the late nineteenth century and the first half of the twentieth century, the United States was the main driver of the global economy. Today, other countries are sharing the locomotive role of global growth with the United States. They are developing centers of excellence that rival those of the United States, at times providing superior capabilities, competitive cost, and the supporting industries that make them attractive to both domestic and foreign players.

Following this chapter, we provide brief descriptions of three promising markets: China, which is expected to catch up with the United States as the world's largest economy sometime between 2025 and 2050, although it will continue to lag behind the United States in per capita income, innovation capability, and many other features; India, which is often lumped with China as having the largest world population and home to the most promising emerging economies; and Israel, which despite its security problems displays an amazing entrepreneurial and innovative spirit that make it a hub for new technologies and places it among the highest per capita recipients of foreign investment in the world.

All this does not necessarily imply that the United States will lose its leadership position in the global economy, or that it will cease to be a center for innovation, a global trend-setter, and one of the most stable places from which to conduct far flung operations, or that it will cease to be the foreign investment magnet it is today. Not only should the United States remain all that, it is also likely to benefit from the changes more than many other economies. Nor does the change in global balance imply that U.S. firms will lose their competitive edge as industry leaders in many segments, as viable players in others, and as creators of whole new industries and business lines. Successful U.S. firms that can take advantage of the changes in the global environment and tap the resources (including people) and markets that are globally available while avoiding the pitfalls will not only survive but also strive, as will foreign firms that leverage the innovation capabilities and other benefits of the U.S. workforce and the size and diversity of the U.S. market. Later in this book we show what it takes to be among those winners in this global economy.

Still, the evolution altering the relative size and position of the world economies is nothing short of a paradigm change. In the future, many of the largest and most sophisticated firms will hail from countries other than the United States. Those newcomers will be based not only in the traditional hubs of the European Union and Japan but increasingly in the emerging and developing economies such as China, India, South Korea, and Brazil, to name just a few. Data from the United Nations Conference on Trade and Development (UNCTAD) show that just before the end of the millennium, virtually all the top 100 "transnational corporations" were headquartered in developed nations, especially the United States, Western Europe, and Japan; however, by 2004 the list of such corporations included members from developed nations, namely Hutchison Whampoa (Hong-Kong, China), Petronas (Brazil), Singtel (Singapore), Samsung (South Korea), and CITIC Group (China). We estimate that by 2020, emerging markets will host the headquarters of more than a quarter of the top 100 transnational firms.

What does this sea-change mean to investors? Here is a partial list. First, companies that are little known today will come "from nowhere" to challenge the market leaders. Investors will have to look for those winners, not an easy challenge because they will come from unfamiliar environments not necessarily known for transparency. Second, although developed country multinationals salivate at the prospect of selling in foreign markets, they will face stiff resistance from powerful local and regional players who increasingly venture away from their home turf. This means that rosy prospects for global expansion might not always exist. Some local players, companies such as China's Huawei, have already become formidable competitors (in the case of Huawei, to Cisco) in developing country markets, such as the Middle East and North Africa, and have already made forays into developed country markets, though not always successfully. Many will seek foreign acquisitions as a way to shorten the way up and compensate for their own shortcomings. Third, the realignment in the global distribution of power will threaten firms that remain purely domestic or that have ventured abroad too little or too late. And although industries will continue to vary in their level of internationalization for years to come, it is safe to say that firms who stay behind, or retreat to domestic markets (e.g., Gateway Computers, later acquired by Taiwan's based Acer), are unlikely to fare well. Fourth, as developing economies come of age, they will provide much of the growth in consumption and production capacity. Indeed, for the first time ever, the share of developing economies in attracting foreign direct investment is rising. This trend is likely to influence everything from exchange rates to the fortunes of logistic firms who ferry goods and components along a stretched value chain. Fifth, the coming realignment will threaten the accepted wisdom regarding what role is played by whom in the global production (or service delivery) chain, creating a new business map.

The technological edge of the United States is, by-and-large, taken for granted, and that view may be supported by the R&D advantage the United States has enjoyed for so long (Exhibit 6-1). Offsetting that, however, is the decline in manufacturing activity in the economic mix, and a narrowing of its scope and range. It could undercut the capability to innovate that the United States is known for. Today, the manufacturing sector fulfills the role of an innovation engine, accounting for most of the research and development conducted in the United States. A decline in relative manufacturing might mean a relative decline in R&D capabilities, especially when

combined with the rise of innovation capabilities in other countries
and the migration of some R&D capabilities to other markets.

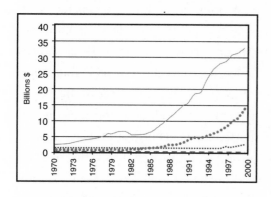

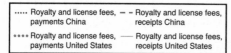

..... Royalty and license fees,   − − Royalty and license fees,
      payments China   receipts China
•••• Royalty and license fees,   ──── Royalty and license fees,
      payments United States   receipts United States

**Exhibit 6-1   Royalty and License Fees Payments and Receipts for USA
and China (Source: Reprinted from Shenkar, Oded, *The Chinese Century*,
Wharton 2004; based on data from the World Bank, 2002 World Development Indicators)**

It should not be taken for granted that it is viable in the long term
to retain high-end manufacturing and research work at home while
outsourcing other manufacturing activities to cheaper locations. One
should not assume that other nations will accept such a division of
labor for long. All indications are that they will not; nor should we
assume that firms will not notice the opportunities to produce
research at a competitive price abroad.

Exhibits 6-2 and 6-3 show the levels of R&D spending in major
economies and the rapid rise of China in terms of the percentage of
GDP devoted to R&D. The percentage growth becomes even more
meaningful when we keep in mind that, first, with growth rates of the
Chinese economy being much faster than those of Japan and the
United States, the dollar increase has been much greater, and, second, given that much R&D expenditure comes in the form of salaries
for scientists and engineers, lower wage levels in China imply much
more research for the dollar spent.

Exhibit 6-2   Global R&D Spending (Source: *R&D Magazine,* Battelle, OECD, World Bank)

	R&D PPP 2005 Billions, $	R&D PPP 2006 Billions, $	R&D PPP 2007 Billions, $	CAGR for Past 2 Years
Americas	369.07	379.69	387.64	2.5%
USA	319.6	328.9	335.5	2.5%
Asia	341.3	361.85	384.01	6.1%
China (Mainland)	124.03	136.3	149.8	9.9%
Japan	124.48	127.84	131.29	2.7%
India	36.11	38.85	41.81	7.6%
Europe	236.09	240.16	244.42	1.7%
Germany	59.68	60.21	60.75	0.9%
France	41.36	42.1	42.86	1.8%
UK	36.72	37.39	38.06	1.8%
Other	31.88	33.76	35.68	5.8%
World	978.34	1015.46	1051.75	3.7%

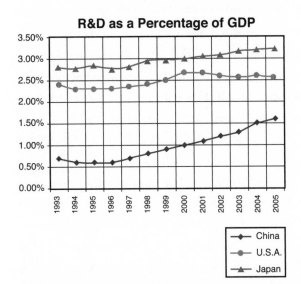

Exhibit 6-3   Growth in China's R&D Expenditures as Compared to United States and Japan (Source: *R&D Magazine,* Battelle, OECD, World Bank)

Data from multiple sources, including the Economist Intelligence Unit and the U.S. Chamber of Commerce in China, among others, indicate that other nations, among them developing countries and in particular China and India, are becoming strong contenders for locating R&D activities. In other words, the old division of labor where high value added activities were located in the developed world and the low parts of the value chain were located in the developing world, may no longer apply.

This important transformation is the result of many existing factors as well as factors that are still evolving and are likely to become more robust in future years. They are as true for manufacturing as for high-tech services such as software and sophisticated banking services. Although cost remains paramount in making the R&D location decision, it is not the only reason. Other reasons for accelerated R&D investment in emerging economies include a growing market and production base, a large pool of science and technology graduates and R&D personnel, preferential government policies, and the availability of top notch talent, as the case of Israel will illustrate.

The economic and investment ramifications are far reaching. First, tomorrow's Microsoft and Google might come from a much broader range of countries than today, and although many of them will list on U.S. markets, not all will. This will reinforce the need to be present in foreign markets where such innovators will co-list or choose as their primary listing. Second, with cost competition and imitative capabilities growing, the sheer ability to innovate will not be sufficient to guarantee performance. This implies that investors should be looking not only for tomorrow's innovators but also for today's and tomorrow's successful imitators, those who take a successful product, service, or business model into another market (for example, Ryanair and Easyjet's replication of the Southwest model in the European market). Third, companies that cannot tap and leverage new sources of innovation and new imitation opportunities, or those lacking in the capability to integrate them into their broader operations and to combine them with lower cost portions of the value chain, will languish behind.

Leveraging Comparative Advantage

Comparative advantage, a centuries old concept, states that each country has an advantage in something, be it oil, labor, favorable climate, and so forth, which provides it with an advantage over other nations in agriculture, manufacturing, or service provision. Although the capabilities that underlie comparative advantage have been extended over the years to include such things as technological skills and the potential for knowledge creation, the basic concept remains intact. What is new today is that globalization and technology permit the splitting of the various elements of the production (or service provision) process across many locations; in other words, "production factors" have become mobile, permitting firms to tap the comparative advantage available in multiple locations. Successful firms are good at leveraging the advantage embedded in various national environments to produce a unique advantage that cannot be easily replicated by others; others excel in imitating their competitors quickly and efficiently, producing a similar product at a lower cost. Both will do well in the new global economy. However many companies that are successful in their home country or region will find it difficult to expand abroad or will be unable to effectively integrate their operations with those of foreign providers and partners. Identifying global capabilities (or lack of) is hence important to investors.

Analyzing National Environments

To many investors, the prominent feature of a national environment is its economic landscape: Economic data conjures images of growing (or stagnating) markets, volatile (or stable) economies, strong (or weak) currencies, high (or low) inflation, and related information that can be interpreted as an input on firm performance, prospects for exchange rate movements, consumer spending, and so on. Although economic numbers are reviewed throughout this book, they are by no means the only information of importance to investors. Political processes, social dynamics, cultural tenets, and similiar elements of the national environment have major repercussions for economic well-being, growth, and, in turn, investment.

The political environment determines the rules by which economic transactions take place, not only because governments oversee economic institutions and influence regulation, trade, and foreign investment policies, among many other elements of the economic infrastructure, but also because politics impact risk (e.g., the prospects for a sudden regime change or reversal of economic policies), prospects for economic liberalization, and the probability of protectionist steps, among many other potential impacts. Understanding those elements is vital to better understanding of economic life and vital for generating accurate forecasts.

The legal environment determines the rules of the economic game, for instance, the protection accorded to owners of intellectual property rights, the rights of minority investors, the extent to which a country has an independent judiciary likely to make impartial decisions and enforce them, and the like. These elements can greatly and variably influence the fortunes of different players, for instance, the ability of multinational players to profit from their established brand names; they also affect the way companies from a given environment play in the international market place, for instance, the extent to which they are likely to be transparent in their dealings.

The social environment refers to a host of elements that make up the social fabric of a country, for instance, social stratification that influences life style and consumption patterns or public attitudes toward foreign investment, which in turn can trigger a change in the regulations governing such investment. For example, resentment regarding foreign influence can encourage governments to narrow the range of sectors open to foreign investment, limit the ownership stake of foreign investors, constrain their capital repatriation rights, or take other steps that can affect their earnings and profits. Social mores influence such things as labor market participation, consumption, and mobility.

Finally, the cultural environment affects much more than is commonly acknowledged, though often with other variables. Culture is an important determinant of the comparative advantage of nations (for instance, members of individualistic cultures tend to be strong in entrepreneurship), and the difference between one's own culture to another culture is also a factor in how comfortable investors are with investments in a particular location. Importantly, it has been established that investors prefer locations closer to home even when investing domestically, the so called "home bias." A study conducted by Joshua D. Coval and Tobial J. Moskowitz in the paper "Home Bias at home: Local equity preference in domestic portfolios" suggests that asymmetric information between local and nonlocal investors drive the preference for geographically proximate investments. The paper points out that the investors can have easy access to information about a firm located near them from employees, managers, suppliers, and customers. This gives an information advantage to investors who invest in local stocks. Further, investors can hedge against price increases in local services or in goods not easily traded outside the local area. Finally, local brokerage firms often encourage local investment that benefits the local community, particularly when personally connected local corporate executives are involved.

International Market Features

We have earlier noted the importance of noneconomic variables such as culture and society for the investment environment. Although the measures used rarely capture the full essence of the investment environment, they offer a first glimpse at the vagaries of a foreign market.

Political Risk

Political risk is the probability of disruption to the operations of a multinational enterprise (MNE) emanating from major political events (for example, a coup), though that risk is usually perceived more broadly to include political, social, and economic events that can have a material effect on the fortunes of firms that are based, operate, or have an ownership stake in a given country, whether by an action of government or not. An arbitrary change in investment conditions (e.g., retroactive change in investment rules, as we have seen recently in Venezuela), the undermining of property rights by the court system, including lax enforcement, are also examples of political risk.

Political risk is a problem for firms and investors who like to have a stable environment in which a company can plan and operate for the long term and where its investment is not subject to the whims of a given regime. Though as a group, developing and emerging economies are characterized by high political risk, developed economies can also suffer. Nondemocratic regimes are also typically prone to political risk (for instance, because of the possibility of a coup), but some authoritarian regimes are quite stable. A case in point is China, whereas in India, democracy introduces a measure of risk associated with a changing regime (who might, for instance, backpedal on economic reforms). An example of a political risk involving a developed country democracy is Canada, where Quebec was at one point close to seceding though this risk has receded in recent years.

The inherent problem in the measurement of political risk is that the political landscape is notoriously difficult to forecast. Change might come as a result of election, but it can also come with a decision by an autocratic ruler, such as in the case of Iraq's invasion of Kuwait. The events of September 11, 2001, drew attention to the risk of terrorism, which is becoming a significant concern for companies. Terrorism not only puts a company's own workforce at risk, but it also endangers its business prospects. Understandably, some industries are more vulnerable than others; for instance, airlines and other industries associated with tourism are more sensitive to terrorist attacks than, say, the high tech sector, as the cases of Israel and India show. At the same time, firms in countries vulnerable to terrorism learn early on how to deal with the phenomenon and are generally more open to invest in world regions considered risky by other investors. Such nations also tend to have firms that develop expertise in various antiterror activities.

Among the strongest manifestations of political risk are expropriation or forced divestment—often but not always with some compensation, although typically such compensation is partial and does not cover the opportunity cost. Milder forms include pressure toward or a formal change in investment rules that forces firms to reduce their stake (e.g., sharing ownership with the government or a local firm). In essence, any change to the "rules of the game" under which firms, and especially foreign players, operate (e.g., arbitrary taxation), and any measure that limits their strategic freedom and autonomy, can have adverse consequences. This includes, for instance, capital controls that limit the repatriation of profit. At the same time, firms and individuals in high political risk nations often seek "safe haven" locations that benefit from the flow.

In addition to examining the national level of political risk, investors should remember the variations among regions and industries within a country. Investors should also ask whether a firm is in a position to tackle, avoid, or mitigate the risk. To mitigate political risk, firms take such measures as the following:

1. Minimizing outright investment
2. Leasing rather than buying
3. Relying on government incentives, where available
4. Signing bilateral or multilateral treaties that protect foreign investment
5. Identifying or creating reciprocal settings where investment from the host country can be seized in case of expropriation

6. Avoiding high-visibility acquisitions, especially of firms or key assets that are viewed as national icons

7. Reducing capital exposure by utilizing host country financing, accelerating profit repatriation, and developing a staggered technology transfer policy

8. Sourcing locally, reducing the host country incentive to harm the foreign firm

9. Establishing strategic alliances with a local partner, thus reducing the foreign investor outlays and pacifying nationalist sentiment

10. Using agencies such as the Overseas Private Investment Corporation (OPIC) that insure companies against political risk

11. Building political support at home and in the host nation through lobbying, public relations, and a proactive social responsibility

12. In general monitoring political and economic development to prepare, avoid, or counter intervention

Such mitigating measures are rarely taken into account by investors but should be looked at closely.

Corruption

Some level of corruption exists in all nations; however, levels vary widely (see Exhibit 6-4, 6-5, and 6-6). To investors, the existence of a high level of corruption implies, for instance, that the numbers that we see are less likely to actually reflect the financial situation of a company.

A special risk is related to the Foreign Corrupt Practices Act, which dates back to 1973 and has criminalized the payment of bribes abroad by U.S. firms (or the U.S. subsidiaries of foreign firms) and its more recent counterpart in other OECD nations. The upheaval at Siemens where the German authorities have been investigating an endemic bribe payment is a good illustration of the risks to investors from such practices. Understandably, firms who operate in high corruption countries are more at risk.

Exhibit 6-4   Bribery across Countries (Source: Adapted or reprinted from Bribe Payers Index. Copyright 2006 Transparency International: the global coalition against corruption. Used with permission. For more information, visit http://www.transparency.org.)

Rank	Country/Territory	Average Score
1	Switzerland	7.81
2	Sweden	7.81
3	Australia	7.59
4	Austria	7.5
5	Canada	7.46
6	United Kingdom	7.39
7	Germany	7.34
8	Netherlands	7.28
9	Belgium	7.22
10	United States	7.22
11	Japan	7.1
12	Singapore	6.78
13	Spain	6.63
14	United Arab Emirates	6.62
15	France	6.5
16	Portugal	6.47
17	Mexico	6.45
18	Hong Kong	6.01
19	Israel	6.01
20	Italy	5.94
21	South Korea	5.83
22	Saudi Arabia	5.75
23	Brazil	5.65
24	South Africa	5.61
25	Malaysia	5.59
26	Republic of China (Taiwan)	5.41
27	Turkey	5.23
28	Russia	5.16
29	China	4.94
30	India	4.62

Exhibit 6-5   Least Corrupt Nations (Source: Adapted or reprinted from Corruption Perceptions Index. Copyright 2007 Transparency International: the global coalition against corruption. Used with permission. For more information, visit http://www.transparency.org.)

County Rank	Country	2007 CPI Score	Survey Used	Confidence Range
1	Denmark	9.4	6	9.2–9.6
1	Finland	9.4	6	9.2–9.6
1	New Zealand	9.4	6	9.2–9.6
4	Singapore	9.3	9	9.0–9.5
4	Sweden	9.3	6	9.1–9.4
6	Iceland	9.2	6	8.3–9.6
7	Netherlands	9	6	8.8–9.2
7	Switzerland	9	6	8.8–9.2
9	Canada	8.7	6	8.3–9.1
9	Norway	8.7	6	8.0–9.2

Exhibit 6-6   Most Corrupt Nations (Source: Adapted or reprinted from Corruption Perceptions Index. Copyright 2007 Transparency International: the global coalition against corruption. Used with permission. For more information, visit http://www.transparency.org.)

County Rank	Country	2007 CPI Score	Survey Used	Confidence Range
168	Laos	1.9	6	1.7–2.2
172	Afghanistan	1.8	4	1.4–2.0
172	Chad	1.8	7	1.7–1.9
172	Sudan	1.8	6	1.6–1.9
175	Tonga	1.7	3	1.5–1.8
175	Uzbekistan	1.7	7	1.6–1.9
177	Haiti	1.6	4	1.3–1.8
178	Iraq	1.5	4	1.3–1.7
179	Myanmar	1.4	4	1.1–1.7
179	Somalia	1.4	4	1.1–1.7

The next chapter focuses on three countries that appear to have solid growth prospects. They are China, India, and Israel. Israel faces much steeper external political hurdles than China and India and is a much smaller country. Still, it offers lessons about the sources of growth and characteristics required to sustain it.

7

Three Emerging Countries

In this chapter we present three examples of emerging economies and the role they are likely to play in the global economy. The first two, China and India, are often portrayed as the two rising powers of the global economy. The third, Israel, is an example of a small nation that plays a vital niche role in the global economy.

China

The Chinese economy continues to grow at close to double-digit levels, defying western skeptics who opined at the time that it was impossible to develop a thriving free market without a democracy. China has shown that it is not only possible to have a thriving economy under a totalitarian regime, but also that the combination produces a new breed of competitors that use different ground rules to establish a market advantage. Chinese firms, for instance, are among the world's most advanced imitators, often copying the designs and products of their advanced counterparts and relying on a multitude of factors, not only cheap labor, to establish a tremendous price advantage—the so called China Price. Low, but rapidly rising, R&D expenditures, lax regulations (environmental, safety, and so on), subsidies and rebates, low capital costs, favorable exchange rates and low margins lead to a significant price advantage. The ramifications are evident: For instance, between 1996 and 2002, U.S. imports of Chinese household furniture rose more than six-fold from $741 million to

$4.8 billion. U.S. imports from China, by then the world's leading maker and exporter of wooden furniture, rose 75% between 2000 and 2002. The U.S. consumer market has also shown an insatiable appetite for Chinese products—from bicycles, coats, and Christmas ornaments to TVs and DVD players. In 1992, China had less than 10% of the U.S. electronic market. By the end of the decade, that had more than doubled. The ramifications have been a rapid loss of market share and margins for competitors who have failed to effectively counter the onslaught via outsourcing, automation, shift to premium markets, and the like. The Chinese exports have also improved the fortunes of discount retailers worldwide who now have cheaper and more varied product sources.

Exhibit 7-1 shows movement in the Yuan-Dollar exchange rate that has often been cited as one of the major reasons behind the China Price by making Chinese exports relatively cheap in export markets and rendering foreign imports relatively expensive in the Chinese market. Because the Yuan is not freely traded, goes the argument, it is held artificially weak by the Chinese government; although as Exhibit 7-1 shows, it has been slowly strengthening. The expected revaluation of the Yuan is unlikely to bring about a dramatic change in the trade picture between China and the United States. The relationship with the EU depends in part on how the Euro trades relative to the dollar. Investors might benefit from an increase in the dollar value of their Chinese securities, while at the same time they might be hurt from declining competitiveness of Chinese firms in the global market place.

Because Chinese products have a high import content (in other words, Chinese firms import components and inputs that they put into the final product they assemble, meaning their added value is quite limited), a revaluation of the Yuan will have a limited impact because the prices of imported inputs will go down. In addition, a revaluation will bring benefits for Chinese firms not currently considered by the U.S. government and media. First, a revaluation will actually increase the competitiveness of Chinese firms as players are forced to consolidate and those who remain in the game become "leaner and meaner." (This is what happened in Japan in the 1980s.) Second, a revaluation of the Yuan will hasten talent migration lured by the prospects of higher relative pay, a critical element in a knowledge-based economy. Third, a revaluation will lower the prices of overseas assets, thus accelerating foreign acquisitions by Chinese firms seeking not only new markets but also advanced technologies. No wonder, Chinese outward foreign investment is growing by leaps and bounds (see Exhibit 7-2).

Among the targets for the next wave of Chinese acquisitions will be firms in near-commodity areas with know-how, established brands, and strong distribution; firms with unique and complex technologies that can be easily unbundled; firms where the value added has been moving toward suppliers (e.g., automotive), energy firms, and retailers. Although such acquisitions are critical to the attempt by Chinese firms to become truly global firms, they are likely to face tremendous integration challenges. Cross-border M&A are extremely problematic under the best of circumstances. (The majority of such transactions return negative equity to the shareholders of the acquiring firm.) Add to that the lack of experience of Chinese firms in conducting foreign (and sometimes even domestic) acquisitions and the investment risk becomes clear.

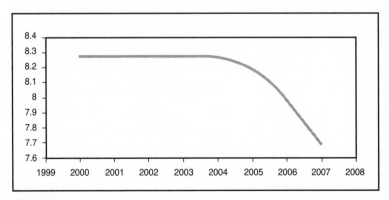

Exhibit 7-1   Yuan—Dollar Historic Exchange Rates (Source: exchange-rates.org)

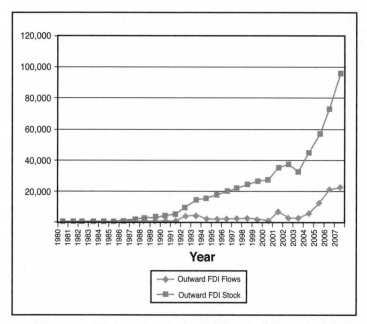

Exhibit 7-2   China Outward Foreign Direct Investment (FDI) Flows and Stock (Source: Calculated from data of the China Statistics Bureau and UNCTAD 2007-09)

Still, Chinese firms suffer from many underlying weaknesses. The need to copy, for example, is driven as much by the inability to innovate as by the desire to lower cost by skimping on development costs and the immediate need for economic growth. The recent problems with defective products from China show not only a lack of regulatory oversight but also just how intense the price competition is. Desperate to cut another nickel from the price of a product for fears of being dropped by a demanding buyer abroad and a price-sensitive customer at home, quite a few Chinese manufacturers have been driven to cutting corners, using a cheaper substitute to anything from a toothpaste ingredient to a toy's paint. Many others maintain razor thin margins or are sustained by local authorities eager to sustain employment and show they meet central government targets for economic growth.

Other macro problems abound. To continue its march forward, China needs to transform its banking sector, diffuse a social security crisis, and respond to discontent on the part of rural workers and others at the very bottom of the Chinese economic ladder. Fears of unemployment and resulting unrest will drive a continuous feed of its export engine, but the same fears will drive it to avert a possible trade war. In the meantime, a recent scare regarding defective products might put a dampner on growth, as manufacturers regroup to improve quality and safety standards and convince an increasingly skeptic clientele that the products made in China are safe. Still, with China holding a commanding lead in many product lines, it is difficult to find substitutes who would take on any slack. For instance, China now accounts for roughly 80% of the toys imported into the United States and the EU, so a lead paint scare notwithstanding, it is likely to remain the industry leader for years to come, even as cheaper locations begin capturing the lowest parts of the value chain. After all, China's advantage is anchored not only in cheap labor and lax regulation but also in the presence of supporting industries and a helpful government assisting with infrastructure development while turning a blind eye to intellectual property rights (IPR) violations.

As Exhibit 7-3 shows, Chinese firms have actually fallen behind when it comes to developing, making, and especially marketing and distributing export quality products. The Chinese government is determined to arrest this trend, among other means, by leveling the playing field, for instance, by abolishing the tax advantages enjoyed by foreign investors. Still, the inability to innovate continues to hamper the prospects of Chinese firms, many of which can capture only a small portion of the profit accrued to the middlemen and retailers who sell the products they make.

The question of whether China can overcome its weak innovation capabilities remains open. The country's R&D investment as a proportion of GDP is rising, although, it still lags considerably below that of advanced nations. Chinese firms compensate partially by expropriating others' technology and partially by using generation-old technologies while competing on price. The government continues to provide incentives to foreign investors who are willing to transfer advanced technologies. But, there are also signs that the Chinese are making strides. China ranks second only to the United States in

publishing technical papers in nanoscience and nanotechnology and
is catching up in other scientific areas (see Exhibit 7-4).

**Exhibit 7-3 China's Exports and the Share of Foreign Affiliates.
Percentage Share of Foreign Invested Enterprises in China's Exports.
(Sources: UNCTAD, Chinese Sources [rounded estimates]; authors'
forecast)**

Year	Percentage
1987	10
1992	20
1995	30
1997	40
2001	50
2005	58 (ranging from 28% in textiles to 84% in electronics/IT)
2015	40 (forecast)

**Exhibit 7-4 Perceived Technology Capabilities (Top Four Rankings)
(Source: 2007 Global R&D Report [Battelle])**

	1st	2nd	3rd	4th
Aerospace Technology	USA	Japan	China	India
Pharma Discovery & Development	USA	Japan	India	China
Biotechnology	USA	Japan	India	China
Nanotechnology	USA	Japan	India	China
Information Technology	USA	Japan	India	China
Photonics	USA	Japan	China	India
Academic Basic Research	USA	Japan	India	China
Automation/Robotics	Japan	USA	China	India
Telecommunications	Japan	India	USA	China
Energy Research	Japan	USA	India	China
Electronics Research	Japan	USA	India	China
Automotive Development	Japan	USA	China	India

To investors, the issue is not only how the Chinese stock market
performs or how Chinese firms listed in foreign markets perform, but
also what would be the collateral impact of China's rise. For example,

China's rise has the capacity to devastate labor-intensive industries such as garment making in other nations, both developing (e.g., Mexico, Bangladesh, Lesotho) and developed (e.g., Italy) because China is moving upward into more expensive designer goods without relinquishing the entry level. Non-China producers of labor-intensive goods who lack the sophisticated supply chain with which to leverage production in China and other foreign locations and have reached their automation limits will find themselves priced out of the market. Near-commodity producers such as makers of appliances and non-tech automotive components might also find themselves out of luck. The same is true for producers who cannot defend against the assault on their intellectual property rights.

At the same time, many industries can benefit from China's rise. Examples include raw material producers, infrastructure builders and equipment makers (e.g., Caterpillar), agricultural producers (e.g., soybeans, while some growers, such as those of apples, will actually suffer from surging Chinese exports), aircraft makers, for which China (and in time India) has become the most promising market, learning and training providers, logistic providers, technology players (but only if they can build effective defenses against leakage and expropriation) and financial services, both banking and insurance (and, eventually, brokerage).

India

Deutsche Bank estimates India's growth between 2006 and 2020 to average more than 6 percent, higher than that of other emerging markets, including China. Assuming it is sustained, that growth level will almost triple the size of the economy by 2020 from its 2002 level (in terms of purchasing power parity). GDP per capita, which together with per capita income level is a key measure of the standard of living and consumer power, is projected to more than double during the same period (see Exhibit 7-5).

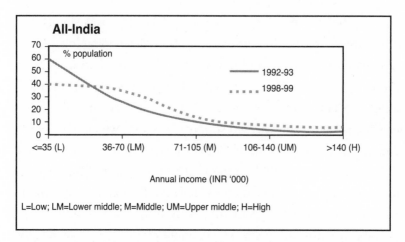

Exhibit 7-5   Distribution of Population in India as per the Annual Income (Source: Deutsche Bank Research on "India rising: A medium-term perspective," Press Conference, Frankfurt, May 19, 2005)

The emergence of a substantial Indian middle class is important not only for its consumer implications but also for what it means in terms of social stability and the prospects for continuous improvement of education, a common demand among members of the middle class. Unlike China, whose population will rapidly age due to the one child policy, India is slated to maintain its high ratio of young population (roughly one-third are under 15 and only 5% are over the retirement age of 65), implying ample labor supply (including a large contingent of educated workforce), and rosy prospects for purveyors of age-sensitive goods (e.g., toys).

On the weaker side, the level of foreign direct investment in India is still low, vastly trailing China. The low amount reflects the unease many would-be investors have with the notorious Indian bureaucracy, corruption, and other obstacles to the conducting of efficient business. Yet, there are many reasons to believe that this will improve over time (Exhibit 7-6).

FDI Confidence Index®

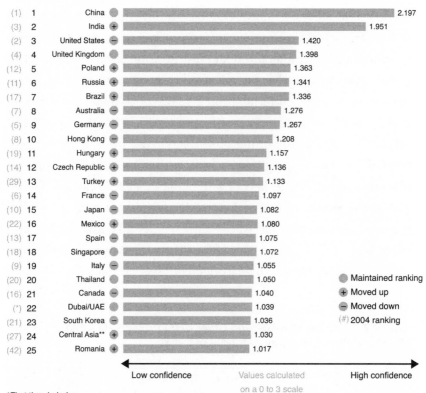

Top 25, December 2005

(1)	1	China ●		2.197
(3)	2	India ⊕		1.951
(2)	3	United States ⊖		1.420
(4)	4	United Kingdom ●		1.398
(12)	5	Poland ⊕		1.363
(11)	6	Russia ⊕		1.341
(17)	7	Brazil ⊕		1.336
(7)	8	Australia ⊖		1.276
(5)	9	Germany ⊖		1.267
(8)	10	Hong Kong ⊖		1.208
(19)	11	Hungary ⊕		1.157
(14)	12	Czech Republic ⊕		1.136
(29)	13	Turkey ⊕		1.133
(6)	14	France ⊖		1.097
(10)	15	Japan ⊖		1.082
(22)	16	Mexico ⊕		1.080
(13)	17	Spain ⊖		1.075
(18)	18	Singapore ●		1.072
(9)	19	Italy ⊖		1.055
(20)	20	Thailand ●		1.050
(16)	21	Canada ⊖		1.040
(*)	22	Dubai/UAE ●		1.039
(21)	23	South Korea ⊖		1.036
(27)	24	Central Asia** ⊕		1.030
(42)	25	Romania ⊕		1.017

● Maintained ranking
⊕ Moved up
⊖ Moved down
(#) 2004 ranking

Low confidence   Values calculated   High confidence
on a 0 to 3 scale

*First time in Index
**Central Asia includes Azerbaijan, Belarus, Kazakhstan, and Turkmenistan

Exhibit 7-6 FDI Confidence Index—Attractive FDI Locations in the World (Source: Foreign Direct Investment Confidence Index, Copyright A.T. Kearney, 2005. All rights reserved. Reprinted with permission.)

India also suffers from poor infrastructure, the result of its late entry into the reform era and the complex, political, and corruption-prone approval process, among other factors. However this can also be viewed as an opportunity, with massive investments and expertise needed in such realms as new airports, where ancient infrastructure is a bottleneck to a liberalized and fast-growing airline industry. The power sector in India has been marred by continuous shortages. The country is currently suffering from a 12.8% peak-time power deficit. India's peak load in 2006 was estimated at 115,705 MW, but ministry officials say up to 30% of the power is derived from illegal connections or lost due to aging transmission grids. The Indian government plans on adding 100,000 MW of generation capacity by 2012—(77,000 MW in the public sector and 23,000 MW from the private sector) but it is not at all clear that this will be sufficient. Road networks have also fallen way behind growth in traffic with budgets for expansion and maintenance continuing to be inadequate (see Exhibit 7-7).

**Exhibit 7-7   Status of NHDP and Other NHAI Projects (in Kms)
(Source: National Highway Authority of India)**

	GQ	NS-EW	Port Connectivity	Others	Total
Total	5846	7274	356	777	**14253**
Completed	3121	653	69	194	**4037**
Under implementation	2725	410	229	121	**3485**
To be awarded		6211	58	462	**6731**

Like all economies, India is vulnerable to downturns in the global economy and to those of its own. Even more than China, India is a fragmented nation with regions differentiated by dialects, culture, and many other factors (e.g., minority population) in addition to economics. That India is a stable democracy is often noted as a plus, but it also implies coalition politics with its attendant negatives, such as an opaque decision-making process.

India is often noted for the number and quality of its workers, the result of both a large population and an education system that despite its problems includes many good and sometimes excellent institutions such as the Indian Institutes of Technology, Indian Institutes of Management, Banaras Hindu University, All India Institute of Medical Sciences, National Institute of Technology, Indian Institute of Science, and the Indian School of Business. For instance, the International Institute of Management Development (IMD) report shows India with one of the highest availability of skilled labor in the world, as shown in Exhibit 7-8.

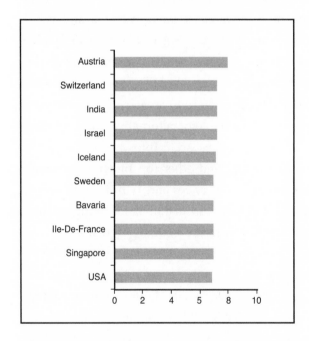

Exhibit 7-8   Labor Market—Top 10 Countries with Availability of Skilled Labor (Source: IMD Report 2006)

The industries that are often noted as likely to thrive in India and integrate into the global economy are mostly in the service sector, including IT outsourcing, software development to maintenance, and call centers. However certain manufacturing industries are also likely to thrive, including, but not limited to, autos and automotive components, pharmaceuticals, especially generic drug makers. In 2006, Indian companies announced 125 foreign acquisitions with a value of nearly $10 billion. That is roughly eight times the 2000 figure. However, in the first 5 months of 2007, the value crossed $15 billion. India's leading drug maker Sun Pharmaceutical Industries aims to buy Israel-based generic drug producer Taro for $454 million. Sun Pharma offered $7.75 per share for Toro's equity valued at $230 million.

Although most Americans focus on investment in India by U.S. companies (and also vice versa), it is worthwhile to observe India's growing relations with other economies, such as China and Israel, which provide for interesting synergies. For instance, in December 2002, India and Israel entered into an alliance to produce and market the Advanced Light Helicopter Dhruv (ALH), whereas Indian and Israeli companies cooperate in numerous areas such as computer software and hardware, nanotechnology, alternative fuels, agriculture, animal husbandry, and space research. Infosys, the Bangalore-based software services company, and other top Indian outsourcing rivals, including Tata Consultancy Services and Wipro Technologies, are doing application development and maintenance work in China as they grow rapidly to keep up with the booming demand from the West for their services. In October 2007, a new joint venture facility between Tata Consultancy Services (TCS) and three Chinese partners was built in Zhongguancun Software Park, the Chinese capital's showcase high-tech zone. The TCS (China) building is the physical embodiment of the first example of the long-hyped potential for Sino-Indian collaboration in information. Further, Tata Tea Ltd. has formed a joint venture with China's Zhejiang Tea Import and Export Company to manufacture and market tea and allied value-added products in China. As another example, Bharat Forge Ltd. (BFL), India, the world's second-largest manufacturer of automotive forgings, has signed a joint venture agreement with China-based FAW

Corp. The Indian company will hold a 52% stake in the new company, known as FAW Bharat Forge, which will manufacture forged auto components.

Israel

Given its difficult geopolitical situation and constant security risk, some would be surprised to find Israel designated as a promising emerging market. Unlike India and China, which have the largest populations in the world, Israel is a small country of seven million inhabitants surrounded by largely hostile neighbors. For the last two decades, the Israeli economy underwent major liberalization, shifting from hybrid socialism to an unabashed free market. At $20,000 per capita, Israelis are positioned at the tail end of West European nations but place higher than that of eastern and central Europe. If current trends continue, however (GDP growth rates exceeded 5% in 2005, 2006, and 2007, considerably higher than that for the United States and Europe), Israel will be among the ranks of rich West European economies. Lower government and public debt and lower capital expenditure are among the positive trends in the Israeli economy in recent years. Inflation, once a staple and at one point running at 3 digits, has dropped dramatically and is now within U.S. and European standards.

Where Israel excels is in technology start-ups. The country is home to more than 100 venture capital firms, and the number of Israeli firms on the NASDAQ is second only to the United States. The country is among the highest if not the highest per capita destination for FDI in the world—if we exclude such destinations as Luxemburg where foreign investment is mostly routed through its financial center on the way to other destinations. In 2006, FDI in Israel approached $15 billion, whereas in 2007 it was close to the $20 billion mark. FDI in Israel benefits from R&D expenditure that is among the highest in the world (Exhibit 7-9), and from a highly

skilled workforce that is strong in entrepreneurial and inventive capabilities as evidenced by a high level of venture capital investment
(Exhibit 7-10).

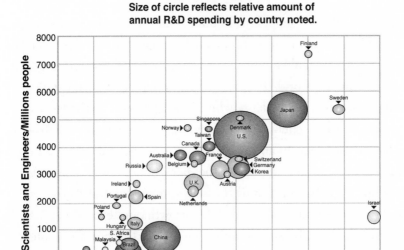

World of R&D 2005

Size of circle reflects relative amount of
annual R&D spending by country noted.

**Exhibit 7-9   R&D Expenditures of Israel (and Other Developed Nations)
as a Percentage of GDP (Source: Global R&D Report, 2007 [*R&D
Magazine* and Batelle])**

As of 2007, 101 (AMEX has six companies listed that are not
added in the 101 count) Israeli firms were traded on U.S. stock
exchanges, the highest number of any foreign nation, and two—
Check Point Software Technologies Ltd. (CHKP), Teva Pharmaceutical Industries Limited (TEVA)—were on the Nasdaq-100 index.
More than 60 Israeli firms are listed on European exchanges, and 39
Israel firms are listed both on the Tel Aviv and NYSE or other foreign
exchanges.

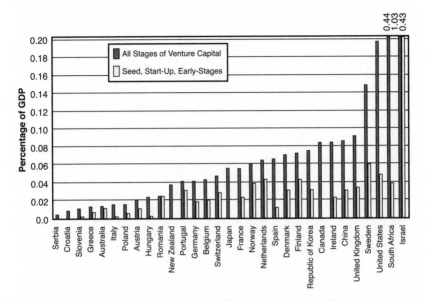

Exhibit 7-10   Venture Capital Investments as a Percentage of GDP, by Stage of the Company (Source: NVCA and EVCA, and national venture capital associations. Figure reprinted by permission as it appeared in the *Global Entrepreneurship Monitor 2009 Executive Report* by Niels Bosma and Jonathan Levie.)

Enhancing the growth prospects of all three countries is their relatively strong balance sheets. Their public sectors are not "developed" in the sense obligations are not absorbing significant amounts of each country's GDP and beginning to constrain growth prospects. Their private sectors trend toward more disbursed decision-making and economic participation instead of becoming more concentrated. Each country should continue to grow faster than the global economy.

8

Private Sector Composition

Investments are categorized as equities, fixed income, money market instruments, alternative investments, and so on. These are the basic categories used for asset allocation. Investing might be done through an investment advisor, in a mutual fund, in an exchange traded fund (ETF), or through some other channel. Whatever the type of investments made or channels used, if those investments aren't backed by a government or a hard asset, the investments will almost always involve the debt or equity of companies. This chapter is about better understanding companies; where those companies fit in the global economy and the global markets; and if their characteristics are compatible with your investment goals.

As a starting point for differentiating these companies, we use the Global Industry Classification Standard (GICS) developed by MSCI Barra and Standard & Poor's (S&P) as a basis for discussing company fundamentals. S&P uses GICS to classify every company in its indexes, and we use S&P's indexes for some additional perspective. Not all company equities are suitable for your investment goals.

The Standard & Poor's 500 Index is used as a benchmark for more than $1.5 trillion of assets under management, and it is the most actively indexed fund. It consists of 500 of the largest companies by market capitalization headquartered in the United States, and they represent about 75% of the market capitalization of companies in the United States. Similarly, the Standard & Poor's Global 1200 consists of 1200 of the largest companies by market capitalization in the world and is estimated to represent about 70% of the global equities' market capitalization. The composition of the indexes changes regularly because companies merge, get acquired, get into trouble, and change. Regardless of the changes, all companies in these indexes come from one of ten sectors meant to reflect the composition of the broader economy. These ten sectors are then broken down into 24 industry groups, which consist of 67 industries, and those industries include 147 subindustries. A list of the industries and subindustries can be found on the Standard and Poor's Web site. This chapter focuses principally on the ten sectors and 24 industry groups.

Company Characteristics

Understanding the basics of a company is a step to making a better investment decision. Is it positioned to benefit from global growth opportunities or to create other growth opportunities, or is it dependent on regional economic fortunes? Where does the company fit in terms of risk profile and investment style? This chapter focuses on several characteristics such as a company's sources of growth, capital intensity, valuation, and typical investment themes.

Sources of growth–Often company equities are labeled growth stocks because of their historic performance. This misses the point. The most valuable growth is organic growth and that is driven by innovation and the economic environment. Other sources of growth in order of attractiveness are a business model followed by financial management and productivity advances. Identifying emerging organic growth opportunities should provide some of the best equity investment opportunities. We also discuss pricing power as a subset of a sector's growth equation.

Capital intensity–Some companies must retain much of their earnings for reinvestment if they are to sustain their growth. They are capital-intensive. Others reach a critical mass and can utilize a substantial portion of their earnings in dividends and stock buy-back or in acquisitions. These are less capital-intensive. Companies just reaching that critical mass point should provide good fixed income investment opportunities because they would likely reduce leverage.

Valuation–Here we focus primarily on estimated P/Es and some dividend yields for the S&P 500.

Investment themes–This is meant to give an idea of what investors expect from the sector.

The Sectors and the Industry Groups

The S&P Global 1200 Index market cap approaches $22 trillion compared to more than $10.5 trillion for the S&P 500 (March 2010). As shown in Exhibit 8-1 and Exhibit 8-2, Financials, Materials, Telecom, and Utilities are the components of the Global Index, whereas Health Care, Technology, Industrials, and Energy are relatively larger parts of the S&P 500.

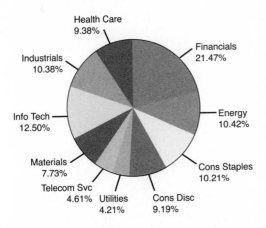

Exhibit 8-1   S&P Global 1200 Composition (Source: Standard & Poor's)

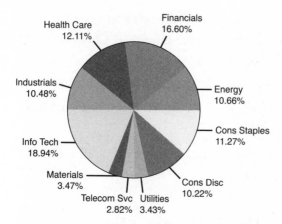

Exhibit 8-2   S&P 500 Composition (Source: Standard & Poor's)

Sectors

Consumer discretionary is composed principally of those companies that provide goods and services considered just that—discretionary consumer purchases. It consists of 5 industry groups, 12 industries, and 35 subindustries. The five industry groups are

1. Automobile components
2. Consumer durables and apparel
3. Consumer services
4. Media
5. Retailing

It is not the largest sector in terms of market capitalization, but it is one of the most fragmented sectors. This means the typical company of this sector has a smaller market capitalization compared to companies in other sectors. Not surprisingly, this sector is a larger component of developed country markets than emerging markets. This is because the consumer economy is much further along in its evolution in developed countries, and their economies tend to house auto and media related companies.

**Exhibit 8-3 Consumer Discretionary Represen-
tation in Global Indexes (Source: Standard &
Poor's)**

	Percentage of Market Capital
Global	10.0%
United States	10.2%
Europe	7.3%
Japan	19.7%
Asia	6.7%
Latin America	3.5%

The best growth opportunities appear to reside outside the United States, and especially in the emerging markets where the middle class is beginning to grow in earnest and should dwarf that of the United States in the next decade. For instance, India's middle class is growing and estimated to already exceed 200 million, whereas the middle class in China is approaching 300 million. For comparison purposes, the population of the United States is about 300 million.

There is also a trend working against the growth prospects of the sector in the United States—nondiscretionary items are taking an increasing share of disposable income, as shown in Exhibit 8-4. The key to growth for many companies is the attractiveness of their offering. This implies weak pricing power, resulting in a weak outlook for most consumer discretionary companies. Based on the history of the United States, it will take decades for consumer discretionary items to reach full saturation in the developing economies.

Capital intensity for the sector is high and dividend yields are generally low. Many companies need to reinvest a substantial portion of their earnings in store expansion and identifying the correct fashion trends. The latter is a more volatile proposition at best. Still, others are saddled with high debts and restructuring pressures.

Valuation levels tend to be higher than other sectors reflecting the sector's composition. It tends to include many companies with

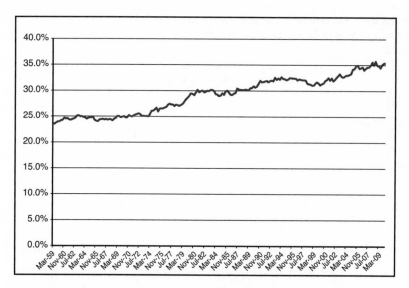

Exhibit 8-4   Nondiscretionary Spending to Personal Disposable Income (Source: Bureau of Economic Analysis)

higher growth expectations, and companies with more volatile earnings and in the process of transition. For instance, the pain of the recent financial crisis was reflected in negative results of many parts of the sector—auto companies took large write-offs and two were taken over, while homebuilders saw their earnings plunge from record levels to losses.

Typical investment themes for consumer discretionary companies include growth at an attractive price, new growth opportunities tied to new market opportunities and products, and turnaround stories. Value, attractive dividend yields, and strong cash flow generation are themes that should be less prevalent. In developing markets, this sector should grow relatively faster.

Consumer staples companies produce and sell consumer basics. This means producing products such as food, beverages, and tobacco. The distribution outlets included in the sector are drug stores, supermarkets, and others. These products are considered noncyclical, and the performance of the companies is expected to be less volatile and more consistent. For investors, the investment attraction of many of the companies in the sector is the relative consistency of their performance, and the expectation that there is greater predictability in their performance.

The sector consists of 3 industry groups, 6 industries, and 13 subindustries. The three industry groups are

1. Food and staples retailing
2. Food, beverage, and tobacco
3. Household and personal products

Like the Consumer Discretionary sector, the best growth opportunities for Consumer Staples' companies appear to reside outside the United States, especially the emerging markets (Exhibit 8-5). In most developing countries, the penetration level of most products is high, and increased share often comes from the introduction of new products or from lower pricing models from companies such as Wal-Mart. Growth is more dependent on increased volume and financial management as margins remain under pressure.

Exhibit 8-5   Consumer Staples Representation in Global Indexes (Source: Standard & Poor's)

	Percentage of Market Capital
Global	11.1%
United States	11.3%
Europe	12.2%
Japan	5.8%
Asia	1.8%
Latin America	11.0%

Capital intensity for the sector is modest with the smaller cap companies more likely to reinvest their earnings because of organic growth opportunities. The larger cap companies, however, should continue to use most of their earnings to support rising dividend payments, share repurchase programs, and acquisitions. To the extent large cap companies reinvest a portion of the free cash flow beyond what is required for maintenance purposes, the bulk of those investments should be made in the developing countries.

Valuation also tends be among the highest of any sector. Using estimated earnings per share (EPS) for 2011, the Consumer Staples sector recently traded at 13.7 times estimated earnings, which is the second highest valuation after that of the Industrials sector. Relative to that sector, growth expectations are less but so is expected volatility. Three-year earnings' growth through 2011 is expected to be 8.0% compared to 24.1% for the S&P 500 and a decline for Industrials.

Investment themes include global growth opportunities, consolidation, and defensive growth. Value and attractive dividend yields are less prevalent themes.

Energy includes the major oil companies, the companies making the equipment to find oil and natural gas, exploration companies, refiners, storage and transportation companies, and coal and related companies. It is one of the largest sectors and includes some of the largest companies in the world based on market capitalization. The absence of large amounts of natural resources and the resulting absence of a more significant energy business presence is evident in the sector's market cap share of the Asian and Japanese indices (Exhibit 8-6). This is one of four sectors not disaggregated at the industry group level.

Exhibit 8-6   Energy Representation in Global Indexes (Source: Standard & Poor's)

	Percentage of Market Capital
Global	11.3%
United States	10.7%
Europe	11.2%
Japan	1.0%
Asia	6.3%
Latin America	13.7%

In the energy sector/industry group, there are two industries and seven subindustries. The two industries are

1. Energy equipment and services
2. Oil, gas and consumable fuels

Historically, most energy companies were considered to be value stocks. Earnings forecasts seem to be among the most difficult to build because of the more volatile nature of energy prices. Still, between 2004 and 2006, the energy sector delivered the most robust earnings growth of any sector in the S&P 500—34.0%. The source of the growth was organic, triggered by an era of growing global energy demand preceded by a period of underinvestment that lasted more than a decade. Energy demand is expected to remain strong. As a result, pricing power should remain strong for companies providing the tools needed to find and develop new sources of energy. Because energy costs are consuming a growing share of resources and the concerns surrounding the environmental impact are growing, the demand for alternative forms of energy should rise and keep investment levels in this space elevated.

Capital intensity for the sector is high. Many companies need to reinvest a substantial portion of their earnings in capital expenditures, production, and R&D. However, the integrated oil companies also generate sufficiently large levels of free cash flow and should continue to repurchase a meaningful amount of their shares.

The energy sector's performance has been highly correlated with the price of oil, and its valuation tends to be among the lowest in the S&P 500. At 11.6 times 2011 estimated earnings, its P/E ratio was the second lowest in the S&P 500.

Value, global growth, the rising price of energy, continued growth in exploration budgets, and the alternative energy sources should continue to be some of the most popular investment themes in the sector. However, like any investment delivering attractive results over a long period of time, the sustainability of those returns will increasingly be questioned.

Financial services represents the largest global sector and the largest source of corporate earnings in the United States. Since the early 1980s, the financial services sector's share of U.S. corporate profits grew, as shown in Exhibit 8-7.

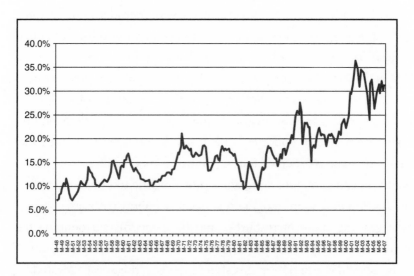

Exhibit 8-7   Financial Profits as a Percent of Total Corporate Profits (Source: Bureau of Economic Analysis)

Some of the sources of superior growth were the end of the Great Inflation of the 1970s; the Digital Age that began in earnest in the 1980s; the maturing of the baby boom; a series of financial innovations;

and the opening of the global economy. Between September 1984 and June 2007, the contribution of profits from the financial services sector went from just under 10% to almost 32%. The sector consists of 4 industry groups, 8 industries, and 24 subindustries. The four industry groups are

1. Banks
2. Diversified financials
3. Insurance
4. Real estate

Financial services represent a large part of the global equity markets (Exhibit 8-8) and benefited from the tremendous growth of global capital markets. The traditional banking structures of the 1980s continued to give way to more specialization and greater market orientation. That trend should continue.

Exhibit 8-8   Financial Services Representation in Global Indexes (Source: Standard & Poor's)

	Percentage of Market Capitalization
Global	23.4%
United States	16.6%
Europe	24.1%
Japan	16.1%
Asia	31.4%
Latin America	22.4%

Capital intensity for the sector is high. In fact, the Financial Services sector is one of the more capital intensive sectors. Unlike nonfinancial sectors, the investment requirements are tied much less to traditional capital expenditures and instead to the taking and assumption of risk. Risk comes principally in the form of making loans, making markets, and providing insurance.

The nature of the risk taken by the majority of the companies in the sector is difficult to assess, and many companies have business models operating close to peak profitability with, at best, modest growth prospects. As a result, the P/Es of this sector tend to be among the lowest, whereas dividend yields tend to be among the highest because of a relatively high payout ratio.

Value, yield, consolidation, and new business models should be the more constant investment themes for this sector. Growth opportunities in the sector should be tied to processing and asset management businesses, and growth opportunities provided by the growing financial needs in developing countries. For the processing and asset management businesses, capital requirements are much more modest, capital turns faster, and returns on equity (ROEs) should be much higher.

Health care costs are nondiscretionary and consume more than 15% of personal disposable income in the United States, as shown in Exhibit 8-9. That trend is expected to continue.

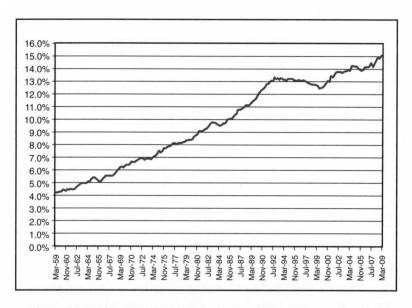

Exhibit 8-9   Health Care Spending as a Percent of Personal Disposable Income (Source: Bureau of Economic Analysis)

The sector provides the products, services, facilities and some of the financial support to meet the growing demand for health care. The sector consists of two industry groups, six industries, and ten subindustries. The two industry groups are

1. Health care equipment & services
2. Pharmaceuticals, biotechnology & life sciences

Because health care is often controlled by governments outside the United States, the sector is not as well represented globally (Exhibit 8-10). Pricing power is stronger in this sector than most, but there seems to be growing resistance to the rising costs as the largest consumer of health care based on age cohorts, over 65, is also the one most likely to be living on a fixed income.

Exhibit 8-10   Health Care Representation in Global Indexes (Source: Standard & Poor's)

	Percentage of Market Capitalization
Global	10.2%
United States	12.1%
Europe	10.4%
Japan	5.4%
Asia	0.0%
Latin America	0.0%

Capital intensity for the sector is modest. Early stage companies such as small and mid-cap bio-tech companies need huge capital until they receive approval for their drug. The large cap pharmaceutical companies generate lots of free cash flow, buy back their stock, have relatively high dividend yields, and are likely to consider further acquisitions. This disparity between firms is a characteristic of this sector. There is a mix of companies needing capital to develop products, whereas others will be more active capital managers, such as the larger cap pharmaceutical companies.

Valuation tends to be middle of the range compared to other sectors. However, despite the rising healthcare cost trend, the sector's earnings growth was weaker than most sectors in the middle of the past decade. This was because some of the larger companies passed their point of peak profitability and could not generate sufficient volumes to maintain strong earnings growth while also offsetting the declining margin. The classic growth companies of yesteryears, large cap pharmaceutical companies are now considered value stocks. Companies with smaller capitalization tend to trade at much higher valuations as a group because many have no earnings. The health care sector is often the highest valued sector based on earnings in the S&P MidCap 400 and S&P SmallCap 600 because many of its companies are not yet profitable.

Despite the changing view of some of the sector's dominant companies, one of the major themes for the healthcare sector is growth. The source of the growth should tend to be the mid-cap and small-cap companies. They also tend to be considered acquisition targets for larger cap healthcare companies looking to reinvest their excess cash flow. The other theme is value, which is usually found in large-cap pharmaceuticals, managed-care companies, and health services. The sector's net profit margin, at more than 10% is relatively high.

Industrial companies are part of a sector that is one of the prime beneficiaries of the global expansion. They provide everything from airplanes, farm equipment, power generation equipment, and the transportation to move goods and people from one place to another, and help put in place the infrastructure necessary to support the growing global economy.

The largest companies have tremendous global reach, and the sector represents more than 20% of Japan's market capitalization (Exhibit 8-11). The sector consists of 3 industry groups, 13 industries and 23 subindustries.

The three industry groups are

1. Capital goods
2. Commercial services and supplies
3. Transportation

Exhibit 8-11 Industrials Representation in Global Indexes (Source: Standard & Poor's)

	Percentage of Market Capitalization
Global	11.2%
United States	10.5%
Europe	9.8%
Japan	20.0%
Asia	5.7%
Latin America	4.0%

Growth opportunities for these companies are driven predominantly by the environment. That is, the tremendous growth generated by many developing countries such as China and India has created a phenomenon we call *infrastructuralization*, which is the need to build the infrastructure of countries for them to evolve into developed countries. That process is an extended one because infrastructure includes more than just roads. It means buildings and cities. According to the website CityMayors, China already has 12 of the world's 50 largest cities, whereas New York City is the only city in the United States to rank in the top 50. Between 2005 and 2030, a mass migration of China's urban center is expected to occur, as still less than 45% of the country is urbanized, compared to more than 80% for the United States, more than 65% in Japan, and more than 75% in Germany.[1] That population is expected to grow from just more than 550 million to about 1 billion. To support the migration, a great deal of cement, steel, copper, and equipment will be required to make roads and buildings and cities. The investment opportunities are global.

Capital intensity for the sector is high. Free cash flow is used to build new capacity and add new equipment. Dividend increases are common, but the yield of the sector is modest, and it is a compelling reason for investing in it.

The growing global economy is the principal theme driving investment in this sector, and the duration of this cycle continues to exceed expectations. That cycle was also extended because of continued military conflicts and the increased demand for more sophisticated weaponry. The relative value of companies in this sector compared to the expected duration of this cycle is the key issue for investors to address when considering opportunities in this sector.

Information technology companies provide many of the products, services, and new business models that started the Digital Age and are necessary to keep it going. This sector includes Google, Yahoo, Microsoft, IBM, and Apple. It also includes Intel and Cisco. Consider some of what has come from this sector—the Internet, e-mail, cell phones, PDAs, iPads, Blackberries, and PCs. They did not exist 30 years ago.

The sector consists of 3 industry groups, 8 industries, and 15 subindustries. The three industry groups are

1. Software and services
2. Technology hardware and equipment
3. Semiconductors and semiconductor equipment

Many of the companies in the sector are global, and as shown in Exhibit 8-12, the bulk of the companies are headquartered in the United States, Japan, or other Asian countries. For these companies, first-stage growth is driven by innovation, which has been followed by mass adoption. When adoption occurs, continued growth is driven by constant innovation as implied by Moore's Law. That innovation is driven in part by the requirement of many new products for more processing capacity and bandwidth. Still, some of the growth begins to be driven by the environment as economies expand. Regardless of the level of demand, pricing power is fleeting as products lose their novelty and continued innovation is required. Without it, or with a strategic misstep, a company could lose its competitive advantage and, with it, its share of the business.

Exhibit 8-12   Information Technology Representation in Global Indexes (Source: Standard & Poor's)

	Percentage of Market Capitalization
Global	13.6%
United States	18.9%
Europe	3.0%
Japan	14.7%
Asia	26.9%
Latin America	0.0%

Capital intensity for the sector is modest. Like many sectors, capital intensity is greater for the smaller and mid-cap companies. Valuation tends to be one of the highest of any sector; small, mid, or large cap. This reflects the higher growth expectations for the sector and relatively high levels of free cash flow.

Growth from innovation is one of the key investment themes for the sector. Given the higher valuation on expected earnings, investors are also sensitive to changes in earnings outlook. Another important theme is the growing consumer markets outside the United States that are often early adopters of some of the more basic products.

Materials companies are also prime beneficiaries of global growth. This sector is a much larger portion of developing country indexes included in the S&P Global 1200 (Exhibit 8-13). Mining and cement companies are a larger part of the Latin American market, whereas plastic and steel companies are a larger part of the Asian market. One of the four sectors that is also its own industry group, Materials then consists of 5 industries and 15 subindustries. The five industries are

1. Chemicals

2. Construction materials

3. Containers and packaging

4. Metals and mining

5. Paper and forest products

**Exhibit 8-13   Materials Representation in Global Indexes
(Source: Standard & Poor's)**

	Percentage of Market Capitalization
Global	19.8%
United States	10.5%
Europe	9.8%
Japan	8.3%
Asia	8.4%
Latin America	26.9%

Growth is tied to the environment, which has favored the more basic materials part of the sector and the companies more sensitive to the building of infrastructure. The strength of the global economy and its effect on the sector is evident in its earnings growth, real, and expected, since 2004. For the 2 years that ended in 2006, materials companies generated 23% earnings growth and were expected to sustain 24.5% annual growth for the 3 years ending in 2011.

Capital intensity for the sector is modest. Expansion is expensive and done cautiously. The rise in many commodity prices pushed net profit margins more than 10% for many and left companies with a level of free cash sufficient to buy back a lot of stock. This seems to be a preferred course in the sector instead of raising dividends, which is logical because of the more volatile nature of the earning streams.

This is a sector that was recently valued in line with the broader index or at a slight discount. Unlike most sectors, the mid-cap and small-cap companies trade at a discount to many of the large-cap companies reflecting a less developed global business.

Investment themes for the sector include global growth and its effect on demand relative to available supply. Another theme is consolidation because of the high cost of finding and developing new sources.

Telecommunication services companies are the providers of telecommunication services and wireless service. They do not manufacture telecommunication equipment and products necessary to make telecommunications work. This is the smallest sector in terms of number of companies and market capitalization (Exhibit 8-14). There are fewer companies in this sector than there are subindustries for many other sectors. It is the same at the industry group level, with two industries and three subindustries. The two industries are

1. Diversified telecommunication services

2. Wireless telecommunication services

Exhibit 8-14   Telecommunication Services Representation in Global Indexes (Source: Standard & Poor's)

	Percentage of Market Capitalization
Global	5.0%
United States	2.8%
Europe	6.5%
Japan	4.0%
Asia	9.2%
Latin America	12.1%

The growth story resides outside the United States and principally in the developing markets where per capita income levels are rising the fastest. In the United States, growth is tied to extending the business model and taking shares from other companies trying to provide products tethered to lines of communications reaching into American households, which include telephone, Internet, and cable.

Capital intensity for the sector is high because of the need to expand the product offerings just to maintain the customer base. Supporting the stocks is an attractive dividend yield and an improving earnings outlook in the United States.

Utility companies are sometimes called the raw materials companies of this economic age because today's raw material is electricity. For most markets, it is basically a domestic industry, and much of it is regional. This is the last of the four sectors that remain the same at the industry group level. It consists of five industries and five subindustries. For all the global market indexes, Utilities represent less than 10% of an index's market capitalization (Exhibit 8-15). The five industries are

1. Electric utilities
2. Gas utilities
3. Multi-utilities
4. Water utilities
5. Independent power producers and energy traders

Exhibit 8-15   Utilities Representation in Global Indexes (Source: Standard & Poor's)

	Percentage of Market Capitalization
Global	4.6%
United States	3.4%
Europe	6.3%
Japan	5.2%
Asia	3.6%
Latin America	6.3%

Growth comes from energy demand, which remains stronger than expected because of strong global economy and the growing use of technology-related products, whose operation requires lots of electricity.

Capital intensity for the sector is high because of the need to build new plants and make old ones more environmentally friendly. Still, a substantial amount of earnings is paid out in dividends, making the sector one of the providers of the highest dividend yields.

For the last 4 of 5 years, this sector provided stronger than expected earnings growth through 2008. That strong growth is not expected to continue through 2011. For the three year period through 2011, annual compound earnings growth is expected to be just under 2% a year.

Endnotes

[1] 2010 Zoomlion presentation

9

Industry Evolution

A century ago, industry was overtaking agriculture as the main source of economic growth and employment. Many decades later, it was the turn of the service sector to claim a gradually bigger portion of the economic pie, as shown in Exhibit 9-1.

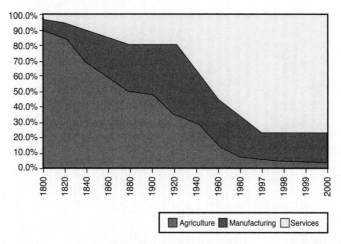

Exhibit 9-1   Changes in U.S. Employment by Sector (1800 to 2001)
(Source: *Historical Statistics of United States: Colonial Times to 1970,*
Susan Carter, Scott Gartner, Michael R. Haines, Alan Olmstead, Richard Sutch, Gavin Wright (editors), Cambridge University Press, 2001)

Today, the service sector occupies the lion share of economic output in not just the United States (Exhibit 9-2), but also in most developed economies where it has become the largest employer. The *Services* sector is also the dominant sector in the global economy, as shown in Exhibit 9-3. In the United States and the European Union, for example, more and more people are employed in tourism, transportation, financial services, and the like rather than in mills and factories. At the same time, the manufacturing sector has been shedding jobs, and surprisingly to some, this has been happening not only in the developed world but also in many developing nations. This change is driven mostly by technological advances, with automation and productivity improvement enabling higher output with a shrinking pool of workers. International trade has been an important contributing factor but still secondary to the impact of technological progress.

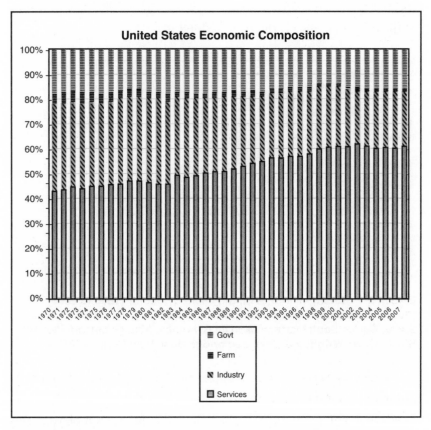

Exhibit 9-2   Share of U.S. GDP by Sector—1970 to 2007 (Source: The World Bank)

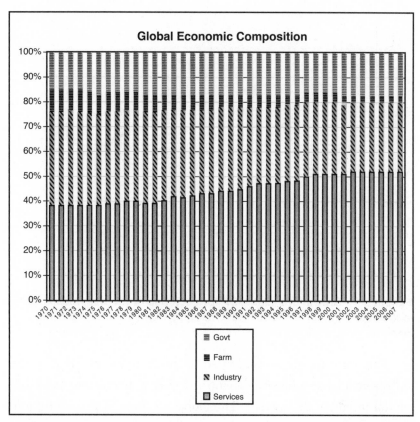

Exhibit 9-3   Share of World GDP by Sector—1970 to 2007 (Source: The World Bank)

Between 1970 and 2007, the global economy grew from less than $3 trillion to more than $55 trillion. In that period, like the U.S. economy, the global economy became more dependent on services and less dependent on manufacturing. The next exhibit, Exhibit 9-4, shows the Indian economy is following a similar path—one that is much less driven by the agrarian economy and much more driven by services.

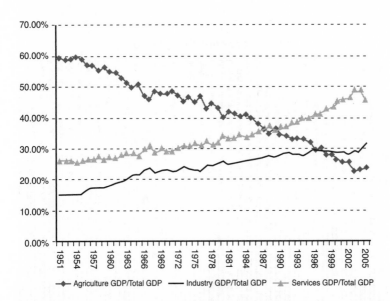

Exhibit 9-4   Growth of Indian GDP for Each Sector (Source: *India's Service Sector Growth—A "New" Revolution* by Rubina Verma, April 17, 2006)

These are trends we identified in the Introduction; that is, the shift from a labor-intensive economy (agrarian) to one that was more capital-intensive (industrial). The global economy is now shifting to a more knowledge- and information-based service economy. The ability to productively employ a growing world population depends on how well the seeds of growth are planted and nurtured. The more unnatural the efforts to achieve that growth, the harder it will be to achieve let alone sustain. Clearly, too much debt is an unnatural source of growth and more likely a source of destruction. What follows in this chapter is a discussion of some specific details about the growth potential of certain industries.

It is important to remember that, like manufacturing, the service sector is quite diverse, including, on one hand, sophisticated fields such as business consulting, and relatively simple fields such as truck transportation on the other (see Exhibit 9-5).

Exhibit 9-5   List of Widely Used Services in the United States (Source: Bureau of Economic Analysis)

Wholesale trade
Retail trade
Transportation and warehousing
Rail transportation

> *Water transportation*
>
> *Truck transportation*
>
> *Transit and ground passenger transportation*
>
> *Pipeline transportation*
>
> *Other transportation and support activities*
>
> *Warehousing and storage*

Information:

> *Publishing industries (includes software)*
>
> *Motion picture and sound recording industries*
>
> *Broadcasting and telecommunications*
>
> *Information and data processing services*

Finance, insurance, real estate, rental, and leasing:

> *Finance and insurance:*
>
> > *Federal Reserve banks, credit intermediation, and related activities*
> >
> > *Securities, commodity contracts, and investments*
> >
> > *Insurance carriers and related activities*
> >
> > *Funds, trusts, and other financial vehicles*
>
> *Real estate and rental and leasing:*
>
> > *Real estate*
> >
> > *Rental and leasing services and lessors of intangible assets*

Professional and business services:

> *Professional, scientific, and technical services:*
>
> > *Legal services*
> >
> > *Computer systems design and related services*
> >
> > *Miscellaneous professional, scientific, and technical services*
>
> *Management of companies and enterprises*
>
> *Administrative and waste management services:*
>
> > *Administrative and support services*
> >
> > *Waste management and remediation services*

Exhibit 9-5   List of Widely Used Services in the United States (Source: Bureau of Economic Analysis)

Educational services, health care, and social assistance:

  Educational services

  Health care and social assistance:

   Ambulatory health care services

   Hospitals and nursing and residential care facilities

   Social assistance

Arts, entertainment, recreation, accommodation, and food services:

  Arts, entertainment, and recreation:

   Performing arts, spectator sports, museums, and related activities

   Amusements, gambling, and recreation industries

  Accommodation and food services:

   Accommodation

   Food services and drinking places

Other services

Understandably, the various sectors require a range of capabilities, from highly paid scientists with advanced degrees to low paid hotel maids. The implication is that some countries will be competitive in certain service sectors but not in others and are therefore less likely to attract value chain activities in the latter areas. Some service subsectors such as software support are mobile; that is, they can be provided at a distance or moved at will to another location; others are not. Among the least mobile are personal care businesses that require service consumption on premises and in many settings (not in the EU for example), trucking. This implies that some service lines are unlikely to integrate into the global economy while others are.

There are natural limits to the shifting of service jobs overseas. Many of them are in industries such as hotels and restaurants, or in public services such as education and health, most of which can never be moved abroad. In Britain, some 60% of all service-sector employment falls into this category. Further, technology might place some constraints on off-shoring. Presently, for instance, customer-service call centers are labor-intensive and wages account for 70% of the costs of a call center in America. That is why companies are rapidly shifting to low-cost destination like India. Firms such as AT&T are working on speech recognition software that might soon be good enough to replace a lot of routine inquiries currently handled in call centers.[1]

In addition to being the primary economic sector in developed economies, the service sector is gaining ground in developing economies. In India, the IT services sector has led the way in reaching foreign markets and grabbing market share.

Even China, "factory to the world," has been shedding industrial employment while increasing service sector employment; although, the process has been uneven with the manufacturing sector growing during certain years. Although many Chinese people continue to move in record numbers from the countryside to the cities, they are increasingly likely to find jobs in construction, transportation, and other service sectors than in manufacturing. Many do find manufacturing employment close to home in enterprises that are often not formally accounted for. A China wide economic census completed in 2005 found under-reporting of some $280 billion of economic output, most of it in the service sector. The discrepancy shows the growing size and share of the Chinese service sector but should also serve as a caution against available numbers and data.

In general, the rise of the service sector and the gradual if partial opening of the sector to international investment promise some fundamental changes of interest to investors. First, they suggest that service providers, from banks and insurance companies to logistic providers and hotel operators will capture a bigger piece of the economic pie, implying higher earnings and valuations. Second, this suggests consolidation among both domestic and international players and, as a result, a continuing wave of mergers and acquisitions. Third,

this means further involvement of the financial sector in manufacturing, for instance, via the acquisition of manufacturing firms by private
equity groups. Fourth, the rise of the service sector suggests a possible change in trade balances and hence in exchange rate movement.
For instance, the United States is competitive in services and runs a
surplus in the service trade while running a huge deficit in the trade
of goods. Other things being equal, this suggests the possibility of an
eventual decline in the overall U.S. trade deficit that has persisted for
roughly three decades.

The Growth of the Financial Services Sector

Within the broader growth in services, financial services grew
rapidly over the last three decades. Banks, insurance companies,
stock exchanges, brokerages, and many other supporting sectors represent a larger share of the economy today as compared to just a few
years ago, as shown in Exhibit 9-6. Exhibit 9-7 gives a sense of the
great diversity within the financial services industry.

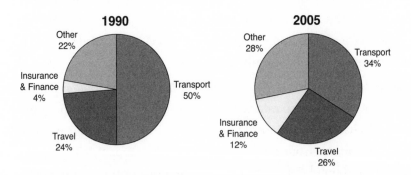

**Exhibit 9-6   Mix of Commercial Services Imports by Developing Coun-
tries (Source: The World Bank)**

Exhibit 9-7   List of Financial Services with SIC Codes (Source: U.S. Department of Labor)

Finance, Insurance, And Real Estate

Major Group 60: Depository Institutions

Industry Group 601: Central Reserve Depository Institutions

6011 Federal Reserve Banks

6019 Central Reserve Depository Institutions, Not Elsewhere Classified

Industry Group 602: Commercial Banks

6021 National Commercial Banks

6022 State Commercial Banks

6029 Commercial Banks, Not Elsewhere Classified

Industry Group 603: Savings Institutions

6035 Savings Institutions, Federally Chartered

6036 Savings Institutions, Not Federally Chartered

Industry Group 606: Credit Unions

6061 Credit Unions, Federally Chartered

6062 Credit Unions, Not Federally Chartered

Industry Group 608: Foreign Banking And Branches And Agencies Of

6081 Branches and Agencies of Foreign Banks

6082 Foreign Trade and International Banking Institutions

Industry Group 609: Functions Related to Depository Banking

6091 Nondeposit Trust Facilities,

6099 Functions Related to Depository Banking, Not Elsewhere Classified

Major Group 61: Nondepository Credit Institutions

Industry Group 611: Federal And Federally Sponsored Credit Agencies

6111 Federal and Federally Sponsored Credit Agencies

Industry Group 614: Personal Credit Institutions

6141 Personal Credit Institutions

Industry Group 615: Business Credit Institutions

6153 Short-Term Business Credit Institutions, Except Agricultural

6159 Miscellaneous Business Credit Institutions

Exhibit 9-7 List of Financial Services with SIC Codes (Source: U.S. Department of Labor)

Industry Group 616: Mortgage Bankers And Brokers

6162 Mortgage Bankers and Loan Correspondents

6163 Loan Brokers

Major Group 62: Security And Commodity Brokers, Dealers, Exchanges, and Services

Industry Group 621: Security Brokers, Dealers, and Flotation

6211 Security Brokers, Dealers, and Flotation Companies

Industry Group 622: Commodity Contracts Brokers and Dealers

6221 Commodity Contracts Brokers and Dealers

Industry Group 623: Security And Commodity Exchanges

6231 Security and Commodity Exchanges

Industry Group 628: Services Allied with the Exchange of Securities

6282 Investment Advice

6289 Services Allied with the Exchange of Securities or Commodities, Not Elsewhere Classified

Major Group 63: Insurance Carriers

Industry Group 631: Life Insurance

6311 Life Insurance

Industry Group 632: Accident and Health Insurance and Medical

6321 Accident and Health Insurance

6324 Hospital and Medical Service Plans

Industry Group 633: Fire, Marine, and Casualty Insurance

6331 Fire, Marine, and Casualty Insurance

Industry Group 635: Surety Insurance

6351 Surety Insurance

Industry Group 636: Title Insurance

6361 Title Insurance

Industry Group 637: Pension, Health, and Welfare Funds

6371 Pension, Health, and Welfare Funds

Exhibit 9-7   List of Financial Services with SIC Codes (Source: U.S. Department of Labor)

Industry Group 639: Insurance Carriers, Not Elsewhere Classified

6399 Insurance Carriers, Not Elsewhere Classified

Major Group 64: Insurance Agents, Brokers, and Service

Industry Group 641: Insurance Agents, Brokers, And Service

6411 Insurance Agents, Brokers, and Service

Major Group 65: Real Estate

Industry Group 651: Real Estate Operators (Except Developers) and

6512 Operators of Nonresidential Buildings

6513 Operators or Apartment Buildings

6514 Operators of Dwellings Other Than Apartment Buildings

6515 Operators of Residential Mobile Home Sites

6517 Lessors of Railroad Property

6519 Lessors of Real Property, Not Elsewhere Classified

Industry Group 653: Real Estate Agents and Managers

6531 Real Estate Agents and Managers

Industry Group 654: Title Abstract Offices

6541 Title Abstract Offices

Industry Group 655: Land Subdividers and Developers

6552 Land Subdividers and Developers, Except Cemeteries

6553 Cemetery Subdividers and Developers

Major Group 67: Holding and Other Investment Offices

Industry Group 671: Holding Offices

6712 Offices of Bank Holding Companies

6719 Offices of Holding Companies, Not Elsewhere Classified

Industry Group 672: Investment Offices

6722 Management Investment Offices, Open-End

6726 Unit Investment Trusts, Face-Amount Certificate Offices, and Closed-End Management Investment Offices

Exhibit 9-7   List of Financial Services with SIC Codes (Source: U.S. Department of Labor)

Industry Group 673: Trusts
6732 Educational, Religious, and Charitable Trusts
6733 Trusts, Except Educational, Religious, and Charitable
Industry Group 679: Miscellaneous Investing
6792 Oil Royalty Traders
6794 Patent Owners and Lessors
6798 Real Estate Investment Trusts
6799 Investors, Not Elsewhere Classified

In emerging economies, economic growth and the rise in per capita income will create tremendous demand for financial services. This is already happening in China and beginning to happen in India. Opening the market to foreign investments in India (FDI limit in private sector banks was raised to 74% in 2004) will create many opportunities for large international banks such as Citibank and HSBC, and possibly for some smaller players as well (see Exhibit 9-8 for a list of local and foreign banks in India). Indian banks, on their part, are likely to consolidate and then venture abroad, possibly tapping ethnic Indian communities at first and then leveraging niches where India is strong, such as IT services.

Exhibit 9-8   List of Banks in India (Source: Reserve Bank of India [Bank-wise gross nonperforming assets, gross advances, and gross NPA ratio of scheduled commercial banks—2009])

Central Bank	Reserve Bank of India
State Bank of India and its associates	State Bank of Bikaner and Jaipur, State Bank of Hyderabad, State Bank of India, State Bank of Indore, State Bank of Mysore, State Bank of Patiala, State Bank of Travancore
Nationalized banks	Allahabad Bank, Andhra Bank, Bank of Baroda, Bank of India, Bank of Maharashtra, Canara Bank, Central Bank of India, Corporation Bank, Dena Bank, IDBI Bank Limited, Indian Bank, Indian Overseas Bank, Oriental Bank of Commerce, Punjab and Sind Bank, Punjab National Bank, Syndicate Bank, UCO Bank, Union Bank of India, United Bank of India, Vijaya Bank
Other scheduled commercial banks	Axis Bank, Bank of Rajasthan, Catholic Syrian Bank, City Union Bank, Development Credit Bank, Dhanalakshmi Bank, Federal Bank, HDFC Bank, ICICI Bank, IndusInd Bank, ING Vysya Bank, Jammu and Kashmir Bank, Karnataka Bank, Karur Vysya Bank, Kotak Mahindra Bank, Lakshmi Vilas Bank, Nainital Bank, Ratnakar Bank, SBI Commercial & International Bank, South Indian Bank, Yes Bank
Foreign banks	AB Bank, ABN AMRO Bank, Abu Dhabi Commercial Bank, American Express Banking Corp., Antwerp Diamond Bank, BNP Paribas, Bank of America, Bank of Bahrain & Kuwait, Bank of Ceylon, Bank of Nova Scotia, Barclays Bank, Calyon Bank, China Trust Commercial Bank, Citibank, Deutsche Bank, Development Bank of Singapore, Hongkong & Shanghai Banking Corporation, JP Morgan Chase Bank, JSC VTB Bank, Krung Thai Bank pcl, Mashreq Bank, Mizuho Corporate Bank, Oman International Bank, Shinhan Bank, Societe Generale, Sonali Bank, Standard Chartered Bank, State Bank of Mauritius, The Bank of Tokyo—Mitsubishi UFJ, UBS AG

Industry Trends and Challenges

Globalization, technological changes, and related changes are changing the fortunes of industries and the fortunes of market players worldwide. We have chosen to illustrate the trends, and their potential economic impact, using brief industry examples for automotive, logistics, and toys. The first industry, automotive, is capital-intensive, suffers from chronic overcapacity, and is in the midst of a dramatic regional shift exemplifying the broader trends described in this book. Logistics is an industry that seems ideally poised to benefit from globalization as a provider of infrastructure and services necessary to keep a global economy humming. The toy industry, traditionally labor-intensive, is still dominated by large developed country players employing developing country cheap labor, but demographics and other developments suggest this should not be taken for granted. Textile and garments are among the oldest industries in the world and have traditionally veered toward lower-cost locations; some are proving however to be much more competitive than others. An even older sector is agriculture, but with food shortages for a larger and wealthier world population looming, it is also undergoing a major transformation. Finally, pharmaceuticals, a technology-intensive growth sector, is also facing major challenges whose resolution will determine winners and losers among national economies and individual firms.

The Automotive Industry

The automotive industry is more than a century old and so are international trade and foreign direct investment in the industry. Almost as soon as the first automobiles appeared on the road, some of the manufacturers (e.g., the Ford Motor Company) began to export their cars and within a few years also opened manufacturing plants abroad to defend against high tariffs. Many of the major exporters of automotive products are also major importers (e.g., the United

States, European Union, Canada, Mexico, and China). The largest volume of trade in automobiles and parts involves trade among the members of the European Union, but this is rapidly changing with Asia rising fast. In 2009, China became the world's largest automobile market, and the Indian market is also growing fast.

The micro-car segment is shaping up as a major Indian battleground, because of the growth in the Indian middle class and its disposable income. High traffic congestion is another reason why India and multinational automotive manufacturers are venturing into low-cost and fuel efficient small cars. Tata Motors, Bajaj Auto, Hero Group, Toyota, Volkswagen, Renault, and Nissan are planning to launch such cars in the price range of $1500 to $5000. Interestingly, Bajaj Auto (in cooperation with Renault) and the Hero Group are primarily two- and three-wheeler manufacturers that have been successful in their industry but are now moving to tap the demand for cheap four-wheelers.

These changing trends carry significant implications for car makers, both local and global. KPMG, a consultancy firm, forecasts that while vehicle sales will grow by 10% to 20% annually over the next few years, the main beneficiaries will be automakers from China and Japan. The winning brands, according to the report, will be Chinese, Indian, Japanese, and South Korean, in that order. North American brands are expected to lose market share, whereas opinions regarding the future of European brands are evenly divided. The report goes on to say that the overcapacity in the industry is estimated at more than 10% or 6 to 10 million vehicles annually. Under these conditions a shakeup is expected, and the recent global financial crisis has merely accelerated the trend. Just before the crisis, Indian maker Tata acquired the venerable Jaguar and Land Rover brands from Ford, and at the time of this writing, Chinese firms have tried to acquire the Hummer brand, completed the purchase of Volvo, and have been involved in other attempted or rumored transactions.

What adds to the complexity in this sector is the tendency of many governments, in both developed and emerging economies, to view automotive as a "pillar industry" because of the large number of other industries affected by it, its employment ramifications, and the fulfill-ment of certain noneconomic objectives. Developed country govern-ments often view automotive as a security-sensitive industry (during World War II, U.S. car makers were cranking out tanks and military vehicles) whereas emerging market governments view it as a ticket to rapid industrialization and development. That the automotive indus-try is one of the main investors in R&D adds to this sensitivity, which amplifies the political and social considerations affecting the industry.

U.S. and European firms have taken a number of steps to con-front the challenges facing them, among them a dramatic increase in outsourced components from lower-cost countries. Another solution has been to move production to a lower-cost location and, in addition to selling in that market, export the product to the home country and other markets (Exhibit 9-9).

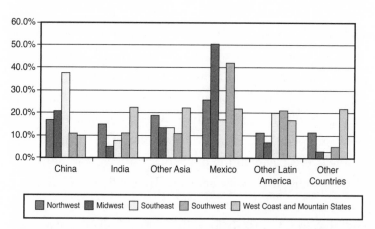

Exhibit 9-9   Percentage of Production Shifts in U.S. Region by Destina-tion Country, January–March 2004 (Source: Bronfenbrenner, K. & Luce, S. [2004]. *The changing nature of corporate global restructuring: The impact of production shifts on jobs in the U.S., China, and around the globe.* **Washington, DC: U.S.-China Economic and Security Review Com-mission)**

In the meantime, the battle goes on for market share in the domestic markets of India, China, Vietnam, Russia, and other emerging market countries that are growing at a fast clip, whereas the U.S. and European markets are stagnating. For instance, the KPMG survey predicts that annual growth in China's automotive market will range between 11% and 20%, whereas developed markets are not likely to move much.

Global Positive Trend—Logistics

If there is an industry that stands to benefit from globalization it is logistics. The need to shift large amounts of goods and components from one country to another is a direct result of the growth in trade and foreign direct investment and the deverticalization of the value chain. To capture the benefits of globalization, companies need to develop an effective supply chain, one that reduces operating cost, improves distribution, and facilitates customer service. Companies with a sophisticated supply chain, such as Wal-Mart, and third-party logistic providers, have been the major beneficiaries of this trend. Efficient management of an increasingly complex supply chain enables logistics-savvy firms to lower procurement and operational costs, whereas at the same time respond quickly to changing consumer trends. Utilizing seamless multimodal transportation and advanced information systems to track and control product and material flow these firms and successful third-party providers can shorten their reaction time, be it to a customer or a supplier, while realizing savings from a direct, flexible, low-inventory supply chain. Consolidation of assembly and distribution in a few key strategic locations around the globe enables firms and providers to gain economies of scale without violating national standards and regulations as long as the regions involved have synchronized their regulatory systems.

Small and medium size players, and sometimes even large companies, turn to third-party logistics providers. In turn, increasing volume and broader customer expectations drive consolidation among logistics providers and domain expansion by the large players. Express shippers such as Federal Express and UPS accelerate their transformation from shipping firms into global logistic providers; although, they operate side by side with specialized and regional logistics outfits that seek to leverage their local expertise. Although the industry is seeing consolidation, new entrants mushroom in markets such as Brazil and China. These new entrants are mostly niche players who offer an intimate understanding of a particular product line (e.g., personal computers) that justifies high premiums and requires such customization that established players might find onerous.

The Toy Industry

Toys have been a classic labor-intensive industry that has been undergoing considerable change in recent years. These changes included a continuous shift of manufacturing to lower cost locations, with China, now making roughly 80% of today's traditional toys, already farming out some low-cost components to neighbors such as Vietnam, Laos, and Cambodia.

This model, where manufacturing moves to a low-cost location while R&D and design remain at home is increasingly tenuous. Large, branded U.S. firms such as Hasbro and Mattel rely on OEMs based in low-cost locations to do the manufacturing of products conceived, designed, marketed, and distributed at home and other global markets. But is this formula sustainable? Let's start with the demographics: The vast majority of the world's children will neither be in the United States nor Europe but rather in Asia, excluding Japan (Exhibit 9-10). (China would have comparatively less children than India because of the One Child policy.) Public spending on education in Asia remains much lower as compared to that in North America and Western Europe, but the numbers will change fairly quickly, especially for emerging markets such as India and China.

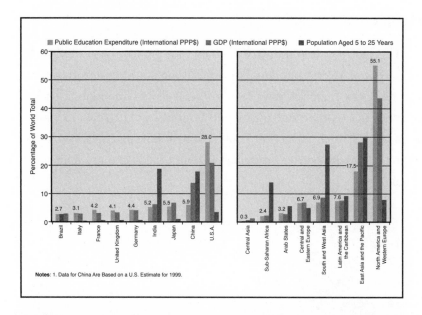

Exhibit 9-10   Global Distribution of Public Expenditure on Education, GDP, and Population Aged 5 to 25 Years, by Region and for Selected Countries, 2004 (Source: UNESCO Institute for Statistics, Global Education Digest 2007)

The U.S. firms that make their toys in China hardly sell them there. This does not bode well for their prospects. Moreover, Chinese manufacturers, who are already making around 80% of the world's toys, are not likely to remain in their assigned OEM roles. They are already doing rudimentary design work and at some point, perhaps after some consolidation in the industry, will start establishing a brand or, faster yet, will acquire an existing brand, which has been a favorite approach of Chinese companies in some other industries. In the meantime, the subcontracting strategy has proven risky in terms of loss of control, as was illustrated in the summer of 2007 when U.S. firms and importers had to recall one toy line after another for excessive lead in their "made in China" toys. Such recall could have far reaching consequences for the bottom line of these companies, because although they can probably shift some of the cost of the recall to the suppliers, the damage to their reputation and the reluctance of customers to purchase any such toys might be far reaching.

Textiles and Garments

The global textile industry is likely to grow from $309 billion to $856 billion. Textile industry is primarily present in areas that have abundant raw material, have low cost as well as skilled labor, have a presence across the value chain, and benefit from a growing domestic market. China, India, the United States, Pakistan, and Brazil are among the major cotton producers (Exhibit 9-11) and are major textile and garment makers.

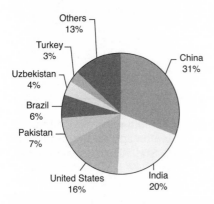

Exhibit 9-11   Global Cotton Production Composition 2007–08 (Source: United States Department of Agriculture)

Textiles and clothing are closely related technologically and in terms of trade policy. Textiles provide the major input to the clothing industry, creating vertical linkages between the two. Textiles however is capital- and technology-intensive, whereas garment making is labor-intensive. International trade in the two sectors is regulated by the Agreement on Textiles and Clothing (ATC) at the multilateral level, whereas bilateral and regional trade agreements typically link the two sectors by rules of origin.

On January 1, 2005, the Multifiber agreement expired and was replaced by the General Agreement on Tariffs. This created an almost immediate shift in the fortunes of various national producers;

for example, China replaced Mexico as the main origin of U.S. garment imports. This sector is politically and socially sensitive because it often provides employment in locations where alternative jobs might be difficult to come by. This is true not only in the developing world but also in rural areas of developed nations such as Appalachia in the United States or rural areas in Italy. Textiles and clothing are also among the sectors in which developing countries have the most to gain from multilateral trade liberalization.

The clothing industry is labor-intensive and offers entry-level jobs for unskilled labor in developed and developing countries. Job creation in the sector has been particularly strong for women in poor countries, who previously had no income opportunities other than the household or the informal sector. Moreover, it is a sector where relatively modern technology can be adopted even in poor countries at relatively low investment costs. These technological features of the industry have made it suitable as the first rung on the industrialization ladder in poor countries, some of which have experienced a high output growth rate in the sector (e.g., Bangladesh, Sri Lanka, Vietnam, and Mauritius). These characteristics, however, have also made it a footloose industry that can adjust to changing market conditions quickly.[2]

Agriculture

Macro Trends

Agriculture should benefit from a growing global economy and population. According to the International Monetary Fund's (IMF) April 2010 *World Economic Outlook,* the pace of global economic growth is expected to accelerate from the economic crisis of 2008:

- World economic growth is projected to increase at a 3.2% average annual rate between 2006 and 2015.
- Strong economic growth in developing countries of about 5% annually is projected through 2015.

- Growth in global population is assumed to continue to slow, to an average of about 1.1% per year compared with an annual rate of 1.7% in the 1980s.

- From 2007 to 2010, oil prices are projected to fall as new crude supplies help offset the rise in demand from Asia. In subsequent years, crude oil prices are projected to rise, but only slightly faster than the broader inflation rate.

Market Trends

Within the United States, we want to highlight a few secular lifestyle trends. They include urbanization, greater use of alternative fuels, and an increased focus on healthy living:[3]

- Urban land amounted to 2.6% of total U.S. land mass in 2002; (but contains 79% of the U.S. population).

- The Renewable Fuel Program of the Energy Policy Act of 2005 mandates renewable fuel use in gasoline (with credits for biodiesel) to reach 7.5 billion gallons by calendar year 2012, nearly double the 2005 level.

- Consumer food prices are projected to rise less than the broader inflation rate.

- Organic farming is one of the fastest-growing segments of U.S. agriculture, with organic food sales reaching $13.8 billion in 2005.

Potential Breakthroughs/Game-Changers

New technologies, structures, and ideas often change the outlook of a business. Here are some that could change the outlook for agriculture:

- Researchers have identified a gene that confers on rice crops the capability to survive extended submersion in water.

- The first drug from a transgenic animal might be nearing approval.

- Experiments in clothing made from a new fiber called Ingeo, derived from genetically engineered corn.

- Vertical farms potentially offer sustainable production of a varied food supply (year-round crop production), and the reclamation of land that has been used for horizontal farming.

Some Trends in Agriculture

Two significant trends occurring in the agricultural sector during the past century involved the increased use of machines and government price supports. These factors combined to encourage operators to increase the size of their farms and gain efficiencies. The purchase of farm inputs, such as machinery, required an increasing amount of capital, and fewer individuals wanted to take on the debt necessary to farm. Large cash outlays for farm equipment increased specialization, and operators began producing larger quantities of a limited number of products. As a result, fewer farms were needed to meet the demand for agricultural products, and a pronounced structural change in the agricultural sector took place. The number of farms declined significantly as compared to the total farm acreage after 1950, thereby concentrating agricultural production in fewer farms (Exhibit 9-12).Total farm and ranch acreage increased steadily during the first half of the twentieth century, due in large part to development in the Great Plains and Far West where land policy encouraged continued conversion of large tracts of arid government lands to agricultural uses. Acreage declined later in the century, when increased production was achieved through efficiency rather than through additional acreage.[4]

In the 1960s, Indian agriculture developed by using more intense agriculture leveraging newer irrigation technologies, modern fertilizers, and a superior seed and crop mix. Such advances also triggered, however, negative byproducts in the form of water and soil degradation that held productivity growth at bay.

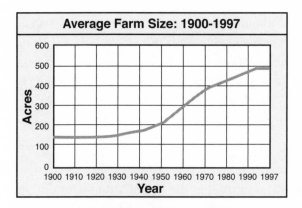

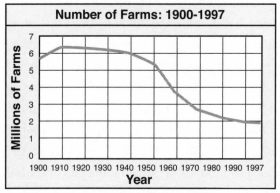

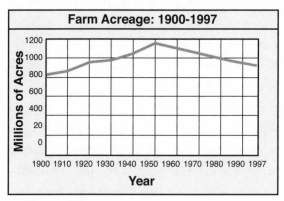

Exhibit 9-12   Structural Change in the U.S. Agriculture Sector (Source: Census of Agriculture)

In the late 1980s, drip irrigation gained popularity with its inherent advantages such as saving water and use in problematic soil. Various research institutes conducted experiments on drip irrigation and made people aware of its benefits. Some manufacturers also conducted their own studies first by importing the materials before venturing into commercial production of drip systems. Today, more than a 60,700 hectare is brought under irrigation covering more than 30 crops. Farmers from various places communicated their experiences of drip irrigation on various crops such as sugarcane, cotton, grapes, banana, pomegranate, vegetables, tea, flowers, and so on. The increase in yield as compared to conventional irrigation methods is from 20% to 100%, whereas saving in water ranges from 40% to 70%.

The results achieved by drip irrigation in a developing country such as India can show many third-world countries optimum utilization of resources for increased agricultural production. India needs to feed more than 1 billion people. An increase of 80 million tons of food grain will be needed in less than a decade (a 50% increase). There are 140 million arable hectares (346 million acres) in India with 41.2 million hectares (102 million acres) being irrigated. The 60,700 hectares (150,000 acres) under drip quoted in the abstract represents merely 0.15% of the irrigated area. In India using drip irrigation, labor savings up to 50–60% can be found; poor quality water and soils can be used; and fertilizer savings of up to 30% are being observed."[5]

Pharmaceuticals

By 2020, the global pharmaceutical market is anticipated to more than double to $1.3 trillion, with the E7 countries—Brazil, China, India, Indonesia, Mexico, Russia, and Turkey—accounting for approximately one-fifth of global pharmaceutical sales. Further, incidence of chronic conditions in the developing world will increasingly resemble those of the developed world,[6] where health expenditures as a percentage of GDP have increased at a fast clip.

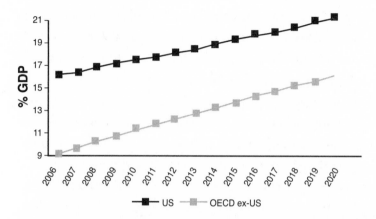

Exhibit 9-13   Health Expenditure as a Percentage of GDP (Source: PricewaterhouseCoopers Health Research Institute. Reproduced with permission of Pricewaterhouse Coopers.)

Some of the major industry changes anticipated are the following:

- Health care will shift in focus from treatment to prevention.
- Pharmaceutical companies will provide total health-care packages.
- The current linear phase R&D process will give way to in-life testing and live licensing, in collaboration with regulators and health-care providers.
- The traditional blockbuster sales model will disappear.
- Many innovative firms will enter the generics segment
- The supply chain function will become revenue generating as it becomes integral to the health-care package and enables access to new channels.
- More sophisticated direct-to-consumer distribution channels will diminish the role of wholesalers.

Although enjoying healthy margins for decades, the established pharmaceutical companies in developed countries are facing a number of major risks:

1. Generics already constitute more than 60% of the U.S. market and more so in many foreign markets. Although pharmaceutical innovators such as Pfizer have now moved to establish

generic divisions, there are serious doubts as to their capability to be successful in a segment that demands strict cost controls and thin margins.

2. The governments of many emerging economies, in which the major growth is expected to occur, have unilaterally suspended intellectual property rights (IPR), forcing the innovators to sell at a fraction of market price or giving the market to generic producers even when they lack a proper license.

3. Pending health-care legislation in the United States might erode margins in the United States, the most lucrative pharmaceutical market.

Endnotes

[1] "Offshoring," Special Report, *Economist*, December 13, 2003.

[2] *SWOT Analysis of Indian Textile Industry* by Vikram Utamsingh, Executive Director, KPMG India Pvt. Ltd., FICCI Textile Conference, September, 2003; *Trends in Japanese Textile Technology* by John E. Berkowitch, September 1996; *The Global Textile and Clothing Industry post the Agreement on Textiles and Clothing* by Hildegunn Kyvik Nordaås, World Trade Organization, Geneva, Switzerland 2004.

[3] Economic Research Service—USDA Agricultural Outlook, April 1998; *Report on Industry Trends*, Global Foresight, Inc. 2006.

[4] *Trends in U.S. Agriculture*, National Agriculture Statistics Service, U.S. Department of Agriculture; *Agricultural Industry Trends and Outlook—78 citations from the AGRICOLA database*, 1990—December 1998, National Agriculture Library.

[5] *Latest Trends in Eco Landscaping* (http://greenlivingideas.com), November, 2007; *Success of Drip in India. An example to the third world in micro irrigation for a changing world: Conserving*

Resources or Preserving the Environment by S. K. Suryawanshi, Proceeds of the Fifth International Micro Irrigation Conference, Orlando, 1995.

[6] *Innovation in the Pharmaceutical Industry—Future Prospects*, by Dr. Franz B. Humer, Chairman of the board of directors and CEO of F. Hoffmann-La Roche Ltd, Zürcher Volkswirtschaftliche Gesellschaft, Zurich, March 16, 2005; *Pharmaceutical industry innovation is more dispersed despite M&A activity, Tufts Center for the Study of Drug Development Impact Report—Analysis and Insight into Critical Drug Development Issues*, Volume 2, June 2000; *Pharma 2020: The Vision Which path will you take?*–PriceWaterhouseCoopers Report, June 2007.

10

The Great Deleveraging

What goes up—must come down.

The capability of many of the world's developed economies to support a rising level of debt relative to their economies and continue the trend of debt growth exceeding economic growth is reaching its limits and might be close to the tipping point. That is, the point when additional incremental debt will begin to be economically destructive. In this scenario, additional debt will coincide with economic decline, which will not be slowed by further leverage—continuing to increase debt faster than the economy grows.

The United States appears to have begun its second period of structural deleveraging in the last 100 years. The first period began in 1930, but debt to GDP did not peak until 1933. From that point, it took 20 years to complete. It began as the economy contracted for 3 years and fell to its lowest level during the Great Depression. During this period, the United States experienced the Great Depression, World War II, and the Korean War. It was a tumultuous period, but over the course of it, the level of debt to GDP was reduced to half.

There were three principal sources of the deleveraging. The first was a contraction of debt across the private sector that started before a sustained resumption of economic growth. The second was economic growth spurred by the preparation and participation in World War II. The final factor was a contraction of government debt after World War II. Almost all the deleveraging occurred in the first decade because of the initial drop in private sector debt, and the resumption of strong economic growth in 1939 as the nation and most other countries anticipated the coming war.

According to a McKinsey & Co. study, the typical duration of deleveraging was 6 to 7 years with the shortest median duration for belt-tightening being 5 years. The McKinsey Global Institute's report, "Debt and Deleveraging: The Global Credit Bubble and Its Economic Consequences," highlighted 32 periods of deleveraging and four ways in which the deleveraging occurred. The four ways were deleveraging by applying measures of austerity; high inflation; defaulting on the debt; and growth—growing the economy faster than debt. Of the 32 episodes, 16 were characterized as "belt-tightening"—austerity; 8 as "high inflation"; 7 as "massive default"; and 1 period was "growing out of debt." The painful results of high inflation and massive default are evident and possible. This chapter focuses on what happens through austerity and growth.

According to the study, that one growth period happened in the United States between 1938 and 1943 when the United States economy grew because of the preparation of an entry into World War II. It was a major part of the long period of deleveraging highlighted earlier in the chapter. Because of the funding requirements of World War II, the level of debt to GDP rose to more than 175% by 1945, only to begin falling again after the war ended, ultimately reaching the 1953 low.

Compared to those 32 periods, the leverage of the U.S. economy is high but not extreme. Like the previous periods of deleveraging, we expect the United States to endure a multiyear period of anemic economic growth while its debt contracts. That debt contraction already started in the private sector, but increases in public sector debt almost entirely offset it. Given the outlook of extended federal government deficits, the process will be challenging.

For the private sector, the deleveraging should include an absolute reduction in debt, and at least, a slowing of the rate of asset and income growth. The public sector deleveraging should be more difficult because it involves not just a reduction of debt, but also a recognition of the obligations of many off-budget entities such as government-sponsored enterprises. Eventually, there will be a downsizing of the relative size of government to the private sector. That can be accomplished through more rapid growth of the private sector, but it is our view that more disciplined management and benchmarking of the public sector are necessary. That requires a review of relative employment levels, compensation levels, benefit levels of public employees, and entitlement commitments.

Exhibit 10-1 shows debt expansion relative to GDP after the end of the Great Inflation. The new equilibrium after the Great Inflation rose toward just over 200%. After 1986, debt to GDP stayed around 225% before drifting up to 250% of GDP in the late 1990s. After that, it rose abruptly to 375%.

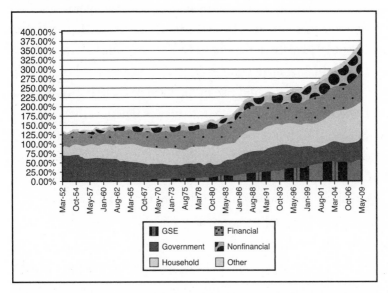

Exhibit 10-1 Debt to GDP (Source: *Flow of Funds*, freelunch.com; authors)

Debt to GDP can continue to rise, but the deleveraging process has already begun. The level of debt to GDP initially depends on how much private sector borrowing contracts and the economy grows because public sector debt should continue to rise. From the peak at the end of the first quarter of 2009, total debt has fallen $280 billion to $52.6 trillion at the end of the third quarter of 2009. The more than $1.25 trillion of debt contraction of the private sector from peak levels is almost entirely offset by increases in public sector debt levels. This has happened before. To get a sense of what lies ahead, it is appropriate to look back and get a sense of what happened.

The Last Deleveraging: 1930–1953

This analysis is based on a different data set that does not completely match the data from the website freelunch.com, which provides quarterly data starting in 1952, whereas this data set provides GDP back to 1790 and debt levels back to 1916. The trends are similar and hopefully, history will not repeat itself. The last major deleveraging that took place in the United States started with the Great Depression in 1930. Although debt to GDP rose until 1932 and 1933, the level of debt began declining in 1930 because of the difficult ecnomic conditions. The rapid rise in the level of GDP between 1929 and 1932 was caused by economic destruction. The leveraging in the United States took place because the economy contracted much faster than debt. Between 1929 and 1933, debt to GDP went from 185% to almost 300%. During that period, total debt outstanding fell 12%, whereas the economy contracted more than 45%.

Before the Great Depression, the corporate sector owed the largest share of debt in the economy. Its debt equaled more than 85% of GDP. Excluding commercial and financial debt corporate debt to GDP exceeded 60%. Unlike the current period, the financial services industry was not a major issuer of debt during this period. Rather, the major contribution by the industry was in the leverage existing in some of the investment products.

In 1932, the level of debt approached 300% of GDP. It would fall to almost 150% in 1953 with the vast majority of the deleveraging taking place by 1943. Relative to the size of the economy, the federal government's debt levels were much lower than current levels in 1932. The private sector was responsible for issuing a much higher share of the outstanding debt. In 1929, the public sector held 16% of total debt, corporations held 46%, and households held 38%. Included in household debt were mortgages for 1–4 family homes (9% of total debt) and for multifamily and similar dwellings (6.9%). Over the next 20 years, the mix would change dramatically.

Although the mix changed, total debt outstanding in 1940 was less than the 1930 level, and not even 15% greater than the 1933 level. Private sector debt would not pass its pre-Depression level until 1947, almost two decades later. The corporate sector debt levels fell 18% before bottoming in 1938 and didn't pass its pre-Depression debt level until 1942. The household sector debt level fell one-third and bottomed in 1943. It passed its pre-Depression peak debt level in 1947. Public sector debt doubled in the 1930s, and it more than quadrupled during World War II. By the end of World War II, public sector debt represented 65.5% of total debt, corporations accounted for 21%, and households accounted for 13.5%. In total, debt growth was slower than GDP growth after 1933, which caused the level of debt to GDP to fall. The growth rate of debt was slower early in the contraction because the private sector debt contraction offset almost the entire increase in public sector debt during the 1930s. Total debt was about the same level in 1938 as it was in 1932.

Through 1945, the Federal Government accounted for more than 100% of the additional borrowing (Exhibit 10-2). It borrowed to finance budget deficits to try and provide stimulus for the economy and to finance the wars. In only three of the years during the deleveraging did the U.S. government run a budget surplus. The private sector could not sustain an economic expansion until after World War II. Most in the private sector became conservative because of the economic destruction caused during the Great Depression. Borrowing was not embraced, nor were credit markets well developed. Home mortgages represented only 4.4% of total debt in 1945. From that

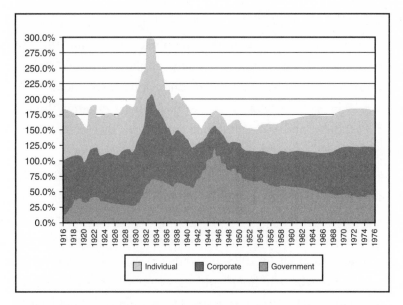

Exhibit 10-2   Debt to GDP during the First Deleveraging (Source: National Bureau of Economic Research)

low point, which was a level of debt that was also less than the amount outstanding in 1929, residential home mortgage debt would more than double in the next 5 years and would more than quadruple by 1953.

Still, in 1953, home ownership was not the norm. Most Americans still rented. The interstate highway system was an idea whose time was about to come. When that idea became a reality, a housing boom started and with it the suburbanization of the United States. From 1953 on, the annual growth rate of debt regularly exceeded the growth rate of the economy.

It would be the longest and most pronounced period of deleveraging in the United States in the past century, and the deleveraging took place in different phases. The first phase was triggered by the private sector contraction, then economic growth, and eventually the contraction of federal government debt after World War II. Contributing to the process were defaults and a great deal of austerity in the private sector.

The Next Deleveraging

With a debt to GDP ratio at more than 375%, the United States economy is supporting its highest ever level of debt. Perhaps more troubling is the level of debt to national income of more than 425%. The need to reduce the debt is real, and the process began in the second quarter of 2009. As laid out by McKinsey, most of the alternatives are not attractive, and they take a great deal of time, often more than 10% of the typical person's working life. Deleveraging should involve a combination of factors including reducing debt levels, growing the size of the economy faster than debt grows, strengthening balance sheets by raising more equity, writing off debt, improving margins, and increasing the level of wealth as reflected by rising equity markets. With the current level of debt, higher interest rate levels will only increase financial burden and financial risk, while making it harder to reduce leverage. What follows is a review of recent leverage levels, the financial condition of the major economic sectors, and prognostication on the paths that lie ahead.

The pressures to deleverage are greatest in the public sector and the financials sector. The process is already taking place in the financials sector, but as of this writing, the public sector continued to take on more debt and increase the leverage of, and risk to, the economy. The public sector includes the federal government; state and local governments; the government sponsored enterprises such as Fannie Mae, Freddie Mac, and the Federal Housing Administration (FHA); and the Federal Reserve. The household sector's process of deleveraging began in 2008 and should continue for several years.

The most likely path for the deleveraging process starts with a continuation of the private sector deleveraging, which has already shed close to $1 trillion as of this writing, or 3% of its debt. The largest amount of the deleveraging took place in the financial sector's shadow banking system as funding for asset back securities fell 20% from peak levels through the third quarter of 2009, or almost $750 billion, which already contributed to a decline of $1 trillion from peak levels. The next largest change took place in the household sector with almost $250 billion shed from its peak level. Debt for nonfinancial corporations was off just less than $150 billion from peak levels, but given the $2.3 trillion of debt supporting commercial real estate in the sector, a more meaningful drop is expected. In aggregate, nonfinancial corporations and households should shed at least $2.5 trillion of debt from peak levels reached during the leveraging cycle. Financial companies excluding government sponsored enterprises (GSEs) are expected to shed another $1.5 trillion. In aggregate, we expect the private sector to shed more than $5 trillion of debt from peak levels of more than $34 trillion, or about 15%.

Public sector deleveraging should happen in stages. To start, state and local governments are being forced to retrench and downsize because of constitutional requirements to balance their budgets in an economy not capable of sustaining sufficient tax revenues. The result will be a rationalization of state and local governments, which grew faster than the economy before the recession. From the end of 2001, when an economic recovery was in place, to the end of 2007, state and local government debt grew at a rate of 9% a year. That was during a period of economic prosperity and strong tax revenue growth for state governments of 6.5% a year, well above the growth rate for the economy and personal income. Over the course of the 6-year period, state and local governments collected almost $6.5 trillion of revenues from multiple taxes and fees, and increased their borrowing almost $900 billion to $2.2 trillion. Relative to personal income from wages, rental income, investment income, and proprietor's income, state and local government taxes and fees increased from 12.2% to 13.3% between the end of 2002 and the end of 2008. (Corporate tax collections at the state & local level are usually less than 4% of total revenues collected.)

The next parts of public sector deleveraging involve the GSEs and the Federal Reserve. The GSEs include Fannie Mae and Freddie Mac, and they along with other federal government agencies are responsible for more than $8 trillion of debt. More than $5 trillion of the debt is backed by government guarantee, and the rest is used to finance assets on their balance sheets. The combined balance sheets of the GSEs have no common equity because of the losses caused by the housing crisis. The cost of supporting Fannie Mae and Freddie Mac will likely exceed the cost of supporting the major investment banks. The Federal Reserve balance sheet doubled in size to more than $2 trillion to help improve the liquidity of the financial system. The combined balance sheets of the GSEs and the Federal Reserve exceed $10 trillion. Their combined balance sheets should decline by more than $2 trillion, half of which is expected to take place on the Fed's balance sheet.

The final piece of the deleveraging will have to occur at the federal government level. Current budget projections show the federal government operating at a deficit for the next decade. Aggregate deficits are expected to approach $5 trillion over the next 5 years and exceed $10 trillion through 2020. Spending levels increased more than 10% in 2009 and are expected to stay elevated (Exhibit 10-3). Over the last 50 years, the increase in nominal spending levels was exceeded only during inflationary times and during the Vietnam build-up and the funding of the Great Society and War on Poverty in the mid-1960s (Exhibit 10-4).

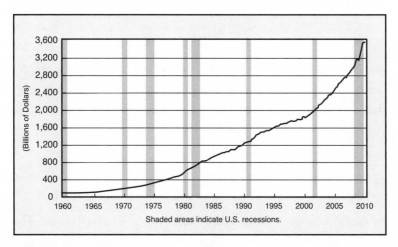

Exhibit 10-3   Federal Government Current Expenditures (Source: U.S. Department of Commerce: Bureau of Economic Analysis; 2010 research.stlouisfed.org)

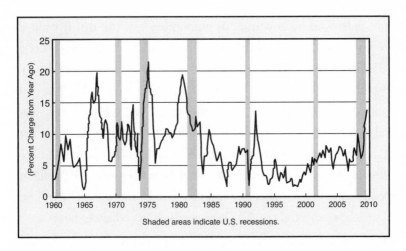

Exhibit 10-4   Annual Change in Federal Government Expenditures (Source: U.S. Department of Commerce: Bureau of Economic Analysis; 2010 research.stlouisfed.org)

The need to reduce the level of government relative to the private sector is reflected in Exhibit 10-5. It shows the relationship of public sector wages and government transfer payments to private wages. It looks at monthly data from January 1993 to December 2009. In a recessionary period, the relationship should increase as the economy becomes more dependent on government activities. Since the recession started in December 2007, the shift upward began and is currently at the high end of its range. Before 1991, it was rare for the ratio to exceed 50%. A rising public burden suggests greater dependence on borrowing to finance government activities; a greater probability of tax increases; increased pressure to reduce government activities; or a combination of the three. The problem with tax increases is that they reduce disposable income of the population paying the taxes. The expectation of a rising level of disposable income is an important ingredient for future economic growth.

Every 1% change in the public burden equals $64 billion. The increase of more than 10% in the ratio from December 2007 caused a $230 billion decline in private wages (−4.3%), an $82 billion increase (7.4%) in public sector wages, and a $403 billion increase (22.7%) in transfer payments. More detail follows on the prospect for deleveraging the nonfinancial private sector and households.

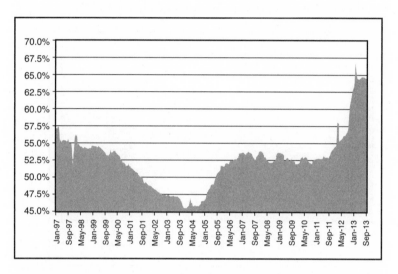

Exhibit 10-5   Public Burden (Source: Bureau of Economic Analysis, authors)

Nonfinancial Corporations

Nonfinancial debt as a share of total debt is at the low end of its range since 1952. That just means borrowing of nonfinancial companies grew at a slower rate than other sectors, especially the financials sector. Relative to historic levels, nonfinancial debt to GDP is at the high end of the range (Exhibit 10-6). The sector includes commercial real estate companies, which borrowed more than $3.4 trillion and are just beginning to reduce their leverage. At the same time, after-tax nonfinancial corporate profits are below peak levels but still strong and capable of supporting more debt (Exhibit 10-7). Total debt for this sector exceeds $11 trillion, whereas net profits after tax approach $600 billion and cash flow exceeds capital expenditures— the financing gap is negative (Exhibit 10-8). Finally, interest costs are about at the median level of the last two decades (Exhibit 10-9).

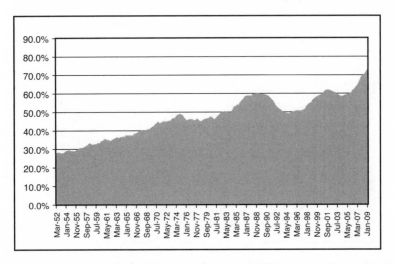

Exhibit 10-6   Nonfinancial Sector Debt to GDP (Source: *Flow of Funds*, authors)

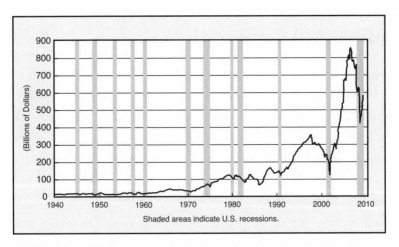

Exhibit 10-7   Net Income of Nonfinancial Corporations (Source: U.S. Department of Commerce: Bureau of Economic Analysis; 2009 research.stlouisfed.org)

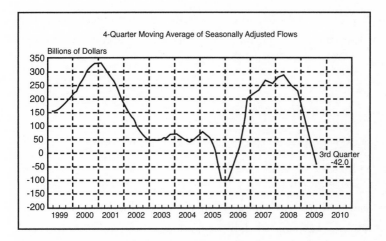

Exhibit 10-8   Financing Gap for Nonfinancial Corporate Business (Source: Federal Reserve Board of Governors)

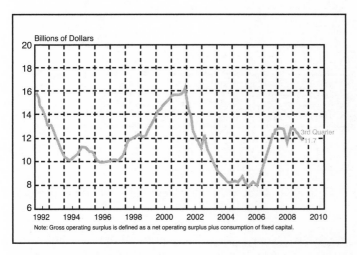

Exhibit 10-9   Net Interest Payments to Operating Surplus for Nonfinancial Corporations (Source: Federal Reserve Board of Governors)

Debt levels peaked in the fourth quarter of 2008 and began to slide a bit. In the 1930s, corporate debt contracted until the war effort took hold. The prospects of an anemic economy and the need for the commercial real estate sector to reduce its leverage mean the level of debt outstanding should continue to decline. During the course of the deleveraging, managements are expected to be more cautious.

Households

Household debt to GDP (Exhibit 10-10) is at the high end of its historic range reflecting the expansion of the growing percentage of households owning a home and the use of greater leverage to finance those houses and borrow against their equity in those houses to support themselves. Household debt peaked at $13.8 trillion in the second quarter of 2008 and since declined more than $240 billion.

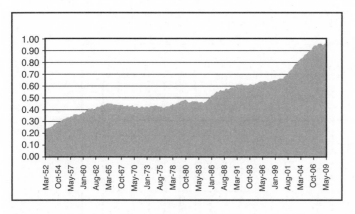

Exhibit 10-10   Household Debt to GDP (Source: *Flow of Funds*, authors)

Household debt service payments as a percent of disposable personal incomes have moderated but remain well above their median level of the last 20 years (Exhibit 10-11). Much of the recent moderation was caused by lower interest rates, which generated lower interest payments. For instance, in September 2007, their annualized level on non-mortgage interest payments was $270 billion, and by December 2009, it had fallen to $199 billion.

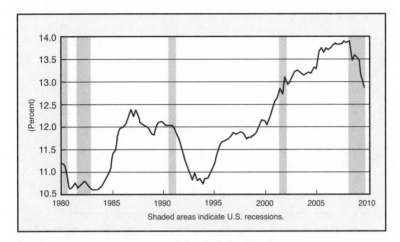

Exhibit 10-11   Household Debt Service Payments as a Percent of Disposable Personal Income (Source: Board of Governors of the Federal Reserve System; 2009 research.stlouisfed.org)

In a difficult economy with challenging employment prospects, it would not be surprising for the debt service ratio to eventually fall toward the low end of the range. This would imply a further reduction in household debt of more than $1.5 trillion and perhaps as much as $2.5 trillion. Relative to total household assets (Exhibit 10-12), a debt reduction of $2 trillion would put the level of debt to total assets closer to 17%, which represented the high end of the historic range until 2008 when the equity market and house prices declined. Debt currently exceeds 20%, largely because debt levels continued rising through September 2008 and then began a modest decline, whereas household assets peaked a year before in September 2007 at $80 trillion and then plummeted to $62.6 trillion in March 2009. They have since rebounded to more than $67 trillion in September 2009 with the prospect of going even higher. However, the likelihood asset levels rebound to $80 trillion in the short term seems remote, and therefore the probability of continued household deleveraging is great. The major source of the decline would be residential mortgages, which represent more than 80% of household debt.

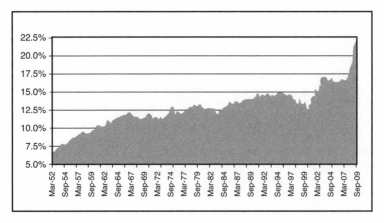

Exhibit 10-12   Household Debt to Assets (Source: *Flow of Funds*, authors)

The factors driving household and nonfinancial deleveraging in the form of debt reduction will be greater risk aversion, less attractive investment opportunities, and tighter credit standards. Ultimately, stronger economic growth is preferred.

Growth

The most attractive path to deleveraging is growth. That means growing the economy faster than debt grows. At the end of the 1930s, economic growth surged because of preparations for World War II and a more accommodative relationship between the administration and the private sector.

The gross domestic product (GDP) is the total of personal consumption expenditures, gross private fixed investment, net exports and government expenditures, and gross investment. The largest factor for the U.S. economy is personal consumption expenditures (PCE) (Exhibit 10-13), which have represented a growing share of the economy since the early 1950s. From a low of about 61%, personal consumption expenditures rose to more than 70% of GDP in 2009. Services were a growing share of those expenditures. They accounted for more than 47% of U.S. GDP in 2009 compared to 25% in 1947.

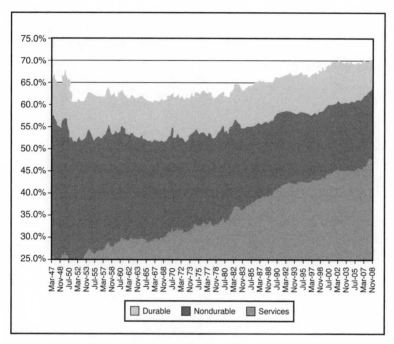

Exhibit 10-13   Personal Consumption Components to GDP (Source: Bureau of Economic Analysis)

Spending on health care was one of the fastest growing parts of the economy since more detailed data was available in 1959. At the end of 2009, health care spending represented more than 11% of GDP. It also represented 25% of spending on services compared to just more than 10% when more detailed data was available from the Bureau of Economic Advisors in 1959 (Exhibit 10-14).

Services are expected to remain a significant part of the economy: a service-based information and knowledge-based economy. Intellectual and human capital will continue to increase in value.

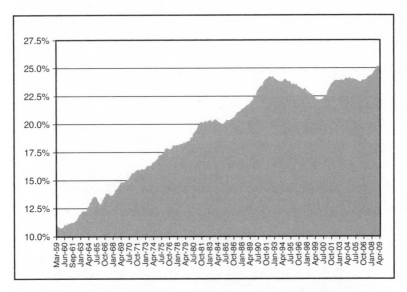

Exhibit 10-14   Health Care Spending to Services Spending (Source: Bureau of Economic Analysis)

Summary

The deleveraging process has started in our opinion, and it started as it started in the 1930s—in the private sector. Like the 1930s, there is an economic shift occurring. This time the economy is shifting to a more information-based, service-oriented economy. Will government policy meaningfully slow the pace of the transition as it did in the 1930s and risk even greater economic destruction, or will policy makers attempt to accommodate a new and not well-known reality? In the 1930s, the prospect of war caused the shift in the policy to one of much greater accommodation and support of the private sector. That accommodation was necessary to create the subsequent economic surge, and it required a substantial increase in government debt to help finance and facilitate the build-out of the infrastructure needed to accelerate the economic transition and become war ready.

This deleveraging process would be helped greatly by an acceleration of economic growth. History does not provide much hope because most periods of economic deleveraging were periods of below-average economic growth, at best. Unlike the 1930s, this period does not appear to be one that would benefit from a further surge in government debt. The economy is already supporting a heavy level of debt, tax levels are already high, and in an economic era more dependent on intellectual capital—the cost of human capital is too high. Eventually, policies will need to be put in place to allow the private sector to grow faster than the public sector. That shift will likely be awkward, and it will involve risk. One source of risk will be a lack of understanding of the economic forces at work by many in policy and decision-making positions. Another source of risk is vested interests not interested in change.

While we cannot know the future, the next two chapters present some tools and rules to help navigate what we believe will continue to be a volatile investment period reflecting the shift in global economic mix we believe is taking place and the greater economic risk many developed countries incurred because of the large levels of debt they have accumulated.

11

Market Signals

Is it a flashing yellow light?

Given an outlook of greater volatility and greater risk, a review of some of the signals that would have helped navigate in the past is the focus of this chapter. For instance, the Tech Bubble and its peak in March 2000, along with the financial crisis of 2008, were both preceded by a number of early warning signs. This chapter presents some classic metrics to use as market signals and to challenge prevailing assumptions about the current outlook. The metrics touch on valuation, past performance, interest rates, current market liquidity, gold, and the dollar. All these metrics can be compiled using publicly available data. They are signals that can be used for other global markets and not just the United States.

Valuation

It is usually better to invest when valuations are low than when they are high. The valuation metric we use the most is the price to earnings ratio—the P/E ratio. Total return on an investment is a function of how much the price of an investment changes and the cash flows it generates. For stocks, the price is a function of changes in earnings and valuation. The cash flow comes in the form of a dividend. The opportunities to generate attractive returns from a point of low valuation are greater than from a point of high valuation, especially when an investor is focused on the broader market and not on an individual stock.

253

Before giving a broader historic perspective, we look at the period following World War II, the period known as the Great Inflation, and the period leading up to 2008.

The period after World War II was one of the two great structural bull markets of the past 60 years. During that bull market, momentum was built on a foundation of low valuation. Investors were not valuing the earnings of the S&P 500 very high. Their expectations were modest, at best. In other words, their expectations for earnings growth were low. Just how low was the market's valuation? It was extremely low. The market traded as low as 5.9 times trailing earnings. At that point, the investment community was small, and the retail investment business was in its infancy. Still, it was a time of low inflation, low interest rates, and the beginning of the baby boom. As detailed in Chapter 3, "Nine Decades of Real Asset Class Returns," it would be the best decade for large cap U.S. equities and an even better decade of equity markets for other countries.

The three components of the attractive returns were multiple expansion, earnings growth, and dividend growth. From the low of 5.9 times earnings, the market's valuation would peak at 22.4 times earnings in 1961. The change in valuation alone generated annual returns of 12.3% for a period of more than 11 years. The market would not be valued higher than that until more than three decades later in October 1991.

In the "Go Go Years" of the 1960s, valuations usually remained above 15.0 times trailing earnings and often went about 17.5 times. With the exception of a few months, the market's valuation stayed above 15.0 times earnings through March 1973. The last effort to keep the valuation even higher was tied to the "Nifty 50."

After March 1973, the market's valuation declined and eventually fell below 10.0 times earnings where it would remain for almost a decade. However, the continuing rise of inflation would pressure stocks and cause the valuation of the market to fall. For almost 4 years that would transcend a bear and bull market, the S&P 500 traded at 7.5 times trailing earnings. Like prior markets, the low end of valuation would prove to be an attractive time to invest (see Exhibit 11-1).

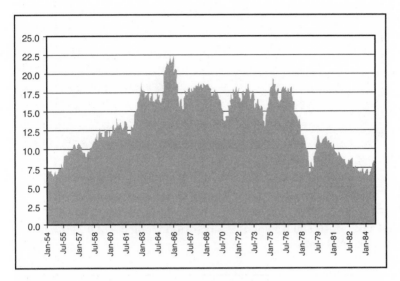

Exhibit 11-1   S&P 500 Trailing P/E—1950 to 1980 (Source: Global Financial Data)

A longer look at the S&P 500 historic P/E (including predecessor indexes—Exhibit 11-2) shows the median P/E for a period of more than 130 years was 14.9 times. Since 1985, the valuation was usually higher than the median. Since the end of World War I, the periods of lowest valuations represented the end of bear markets and the beginning of a bull market. The periods of peak valuations were bad times to invest.

Using a period of more than 200 years, it is clear that investor's chances of realizing attractive long-term annual returns increase if the investment is made at lower valuations. Investing when the market was valued at no more than 10.0 times earnings almost always yielded positive returns over the next 10 years, while investing when the market was valued at 25.0 times earnings, or more, limited 10-year annual returns to less than 15%, and usually well under 5.0% (Exhibit 11-3).

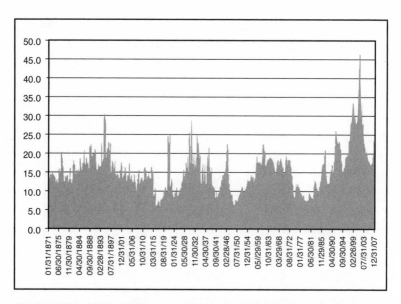

Exhibit 11-2   S&P 500 Trailing P/E Since 1871 Median—14.9 (Source: Global Financial Data)

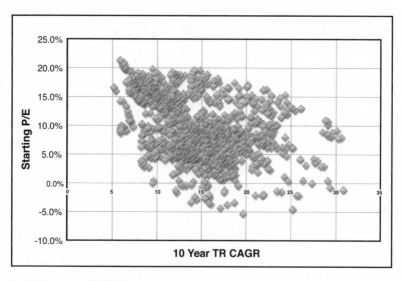

Exhibit 11-3   S&P 500 10-Year Total Return to Starting P/E (Source: Global Financial Data, authors)

A similar conclusion is gained when looking at the 5-year total returns and the starting P/E. An investment made when the P/E was 10.0 times or less almost always generated positive returns and often generated very attractive annual returns. The few times 5-year annual returns exceeded 30% were generated when investments were made at no more than 12.0 times earnings. One of the reasons is simple math. An investment generating an annual return of 30% is worth more than $3.70 for every dollar invested. In almost any economic and earnings growth scenario, the valuation of future earnings 5 years out is much greater than when the initial investment was made at a lower valuation.

Prior Returns

Do we keep riding the same horse?

Success does not always beget success. For 5- and 10-year horizons, equity investments often do better after a period of poor or mediocre returns. Structural bull and bear markets last longer than those time frames, but even they have cycles that go against the secular trend. Just as valuation can help provide a solid market signal to test, so past returns must be understood to help better understand the performance necessary to sustain strong returns over time.

Expanding valuation is often one of the sources of strong returns. At some point, constant multiple expansion is no longer a reasonable assumption. For that matter, robust earnings growth is not an assumption that should be constantly assumed. Add to that group, the assumption of continued strong returns. They are rarely sustained for an extended period. A look at 5-year returns relative to the prior period 5-year returns shows that the robust future returns were preceded by periods of less robust returns.

Exhibit 11-4 shows more than 1,200 periods. It is apparent that strong market performance, where the market more than doubles, is rarely sustained another five years. The market tripled only following periods of sub-10% compound returns, whereas the period of greatest loss followed the periods of best 5-year returns.

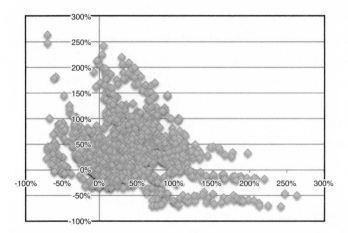

Exhibit 11-4   5-Year Return Versus Previous 5-Year Return (Source: Global Financial Data)

Since 1843, the market delivered annual compound returns over the next 5 years of at least 10% a year over 45% of the time, while generating negative returns for the next 5 years just over 10% of the time, as shown in Exhibit 11-5. That is about how often the market delivered compound annual returns of at least 20% a year. Almost 65% of the time the 5-year compound annual return ended between 0% and 15%.

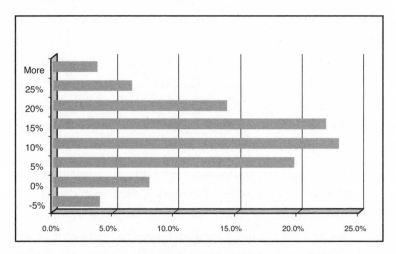

Exhibit 11-5   5-Year Total Return Distribution—S&P 500 Since 1843 (Source: Global Financial Data)

As shown in Exhibit 11-6, the best periods of 5-year returns followed World War II and included 1949 through the end of 1954. They were periods when annual returns almost invariably exceeded 15% and lasted for more than 4 years. The first period lasted from September 1946 through the end of 1954. During that period, the market usually generated annual returns over a 5-year period of at least 20% for investments made between the beginning of 1942 and the middle of 1952.

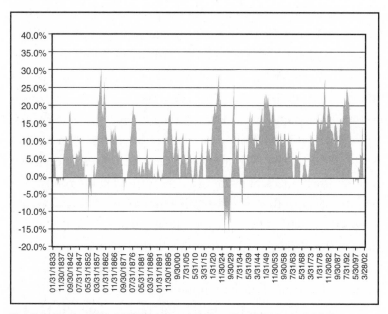

Exhibit 11-6 S&P 500 History of 5-Year Total Return CAGR (Source: Global Financial Data)

Like many periods of attractive investment returns, this one started with low valuations—the trailing P/E was actually less than 6.0 for a few months. It was also a period of low interest rates, low inflation, and ultimately robust economic growth. The Consumer Price Index (CPI) usually stayed below 2.5% and excluding the cost of food, it usually stayed below 2.0%. For the best corporate credits, long-term borrowing rates usually stayed below 3.05% until 1955. Real GDP growth after the recession of 1949 turned up sharply and exceeded 12.5% for a quarter in 1950. Into 1953, real GDP growth exceeded 5.0% for most quarters.

The second period of extended 5-year annualized returns of usually more than 15% started in January 1978 and lasted until September 1985. Over a 5-year period, the S&P 500 total return was usually more than double during the period with the best 5-year return being an increase of more than 250% on the original investment made in 1981.

The Fed would be a catalyst pushing the market higher. Starting in the summer of 1981, it would begin the process of lowering interest rates. The effective Fed Funds rate would go from just more than 20% at the beginning of the summer to just under 10% a year later. The yield of 10-year Treasury Notes would fall from almost 16% to about 10.5% by the end of 1982. The cost of money was coming down because the government was, at last, winning the battle with inflation. Core CPI was about to fall from more than 11.5% to less than 3.5% in the next 24 months. That fall in interest rates and disinflation along with the era's fiscal policy of lower tax rates would lead to robust real GDP growth of more than 8% at the beginning of 1984, and create 10% real GDP growth in five quarters. To summarize, the contributing factors to the attractive returns in this period were the low valuations at the beginning of the period, the eventual period of disinflation and sustained decline in interest rates, the realization of robust real economic growth, and fiscal policy shifts that were increasingly friendly to investors. It was also a period of increasingly disbursed economic power.

The third and final period of strong sustained returns took place for investments made in August 1990 through July 1996. During this period, annual returns of more than 20% for a 5-year period were realized for market investments made between June 1992 and October 1995. This was a period of continued disinflation, low interest rates, looming government surpluses, and strong real GDP growth. It was also a period that began with a healthy amount of investor fear due to the Savings & Loans (S&L) crisis that would reach its peak in the fourth quarter of 1990, whereas its economic effects would linger for more than 2 years. Also occupying the headlines and stunting economic growth was the first Iraq War—Desert Storm. It was the first cable television war with the general population having almost a front row seat to watch it.

With the first Iraq War ended and the S&L crisis resolved, the financial fortunes of the United States shifted abruptly. There were other changes and cable television was only one sign of how much day-to-day life was changing. Quietly, the worldwide web began in 1991 to be followed by the first browser in 1995. During the decade, cell phones became common; fax became old technology; e-mail became available; and Blackberries were invented. With all these new technologies, government surpluses, and an apparent "Peace Dividend," it was not surprising that investor optimism grew. The market multiple on trailing earnings more than doubled in less than nine years, whereas the market's operating earnings would grow almost 130%. The combination of 10% compound earnings growth and expansion of multiples that added more than 8% annually to the growth rate was a potent mixture. It was also unsustainable.

Some expansion of multiples is to be expected from low valuations, or off depressed earnings levels. However, market multiples of more than 30.0 times earnings are rare and almost always followed by poor returns. The strong returns of the 1990s were not just a result of new technologies with attractive growth prospects and better macroeconomic environment, but also a result of a bull market that turned into a bubble—a euphoria. That euphoria was reflected by the market's valuation. At more than 30 times earnings, the market was expecting robust earnings growth with little, if any, acknowledgment of potential risks. There was essentially no allowance for the risk premium.

Most of those risks became evident shortly after the 1990s ended. Investors quickly became concerned about earnings outlook, a weaker economy, and corporate malfeasance. Investors would also become aware of higher than estimated geopolitical risks. What was not evident at first was the deterioration of the nation's balance sheet. After the S&L crisis, the nation's balance sheet was strong and could easily tolerate some more leverage. Chapter 1, "The Great Leveraging," laid out this reckless leveraging process, which rose to peak levels for the country.

Interest Rates and Valuation

The Fed model (Exhibit 11-7) is a straightforward valuation tool comparing the equity market's valuation to that of the 10-year Treasury bond. It is a broad indicator to be used with many other tools. When the ratio is less than 1.00, bonds are more expensive than equities, and when the ratio is more than 1.00, equities are more expensive than bonds. Federal Reserve Board Chairman Alan Greenspan popularized this simple model. To accomplish the comparison, the yield of the 10-year Treasury bond is inverted. So, 10% becomes 10.0; 8% becomes 12.5, and so on.

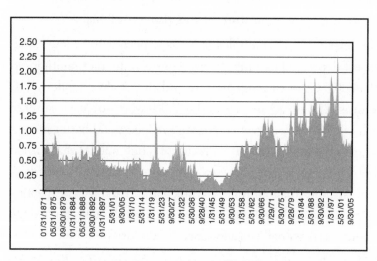

Exhibit 11-7   The Fed Model (Source: Global Financial Data, authors)

Historically, the ratio rarely exceeded 1.00 until the middle of the 1960s. The norm seemed to be 0.75, or less. Government bond yields were controlled during World War II and into the mid-1950s. Still, lingering memories of the 1929 crash kept many investors away from the stock market. Those fears were especially intense after World War II when society and the economy faced an abrupt shift away from a command-and-control war time economy to a more traditional free market system.

Also at that time, the investment business was still in its infancy, and the technology did not exist to make equity investing common-place. The universe of stocks available for investment was much smaller and companies were more involved in capital intensive busi-nesses that warranted a lower valuation. Finally, interest rates were low for most of the period preceding 1965, which meant the Bond P/E was relatively higher as evident in Exhibit 11-8. Only in 1920 did the long-term bond yield stay above 5%, long enough to establish the rate as the average for the year. The long bond yield would not aver-age 5% again until 1968. In the interim, the yield would get under 2% in 1941 and stay below 3% through 1956.

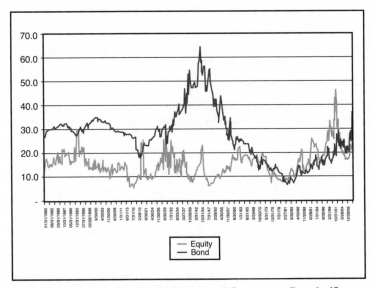

Exhibit 11-8   P/Es for the S&P 500 and Corporate Bonds (Source: Global Financial Data)

The value of a stream of cash flows increases as long-term interest rates fall. The low interest rate environment that persisted through the mid-1960s meant the P/E for debt was usually above 30.0 and almost always more than 20.0. The reverse is also true; when interest rates rise, the value of a stream of cash flows declines. Between 1965 and 1980, the 10-year Treasury constant maturity rate quadrupled from about 4% to about 16% (Exhibit 11-9). The cost of borrowing money became much more expensive, and bonds became a more attractive investment as their yield rose. Of course, investors are less inclined to invest in long-term bonds if they believe rates will continue to rise.

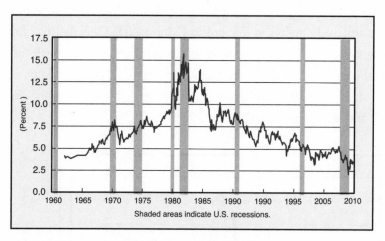

Exhibit 11-9   10-Year Treasury Constant Maturity Rate (Source: Board of Governors of the Federal Reserve System; 2009 research.stlouisfed.org)

The declining interest rate affected housing. Mortgage rates peaked in the early 1980s, and their subsequent fall meant the purchasing power of a borrower increased more than six times. The value of household cash flow was greater because its purchasing power was greater. For the equity market, lower rates are part of an equation that supports higher valuations. The P/E for equities usually stayed below 20.0 times until the 1990s when rates continued to fall, inflation levels trended down, and the level of optimism rose until it morphed into euphoria, and the value-accorded equities rose above 30.0 times earnings.

As Exhibit 11-10 shows, the movements of interest rates and the stock market were often positively correlated. Until 1968, the correlation of the past 10-year's Treasury to the trailing P/E for the S&P 500 seemed to experience regular cycles. The one between 1956 and 1968 showed a negative correlation because interest rates rose, which pushed the Treasury P/E down, whereas the equity P/E rose: The P/Es moved in opposite directions because both reflected the outcome of a strong and productive economy.

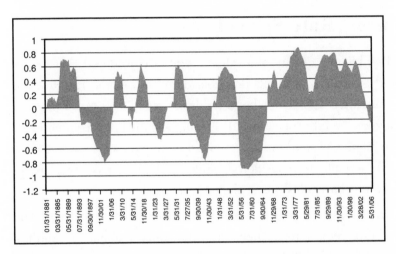

Exhibit 11-10   10-Year P/E Correlation to Interest Rates (Source: Global Financial Data)

Since the end of the 1960s, there was a strong correlation between the yield of the 10-year Treasury and the P/E of the S&P 500. Basically, the stock market moved in the opposite direction of interest rates based on 10 years of monthly data. During the 1970s, interest rates rose to the highest levels in more than 150 years, and stock market valuations fell to near historically low levels. When the recovery of the 1980s was in place, interest rates continued to decline, and the stock market's P/E rose.

The correlation peaked in the last 1970s at more than 0.80, which means that interest rate levels were a major factor in determining the equity market's valuation. In recent years, the correlation turned negative, reflecting the weak economy and reduced role of interest rates in spurring economic activity and instead spurring investors to take on greater risk. The recent experience of Japan raises concerns about the value of low interest rates in an anemic and leveraged economic environment. For almost two decades, Japanese government bonds have yielded less than 2.0%, and yet the Japanese equity market continued to decline and real economic growth was close to 1% a year.

Interest Rate Spreads

The highest quality and safest credit is considered that of the United States government. It is considered to be risk-free. For the same maturity, a corporate bond yields more and the greater the risk, the higher the interest rate paid. The highest quality corporate credits are rated AAA, and the lowest investment grade rating is B. Below that, the credits are considered "junk," or highest risk. As a group, junk credits have a history of much higher losses.

Credit spreads give a sense of the market's risk aversion. The higher the credit spread, the greater the concern about risk and the potential for loss. When credit spreads are narrow, the market is less sensitive to risk. It is differentiating the credit quality of companies less when spreads are narrow than when they are wide. Although AAA is the highest rating for corporate credits, Treasury debt is considered to have even less risk, so there is usually a yield differential between Treasury debt and corporate debt, and government-backed credit such as the GSEs and corporate debt.

Exhibit 11-11 looks at the difference between yields on AAA-rated corporate debt and BBB-rated debt. Not surprisingly, the period of greatest risk aversion was the 1930s. The other periods of greatest differentiation in corporate credit were the late 1970s and early 1980s, and the financial crisis of 2008. In all instances, economic distress was elevated and the three periods represent the top three periods of most extreme economic distress of the last century. In such periods, there was a flight to quality.

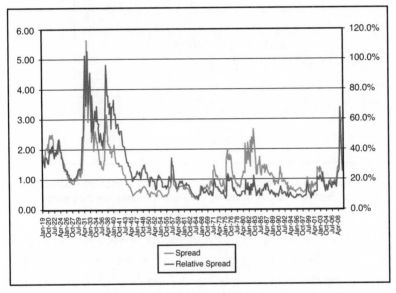

Exhibit 11-11   Credit Spreads Between AAA and BBB Rated Debt (Source: Board of Governors of the Federal Reserve System)

Relative to the 10-year Treasury-Bill yield, the cost of higher risk corporate credit peaked during the recent financial crisis with relative spreads exceeding 550% (Exhibit 11-12). The relative spreads for higher quality credit (AAA) also ratcheted up but not the same way the lesser quality credit changed. Again, like other periods of tremendous economic stress, there was a flight to quality with investors shifting a disproportionate amount of their investment dollars to the safe haven asset—U.S. Treasuries.

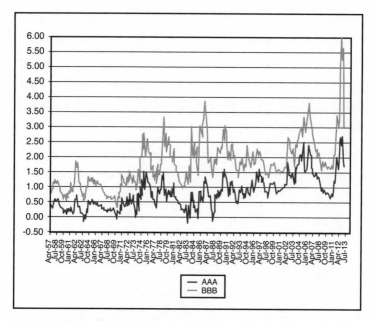

Exhibit 11-12   Credit Spreads to 10-Year Treasury Constant Maturity Rate (Source: Board of Governors of the Federal Reserve System)

When a metric reaches an extreme, there are investment opportunities. From the point of peak spreads, corporate credits provided tremendous investment returns as the process of normalization started.

Liquidity Metrics

The end of the housing bubble and the financial crisis of 2008 highlighted the importance of liquidity metrics. The metrics highlighted the major problem with the markets; the liquidity mechanism was failing. Financial companies would not provide short-term credit to one another and that created the need for government intervention. There are several metrics to highlight and include the TED spread (TED is the acronym formed by using the T in T-Bill and combining it with the ticker symbol for the Eurodollars future contract—ED), the overnight indexed swap (OIS), Libor spread, and the 3-month T-Bill yield.

The TED spread reflects the difference between the 3-month LIBOR (London Inter Bank Overnight Rate) and the yield of the 3-month T-Bill. Normally, the yield is very narrow and reflects the cost for liquidity provided, and perhaps, the risk taken. Historical comparisons are difficult because of the rapid evolution of credit markets over the last 40 years. The markets were less developed in the 1970s, interest rates were much higher and that was reflected in the spread, and risk aversion was on the rise.

What is clear is that the TED spread started showing signs of unease in the first half of 2007 by rising above 0.50% following the failure of Bear Stearns. Then, in the summer, the Carlyse and Bear Stearns hedge funds failed, and the rate stayed above 1.00% until June 2009, almost a year later. When the rate went above 2.50%, it meant the interbank market was effectively closed.

The 3-month T-Bill yield is part of the TED spread equation, and its yield is at the low end of its historic range. Relative to the 3-month T-Bill yield, the TED spread reached its peak during the housing bubble-related financial crisis (Exhibit 11-13). The T-Bill yield was at its lowest point for the period analyzed (Exhibit 11-14), and the spread was close to an all time high. The T-Bill yield in November 2009 was less than 0.10%. The most risk free investment returned almost nothing. The information provided by the 3-month T-Bill is in the extremes. At the high end reached in the early 1980s, the Government was fighting an all out battle to bring down inflation. There were risks to avoid in the early stages of the battle, and opportunities to take as it became apparent the war on inflation was being won. At the low end of the spectrum, the concerns were focused on stimulating economic growth by making the risk-free investment much less attractive.

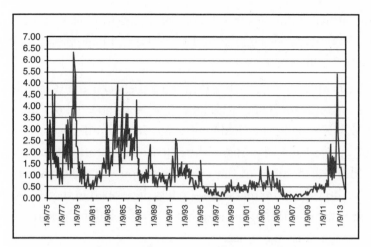

Exhibit 11-13   TED Spread (Source: Board of Governors of the Federal Reserve System)

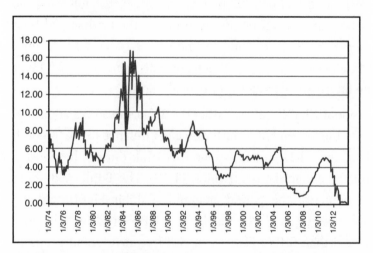

Exhibit 11-14   3-Month T-Bill Yield (Source: Board of Governors of the Federal Reserve System)

The final liquidity metric to consider is similar to the TED spread, and it is the OIS—Libor spread. It measures the difference between the 3-month LIBOR and overnight interest rate swap for the same time frame. Just like the TED spread, this metric reflected the absence of liquidity in the counterparty market, and as a result the spread reached peak levels. It is important to emphasize that the rapid increase in risk premiums reflected first concerns about liquidity and systemic failure. Classic risk aversion was a secondary concern.

Gold and the Dollar

Viewed as a store of value, the price of gold is important to monitor and not just in absolute terms, but also relative to other metrics such as stock market indices. Since the United States got off the gold standard in the 1970s, the price of gold floated freely with the dollar. A rise in the price of gold is usually a sign of a weak currency, the value of the dollar was under pressure. That pressure usually comes from concerns about fiscal and monetary policies and their impact.

Comparing the price of a stock index to gold gives a sense when equity performance is the strongest and weakest. The three most recent structural bull markets are evident in Exhibit 11-15 as are the subsequent bear markets.

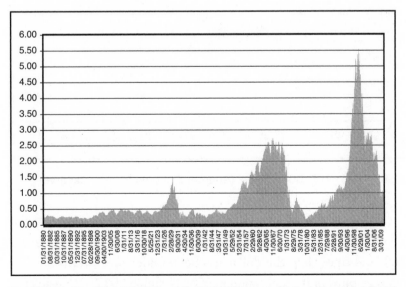

Exhibit 11-15   S&P 500 Priced in Gold (Source: Global Financial Data)

The dollar has been the world's only reserve currency since the end of World War II. Its value was tied to gold until the early 1970s when President Nixon ended the Bretton Woods agreement, thereby canceling fixed convertibility between the dollar and gold. After that, the dollar became a paper currency (a fiat currency) and it lost value. That process continued until the early 1980s when the efforts to stop inflation worked. In the span of almost 4 years, the value of the dollar against other currencies almost doubled only to completely retrace the climb back down with the culmination being the largest one-day market decline on October 19, 1987. On that Black Monday, the market fell almost 23%. That day for the market is evident in the following long-term chart (Exhibit 11-16).

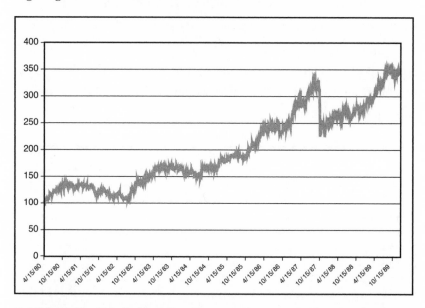

Exhibit 11-16   U.S. Dollar Index (Source: St. Louis Federal Reserve)

The dollar drifted lower into 1995 and then began its most recent bull rally as shown in Exhibit 11-16. That lasted until the beginning of 2002, and since then the dollar has been under pressure. It has lost over one-third of its peak value in 2002 (Exhibit 11-17). It means the performance of many non-dollar investments should have benefited.

Certainly, it means most foreign bonds outperform U.S. dollar denominated bonds as long as the yield on the foreign bond is equal to or greater than the equivalent U.S. bond.

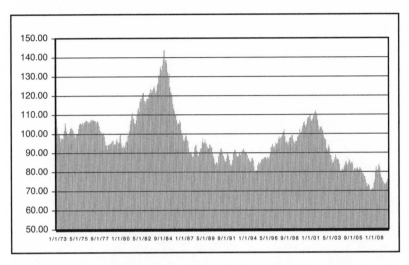

Exhibit 11-17   Trade Weighted Exchange Index of Dollar: Major Currencies (Source: Board of Governors of the Federal Reserve System; 2009 research.stlouisfed.org)

Conclusion

These market signals are just a sample of what an investor can use to monitor the market and determine whether it is in its bull or bear phase. They can also be used to determine how much risk aversion exists and how important interest rates are to the market's performance. Finally, valuation is always important to monitor along with recent performance.

The benefit of using any of these tools would be helped by the observations about some old wisdom. For instance, the following saying is dangerous and a reason to double-check assumptions: "This time is different." In the past decade, that saying was used to support the valuation of technology stocks during the tech bubble and house prices during the housing bubble. There may have been different drivers pushing the respective markets higher, but one thing was still the same; the respective markets were very overvalued and that overvaluation was a sign of trouble ahead. Another saying to remember is "History may not repeat itself, but it does seem to rhyme."

12

Rules of the Road

How about a map?

Assuming deleveraging occurs and leads to a more challenging economic and investing times, most investors will probably not be prepared. One reason is their expectations may be much greater than the types of returns investments delivered over the past nine decades. As shown in Chapter 3, "Nine Decades of Real Asset Class Returns," those returns have not been consistent, and most recently, the long-term equity returns have been negative. In Japan, the stock market is still down over 70% from its peak and 10-year Japanese Government bond yields remain below 2%. There are times to act with greater caution and there are times investors can act more boldly. Structural bear markets are times to act more cautiously, while structural bull markets are times to act more boldly. Fortunately, past structural bull markets usually lasted more than a decade, and, even if the first part was missed, the eventual returns achieved were very attractive. Given the challenges presented by deleveraging and the uncertain policy responses, now is a time to act more cautiously.

Navigating an environment challenged by the financial excesses of the recent past and shedding some of the leverage taken to create those excesses is difficult. Financial pressures and the sense of urgency vary across demographics, from age and wealth to residence and tax status. For people in the lower income groups, financial pressures can be the most severe and most difficult to address. People with lower income tend to be financially less flexible and are generally less familiar with financial options and instruments. Many of them dream of a lucky strike: Studies show that the heaviest lottery players—the 20% of players who provide 82% of lottery revenue—are disproportionately low-income, minority men with less than a college education.[1] If all revenues from lottery games, which exceed $45 billion, were saved, it would increase the personal savings rate from 4.7% to almost 5.5%. Regardless of the income group, income levels tend to increase with age, peaking when people are in their 50s.

Whatever the financial environment, preparing the foundation for a stronger financial future is made easier by following some basic rules. Building a solid financial foundation takes time, persistence, and discipline. The benefits are rarely visible immediately, which makes it tough to withstand the temptation of the instant gratification that comes from spending. Discipline is always important, but more so during difficult times. Applying the following 12 rules should help build a better financial foundation and future:

1. Know your financial self
2. Build a personal balance sheet
3. Understand your risk appetite
4. Develop a savings discipline
5. Preserve principal
6. Develop a spending discipline
7. Diversify your investments
8. Observe some basic investing discipline
9. Identify the nature of the market: structural bull or structural bear
10. Develop a sell discipline
11. Continue your education
12. Beat your financial benchmark

The rules apply to all environments, although the financial and economic environment can change from generation to generation. For people born in 1900 in the United States, the world was filled with promise, and the expectation of a better tomorrow persisted for most of their first 30 years. During that 30-year period, World War I occurred. It caused tremendous destruction, but most of that destruction was overseas. For the United States, it was a time when the country solidified its position as the world's leading economy. By the end of that war, the United States transitioned to a peacetime economy and a new era of consumerism: the Roaring Twenties. During this period, automobiles, radios, and bathtubs were growth businesses; so, too, was housing. Consumer credit became more available as did mortgage financing. The farm economy was in a decline that would continue for decades, reflecting the secular shift away from an agrarian economy. Policymakers, academics, farm advocates, and business leaders were either oblivious to the shift, or, more likely not willing or prepared to accept it. That was unfortunate because many suffered from that transition. Still, the majority of Americans experienced a succession of better times and expected them to continue.

On the contrary, the stock market crashed in 1929, followed by a series of policy mistakes. The expectations and life styles of many born in 1900 and soon thereafter were turned upside down. Aspiring to a better lifestyle as a goal was replaced by economic survival. Unlike the generation of 1900, the generation born in 1935 was relatively small and brought up in difficult times. By the time they became adults, the Korean War ended and the Vietnam War was the burden of a younger generation. The pessimism and modest expectations assumed early in their lives would eventually be challenged by opportunities they never expected. Like the generation of 1900, their expectations about life changed dramatically; they just went in opposite directions.

All generations experience economic and political volatility. Volatility is not the exception; it is the rule. It seems prudent to expect and plan for volatility when structuring a financial plan. It is also important to be realistic and to start by building a strong foundation for your financial house. The benefits of the 1980s bull market and the recent rise of the emerging markets might have obscured the lessons about the disciplines required to save, invest, and build for the future, but they did not alter them.

Know Your Financial Self

This means understanding your financial needs and resources. Start by building a personal cash flow statement. This begins with determining how much you expect to earn next year and how much you expect to spend. Count both job and investment income, including savings and investment properties. On the expense side, the cash flow statement should start with a spending budget. Spending should be broken down into two basic categories: necessities and discretionary items. Necessities include housing, food, medical expenses, education, transportation, clothing, and other commitments such as loan payments. The word necessity does not mean minimum, it means what you believe you are likely to spend in a given year on these items. There is always an opportunity to alter the cost of the necessities, but the first step is to determine how much they cost. The next items to quantify are the discretionary items. These include travel, entertainment, hobbies, and so on. These are expenses that are nice to make but not necessary.

After categorizing expenses, revisit the expected income level, leaving room for savings. The personal savings rate for the United States tended to hover above 7.5% until the mid-1980s but has rarely stayed there since. In 2008, however, the aggregate savings rate on U.S. personal disposable income started rising again, climbing to 5% in late 2009, from a low of 0.8% in April 2008. To finance living costs, more money was borrowed, in part, because less was saved.

Personal savings according to the United States government is the income that remains after personal outlays and taxes (Exhibit 12-1). Outlays are the sum of consumption expenditures, personal interest payments, and transfer payments. Income includes salaries of the public and private sector along with other sources of income such as benefits and income receipts on assets.

The increase in wealth tied to house appreciation and the paydown of a mortgage are not included in the personal savings rate. Nor is any appreciation in a stock portfolio. These are sources of incremental wealth that can be realized when an asset or investment is sold. They are also more volatile sources of wealth than savings. As a result, these sources of wealth cannot be viewed as permanent savings until the gains are realized. Hence, a low savings rate means greater financial risk and less financial flexibility. According to the Federal Reserve's *2007 Survey of Consumer Finance*, the median net worth for families was $120,300 in 2007, a modest increase over the 2004 level of $102,200 and the $101,200 level in 2001. The highest level of median net worth belonged to the 55-64-age cohort. It was $253,700. This was also true in the 2001 and 2004 *Surveys*. However, the 65-74-age cohort achieved the highest median net worth in 1998 at $186,500.

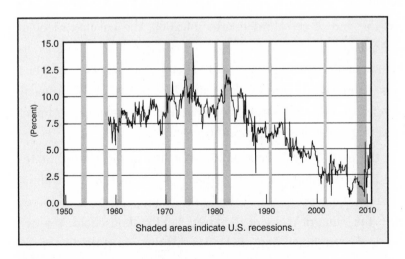

Shaded areas indicate U.S. recessions.

Exhibit 12-1   Personal Savings Rate (Source: U.S. Department of Commerce: Bureau of Economic Analysis)

When building a financial plan, expect costs to rise and avoid making overly optimistic predictions about the level at which income is likely to increase. Always challenge the assumptions underlying any financial projection and try to understand how the outcome changes if the assumptions are altered. To do that, you can build your own simple simulation, or use one of the many simulations available from financial websites. To avoid potential vendor bias, it is generally better to use a third-party simulation and, wherever possible, use multiple simulations to check if you get the same results.

Build a Personal Balance Sheet

Prepare your personal balance sheet. This should include all of the personal assets and personal liabilities. The difference between the two is your financial net worth. For most Americans, their principal asset is their house. Financial assets include deposits, fixed income investments, savings instruments, and equity or equity-like instruments. The tangible assets are predominantly real estate and consumer durable goods such as automobiles, stoves, refrigerators, and computers.

At the end of the third quarter of 2009, the balance sheet of household Americans had total assets of $67.5 trillion. These assets included tangible assets of $23.1 trillion and financial assets of $44.4 trillion. Those assets were funded with $14.4 trillion of debt, mostly mortgages, and the rest was equity. That number includes the financial assets and liabilities of nonprofit organizations.

At the end of 2006, household net worth in the United States reached $64.5 trillion, and liabilities totaled just $13.4 trillion. Because of the subsequent decline in housing prices and the stock market, the value of many of the assets held by household America fell while the liabilities continued to rise. At the end of the first quarter of 2009, the net worth of household America reached $48.5 trillion, a decline of $16 trillion from its level reached in 2006. The value of houses owned by American households aggregated $22.9 trillion at the end of 2006. By the end of the first quarter of 2009, that value fell to $15.7 trillion; a loss of $7.2 trillion of value and more than 30% of the 2006 value. Home mortgages financing those houses totaled $9.8 trillion in 2006 and rose to $10.4 trillion at the end of the first quarter of 2009. In that period the "home equity" of those homes fell from $13.1 trillion to $5.3 trillion.

Corporate equities, mutual fund shares, life insurance reserves, pension fund reserves, equity in noncorporate business, and other assets totaled $37.9 trillion at the end on 2006 and fell to $27.2 trillion at the end of the first quarter of 2009. That is a loss of $10.7 trillion, or about 30%. These assets and the value expected from the eventual sale of a house are the assets most individuals expect to support themselves in retirement. Retirement assets are just that, they are not meant to support current expenses. Their availability should not be assumed until retirement. Also, nonfinancial assets are almost always harder and more expensive to convert to cash than financial assets. They should be valued conservatively on a balance sheet.

According to the 2007 Survey of Consumer Finance, nonfinancial assets represented 66.1% of total assets, which was up from the 64.3% share in 2004 and 57.8% in 2001. The mix of nonfinancial assets in 2007 was vehicles—4.4%; primary residence—48.1%; other residential property—10.7%; equity in nonresidential property— 5.8%; business equity—29.7%; and others—1.3%.

Part of building a strong balance is paying down debt and being cautious when taking on debt. Because most debt is used to finance the purchase of nonfinancial assets, paying it down reduces the carrying costs of those assets and potential financial risk. In 2007, the leverage ratio for all families was 14.9%. The income groups with the greatest leverage were in the 40–59.9 percentile, the 60–79.9 percentile, and the 80–89.9 percentile. The three groups had a leverage ratio of 24.3%, 25.3%, and 23.4%, respectively. Younger people tend to have higher leverage ratios, as do people without a college degree. Relative to the total population, 77% of households have some form of debt, which was up modestly from the 2004 level of 76.4%.

The title of this book contains a warning: Too much leverage creates numerous problems that can burden others; not just the borrower. A strong balance sheet is one of the paths to greater financial freedom and greater personal choice.

Understand Your Appetite for Risk

From the market bottom in 1982 to the market peak in March 2000, equity investors made money on all their investments if they did not sell. The market eventually always went higher. Because the span of the structural bull market lasted almost two decades, the experiences of the market were the only ones for a major portion of investors, and those experiences were often mistaken for lessons. One of the main lessons of the bull market was to buy on weakness. Another was that "buy and hold" was a legitimate investment strategy.

As the market rose, so did the willingness of equity investors to take risk. According to an ICI/SIFMA Equity and Bond Owners Survey, and the Federal Reserve Board Survey of Consumer Finance, the willingness of investors to take risk rose with the rise in the S&P 500. The more rapidly it appreciated, the more rapidly investors' willingness to take risk rose. However, increased confidence does not always lead to the best decisions. When the market turned down, the lessons of the old structural bull market no longer seemed to apply. Instead, there were new lessons learned. One of the principal lessons of the structural bear market is that people do not like to lose money. For most investors the pain and anxiety of losing money is a more intense emotion than making attractive returns.

Assessing an individual's risk profile starts with their age and quantifying their financial obligations. The younger a person, the more risk they can take. Of course, that risk should always be assessed against the expected reward. Whatever the market, a risk assessment should be taken to help better understand an investment's risk–reward profile, and an investor should conduct a realistic assessment of their risk comfort zone.

Develop a Saving Discipline

Benjamin Franklin's adage "A penny saved is a penny earned!" is as true today as it was then. Saving money is a critical component of successful investing and of building a more secure financial future.

First, start with the power of compounding. The earlier an investor starts investing, the bigger advantage they gain. A $1,000 investment compounded at 5% is worth almost $1,630 in 10 years; $2,653 in 20 years; $3,387 in 25 years, and $11,467 in 50 years. If that savings equation is changed to include $1,000 of annual savings at the end of each year, the value changes to $14,207 at the end of 10 years; $35,719 at the end of 20 years; $51,113 at the end of 25 years; and $220,815 at the end of 50 years.

An increase in the interest rate used to compound savings of 1% to 6% increases the amount saved by about 1% in 5 years, almost 5% in 10 years, and 10% over the course of 10 years. For a period of 50 years, the value of that $1,000 initial investment is increased over 60%. If the rate is higher, the impact is proportionately greater. At 8%, a $1,000 investment would be worth $46,902 in 50 years, more than quadruple the value attained if the rate were 5%. If a sum of $1,000 were saved annually and an 8% annual return obtained, the value at the end of 50 years would be $619,672. The message is clear: Save early and save as much as possible. It can reduce the savings burden in later years and create greater financial flexibility.

Based on the Federal Reserve's 2007 *Survey of Consumer Finance*, the peak earning years for most Americans are 45–54. According to the survey, the median income reached $64,500, which is meaningfully higher than the median for years 35–44 of $53,600, and the median income of $49,100 for the next 10 years of 55–64. Assuming this trend for financial planning purposes means that a greater effort to save should be made during this period because that is when most workers will be in their peak earning years. Continuing to experience higher earnings later in life means even greater financial flexibility provided a savings and investing discipline were started early and maintained.

Preserve Principal

The saying "First do no harm!" is appropriate for investors. One of the main goals should be not taking excessive and poorly understood risks with principal, especially principal critical for your basic needs and future.

Investing requires a sense of the risk undertaken to achieve a given reward. No investment provides a guaranteed return, even government bonds. A look back at Chapter 3 and the nine decades of assets class returns provides good examples of the volatility of returns. The pursuit of extraordinary returns often results in extraordinary losses. Different asset classes carry specific risks given their position in the capital and economic structure. The safest asset class is cash because it is the most liquid. For purposes of our analysis, T-Bills are meant to reflect cash. Cash maintains its value in economic environments that are not inflationary. The returns shown in the nine-decade analysis are real returns and indicate that equities usually provide superior returns to fixed income and cash. An inflationary environment hurts fixed income investors. Inflation debases the value of a fixed income security. A look at the real returns of the 1970s shows just how difficult it was to achieve attractive returns during the decade. The prospect of investing in commodities and emerging markets was beyond the reach of most investors at the time. That has changed with the innovation in investment products, greater competition, and globalization. The cost of diversifying one's portfolio is now much lower than it used to be and the range of products is much greater.

With any investment, the best way to start to preserve capital is to understand the investment. Clearly, those who invested with Bernie Madoff did not understand how he invested; they did not even know if he made investments; they just understood that he reported a track record of superior low volatility returns. Those reported returns were far superior to any comparable investment. Probably the best question to ask about something providing a superior return without much apparent risk is, "Is it too good to be true?" The old adage "If it looks too good to be true, it usually is!" is true more often than not. In the process of attempting to preserve principal, try and figure out what are the assumptions behind any investments' expected return and then challenge those assumptions. This process should lead to a better understanding of the risks involved. When dealing with prospective investment managers, avoid those unwilling to explain their strategies and those saying "just trust me." The challenges presented by an economic deleveraging mean even more thought and closer attention to those issues.

Develop a Spending Discipline

The pressure to spend is great for most of us, and compelling; but a more disciplined approach to spending now can lead to more financial flexibility in the future. This is true for individuals, businesses, and governments. One of the great examples of the benefits of controlled spending took place during the administration of President Clinton after the Republicans gained control of Congress. The lesson learned is very basic: keep the rate of spending growth slower than the rate of revenue growth. Doing this over a long period of time should result in a meaningful level of savings. If those savings are well invested, the ability to enjoy a future based on a given level of financial freedom is achievable.

For the United States, a cyclical peak in spending growth was reached in 1990 because of the S&L crisis. Spending growth slowed afterward but was inflated for 2 years because of Desert Storm. However, starting in 1984, the revenue growth rate began to exceed the rate of spending growth and did so in 13 of the next 17 years. The exceptions were 1985, 1990, 1991, and 1992. The last 3 years were burdened by financial crisis, war, and recession. As shown in Exhibit 12-2, the rate of spending growth continued to fall from the early 1990s and would remain low until 2000. That control over spending growth allowed the subsequent pick up in revenue growth tied to the economic recovery that started in 1992, and the surge in revenues from market-driven activities to ultimately create the first federal government budget surplus since 1960 in 1998.

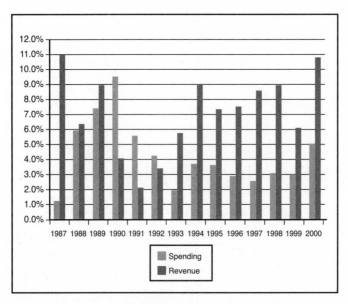

Exhibit 12-2   Annual Growth Rates of Federal Spending and Revenue (Source: U.S. Department of Treasury)

If federal government spending growth were 1% less annually starting in 1961, the federal spending would be more than $1.5 trillion less in 2009, a reduction of almost 40% for 2009 outlays. Instead of running constant deficits, the government would have been in a surplus position starting in 1969. Of course, those surpluses would likely not have materialized: they would have been replaced by lower tax rates, and possibly even less pressure on the dollar. Certainly, the lower level of spending would have reduced the debt burden now facing the United States. By 2009, all else held equal, a 1% reduction in the annual rate of government spending would have freed up almost $10 trillion of funds, or just less than 20% of the current debt outstanding. A 0.5% reduction in the annual growth rate of government spending would have meant 2009 outlays were still almost $1 trillion lower, but the aggregate impact would have been much lower at close to $3 trillion in 2008 and $2 trillion in 2009. Whatever the adjustment, a slightly lower rate of growth for government spending means much less funding pressure over time. Developing a spending discipline is important because it can provide long-term benefits by putting less pressure on the government to tax, and for individuals to borrow, or take excessive risk.

Spending has been a way of life and an economic force. In the U.S. economy, consumer spending was a growing source of economic growth since the mid-1960s, as shown in Exhibit 12-3. Consumer spending has gone from representing a little more than 60% of the GDP to 71% at the end of the third quarter of 2009. For most people, an increasing share of every dollar spent will be spent on services and health care. These are harder to price. The Bureau of Economic Advisors provides quarterly data on the consumption of personal expenditures. The composition of spending has shifted as new products were introduced and existing products became available to more people as a result of price reductions and the expansion of retail channels. (Think of the Sears catalogue and its modern incarnation, online shopping.) Supporting the consumption was financing that became more flexible, widely available, and cheaper as interest rates fell.

The relative weight of different group categories has also been altered. For instance, durable goods, which include motor vehicles and parts, furniture and other durable household items, recreational goods and vehicles and other durable goods, represented more than 10% of GDP in the early 1950s but now represent less than 7.5%. Durable goods should continue to represent a smaller share of GDP and also a smaller share of consumer purchases. The products manufactured are of higher quality and last longer; and global competition is helping to lower their prices.

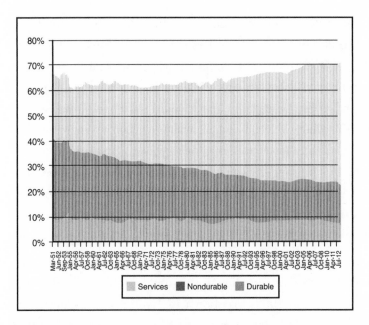

Exhibit 12-3   U.S. Consumer Spending to GDP (Source: Bureau of Economic Advisors)

The biggest shift in consumer spending patterns was from nondurable goods to services, which is shown in Exhibit 12-4. In 1929 and 1930, the food and clothing components of nondurable goods represented almost 33% of consumer spending. By 2008, they represented just 11%, and food includes restaurants. Health care took the biggest share; going from 3% of personal expenditures in 1929 to over 15% in 2008, which represents about 33% of what was spent on services. The growing percentage of spending absorbed by health care reflects the aging population, greater expectations, innovation, greater choice, and a rising cost structure. It also means consumers have less discretionary income after paying for health-care costs, which just reinforces the need to establish a stronger spending discipline. That starts with a budget and prioritizing the spending needs. It is a burden felt by individuals first, then companies, and finally governments.

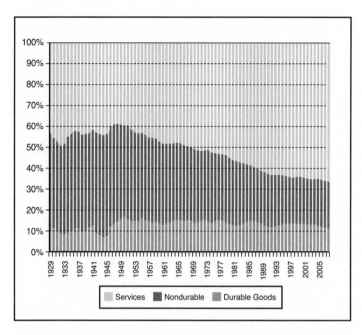

Exhibit 12-4   Composition of Consumer Expenditures (Source: Bureau of Economic Advisors)

The spending pinch means a more price-sensitive consumer and favors companies that provide value at attractive prices. It also means there will likely be consolidation among companies providing consumer discretionary items for those companies to realize cost-savings and other efficiencies.

Diversify the Portfolio

One of the basic lessons of investing and risk management is to diversify. For equity investors, this means reducing exposure to the U.S. equity markets and increasing exposure to other global markets. That shift should be sensitive to valuation and past performance, and it should be done over time.

We have noted earlier in the book how the relative weight of the United States in the global economy is likely to decline. The investment ramifications are obvious even though in the last crisis, global exposure did not provide the diversification it usually does: The market of 2008 was extraordinary in its extremes. Those extremes were caused in large part by a liquidity crisis, which put pressure on most investments and took away many of the benefits of diversification for a period of time. Essentially, most risk assets became highly correlated, which means they performed in a similar fashion—they all went down. And to varying degrees, investors lost money. They lost money because the financial crisis exposed the weakness of many business models and destroyed some businesses and some asset values supporting credit structures.

A liquidity crisis occurs when the basic financial intermediary functions stop working. This includes banks being unwilling to lend to other banks even when the loan is for a short term and backed by security, that is, it is collateralized. It is often called the counterparty trade and as shown in Chapter 11, "Market Signals," liquidity spreads widen out to a point that the liquidity market stopped functioning without government support.

For an equity investor, the market capitalization of the world's stock markets is still well below the level of more than $60 trillion attained at the end of year 2007 (Exhibit 12-5). That value was

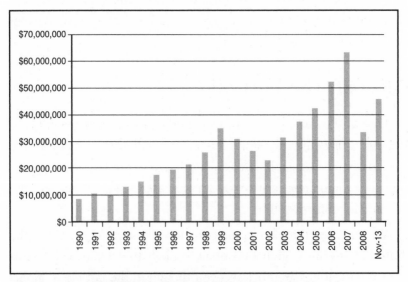

Exhibit 12-5   Market Capitalization of Global Indexes ($mm)
(Source: World Exchange Federations)

almost cut in half during 2008, but it rebounded in 2009 to $45 trillion. The value of the global exchanges now sits higher than in any years but 2006 and 2007. Capturing that performance meant having a diversified global equity portfolio and not one concentrated in any one country.

The importance of diversification is underscored by Exhibit 12-6, which shows the exchanges of Japan and the United State representing a declining share of the world's exchanges. Japan's decline began in 1990, and it was most abrupt through 1997. Since 1997, the strength of the Japanese yen offset some of the weakness in its markets. Still, after two decades, the valuation of Japan's markets slipped from 32% to 8%, a decline in global share of almost 75%. The United States ends about where it started in 1990, at 32% of global market capitalization, and yet since 2000, its share decline was a steep fall from more than 50% to just over 30%.

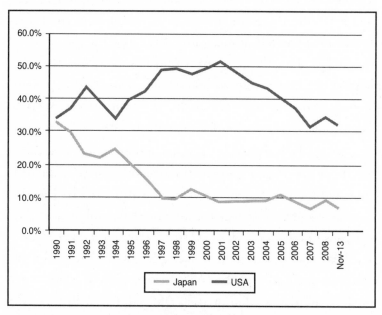

Exhibit 12-6   Value of Japanese and U.S. Markets to Global Markets (Source: World Exchange Federations)

The prospects of many countries with developed economies such as the United States and Japan facing the economic deleveraging imply a continued economic shift toward developing countries and those rich in natural resources. The long-term performance of equity markets should reflect this outlook, and investors with less diversified portfolios should shift their equity weightings accordingly.

Identify the Market Phase—Structural Bull Market or Structural Bear Market

Chapter 5, "Bull and Bear Markets," highlighted the changing nature of markets and how fortunes changed between bull and bear markets. It is important to attempt to identify a structural bull and bear market phase; however, it does not seem realistic to anticipate bull and bear market cycles.

Over the course of the 100 years following 1901, the large-cap equity market in the United States was in a structural bull market for 54 years and a structural bear market for 46 years. Over the course of the structural bull markets, investment gains occurred from the beginning to the end of the structural bull market with periodic opportunities to buy on dips. Identifying the bear markets successfully helps protect capital by avoiding significant losses.

Bear markets did not provide the same opportunities. Investment strategies should be altered based on the structural phase of the market. A buy-and-hold approach can work in a structural bull market but can cause significant financial stress in a structural bear market. That is because the market bias of a structural bull market is up. A structural bear market is a more vulnerable market because of the economic and political excesses of previous periods. The Great Japanese Bear Market started in 1990 and more than two decades later it is still almost 70% lower. Investor attempts to pick the market's bottom have failed. The issues facing the country include deflation, a shrinking population, a rising level of government debt to GDP, and an anemic economy that has produced almost no job growth in the past two decades.

In the United States, the bear market tied to the Great Depression kept the index below its 1929 level into 1952. It was a period that included two of the S&P 500's best one-year performances and two of its three worst performances. The volatility of its performance meant that on a total return basis, it reached its 1929 high around the end of World War II. Still, investing over the course of the next 20 years presented few extended periods of sustained positive returns. The most extended period came as the fortunes of World War II shifted and investors became more confident in an Allied victory. Given the time, investing was the avocation of very few people. When the war ended, markets began to churn and fell 20% before beginning a period of, at best, single-digit annual gains. During the bear market of the 1960s and the 1970s, the market went sideways for about a decade, and that was before factoring in the effects of inflation but including dividend yields. For the 10-year period, the equity index was down.

The sustained periods of attractive returns from a structural bull market begin when the issues releasing the bear are addressed. Part of the process is revaluation. Another is the prospect and ultimate reality of a growing low-inflation economy.

During the structural bull market of the late 1940s through mid-1960s, there was a period of more than 10 years before the end of the bear market in which investors sustained compound annual returns over 10-year periods of more than 15%, which is a quadrupling of an investment before taxes (Exhibit 12-7). The other period of sustained 10-year compound returns started in the late 1970s and lasted into the 1990s. These were periods of extremely attractive returns when buy-and-hold did work and worked very well. They were the exception to history, not the rule.

Again, there are some of the major points about the conditions and shifts occurring at the beginning of a bull market. They include low valuation levels, well-controlled or declining inflation levels, and the prospect of accelerating and sustained real GDP growth. One other point is economic participation becomes more disbursed, which represents a reversal of trend toward concentration.

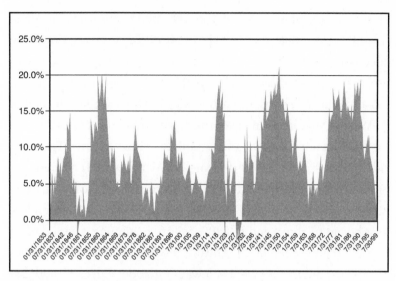

Exhibit 12-7   S&P 500: 10-Year Total Return CAGR Returns by Year of Investment (Source: Global Financial Data)

Apply Basic Investment Disciplines

Identifying the nature of the market should help better protect principal and identify the opportunities to invest more aggressively. Applying some basic investment disciplines should help enhance performance.

Valuation–Low valuation is a better place to start from than a high valuation. As shown in the Chapter 11, returns are usually better from the base of a low valuation than from the base of a high valuation. The valuations to focus on are the price-earnings ratio, price-to-tangible book value, price to sales, and dividend yield. These valuations should be viewed on a relative and absolute basis.

Performance—Strong performance is difficult to sustain, and expectations that it will be sustained should be challenged. Exhibit 12-8 provides the annual returns of the S&P 500 Index and its predecessor indexes since 1825. What is apparent is how rarely one strong year was followed by a similarly strong year, and how a really bad year was rarely followed by a similarly bad year. There is an exception to this observation, and that is what happens after a stock market bubble bursts.

Exhibit 12-8   S&P 500 Annual Return Distribution Since 1925 (Source: Global Financial Data)

40%+		20 to 40%		0 to 20%		0 to -20%		Worse than -20%	
				1901	19.8%				
				1944	19.7%				
				1905	19.7%				
				1972	19.0%				
				1909	18.9%				
		1995	37.6%	1986	18.7%				
		1975	37.2%	1979	18.6%				
		1927	37.1%	1952	18.5%				
		1945	36.5%	1949	18.1%				
		1915	35.5%	1988	16.6%				
		1997	33.4%	1964	16.4%				
		1938	33.2%	2006	15.8%				
		1936	32.8%	1921	14.6%				
		1980	32.5%	1971	14.3%				
		1985	31.7%	1965	12.4%				
		1989	31.7%	1959	11.9%				
		1955	31.4%	1926	11.1%	1939	-0.9%		
		1904	31.0%	1968	11.0%	1953	-1.1%		
		1950	30.6%	2004	10.9%	1934	-2.3%		
		1991	30.5%	1993	10.1%	1990	-3.1%		
		1925	29.5%	2010	9.8%	1914	-3.7%		
		2003	28.7%	1916	8.9%	1981	-4.9%		
		1998	28.6%	1912	8.0%	1977	-7.2%		
		1922	27.8%	1992	7.6%	1910	-7.9%		
		1961	26.8%	1906	6.8%	1946	-8.2%		
		2009	26.5%	1956	6.6%	1969	-8.5%		
		1943	25.8%	1978	6.6%	1962	-8.8%		
		1924	25.7%	1984	6.3%	1932	-8.9%		
		1918	25.6%	1911	5.7%	1929	-8.9%		
		1951	24.6%	2007	5.5%	2000	-9.1%		
		1967	23.9%	1987	5.3%	1913	-9.6%		
		1976	23.9%	1947	5.2%	1940	-10.1%	2002	-22.1%
		1996	23.0%	1948	5.1%	1966	-10.1%	1930	-25.3%
1933	52.9%	1963	22.7%	2005	4.9%	1957	-10.9%	1917	-25.3%
1954	52.4%	1983	22.6%	1902	4.9%	1941	-11.8%	1974	-26.5%
1935	47.2%	1982	21.5%	1923	4.2%	2001	-11.9%	1907	-29.6%
1908	44.5%	1942	21.1%	1970	3.9%	1903	-14.6%	1937	-35.3%
1958	43.3%	1999	21.0%	1994	1.3%	1973	-14.7%	2008	-37.0%
1928	43.3%	1919	20.7%	1960	0.5%	1920	-19.7%	1931	-43.9%
40%+		**20 to 40%**		**0 to 20%**		**0 to -20%**		**Worse than -20%**	

After a bubble bursts, the stock market usually takes more than 2 years to bottom. After 1929 and 1930, the market took 30 months to bottom. The market of 1929 was followed by 1930 (down more than 30%), 1931 down more than 50%, and 1932 down more than 10%. The Tech Bubble was followed by a more than 10% down year in 2000, more than 20% in 2001, and more than 30% in 2002.

Fear and Greed—Pay attention to investor sentiment. Consensus is hard to sustain and when consensus is strongest, the impact of a surprise is greatest. Strong market performance builds growing levels of confidence over time. They also attract more and more money. At some point the next buyer is hard to find. It is probably time to sell or at least hedge positions.

On the other hand, when fear is highest, investment opportunities are often greatest. These are periods that often create great gains and result in investors saying, "The easy money has been made." It was not easy at the time, only in retrospect.

Pay attention to the fixed income markets—Credit signals can foreshadow difficult times ahead for equities. When credit spreads start to widen, it can be a sign of growing risk aversion and potential economic difficulties. If liquidity spreads start to widen, it is an even more cautionary indicator.

Nothing goes up forever—The Tech Bubble, the 1929 market, the housing market, the Japanese market of the 1980s, oil in the 1970s, technology in the late 1990s, all seemed to defy gravity with their ascent. As they kept rising, these markets attracted more and more investment dollars. The good times did not and could not last. The best move was to short the equity market, the second best was to sell.

Have a Sell Discipline

Preserve principal, pay attention to the economy and various market signals, and develop a sell discipline. This is perhaps the hardest part of investing. It is easier to make an investment than it is to part with an investment. Making an investment is much easier for most investors than getting out of an investment, because selling creates multiple opportunities for regret. For instance, there is the regret created when an investment goes higher after you have sold it. The potential for this regret often causes investors to take the path of least resistance, and that is to do nothing.

Start by accepting that it is impossible to know everything about an investment and that usually the market knows more. One approach is to sell if an investment falls by a certain amount. That amount is usually a percentage of your initial investment. It can be a level relative to the performance of an index or the rest of the group. The idea of a sell discipline for an investment losing value is to limit the downside of the loss and avoid the potential of a much larger loss in hopes of things changing. A great many investors maintained positions in a number of the financial stocks such as Bear Stearns, Lehman Brothers, and Citigroup anticipating the financial environment would return to normal, that assets were undervalued, or that the problems were not as large as feared.

A sell discipline used when prices are falling is meant to reduce losses and preserve capital. The other side is a sell discipline in place to take advantage of when an investment performs extraordinarily well. It is meant to take some of the profits and reduce any emerging concentration and substantially reduced level of diversification that might occur if one investment materially outperforms others.

Education, Get More

Government statistics make the point: People with more education do better financially and are somewhat less exposed to effects of harsh economic volatility. In 2007, the median net worth of a household headed by a college graduate was $280,800. That was more than triple the level of the net worth of a household headed by someone with some college education or someone that was a high school graduate. Relative to households headed by someone lacking a high school diploma, the college graduate household net worth was 8.5 times greater in 2007.

The employment statistics reinforce the benefit of getting more education and some of those findings are summarized in Exhibit 12-9. According to the Bureau of Labor Statistics, people with a bachelor's degree and higher have a much lower unemployment rate than the other three groups. This is shown in the following tables from the employment report released in December 2009.

Exhibit 12-9   Employment Rate Summary Based on Level of Education (Source: 2007 Survey of Labor Statistics)

Unemployment Rate	Nov 2008	Nov 2009
Less than a high school diploma	10.6%	15.0%
High school graduates, no college	6.9%	10.4%
Some college, or associate degree	5.5%	9.0%
Bachelor's degree and higher	3.2%	4.9%
Participation Rate	**Nov 2008**	**Nov 2009**
Less than a high school diploma	47.2%	46.3%
High school graduates, no college	62.3%	61.7%
Some college, or associate degree	71.6%	70.4%
Bachelor's degree and higher	77.7%	77.5%
Employment-Population Rate	**Nov 2008**	**Nov 2009**
Less than a high school diploma	42.2%	39.4%
High school graduates, no college	58.1%	55.3%
Some college, or associate degree	67.7%	64.1%
Bachelor's degree and higher	75.3%	73.7%

In all cases, the higher the level of education level attained, the lower the level of unemployment and the greater the percentage of participation and employment-population rate.

Finally, the past four Surveys of Consumer Finance show the median pretax income levels are much higher for college graduates, as shown in Exhibit 12-10. They also show that group of people saved more, which is shown in Exhibit 12-11.

Exhibit 12-10   Income Summary Based on Education Level (Source: 2007 Survey of Consumer Finance)

Median Income Level (000)	1998	2001	2004	2007
No high school diploma	$19.8	$19.8	$21.3	$22.2
High school diploma	$37.2	$39.7	$39.3	$36.7
Some college	$45.2	$47.9	$45.1	$45.6
College degree	$70.0	$79.4	$80.5	$78.2

Exhibit 12-11   Savings Summary Based on Education Level (Source: 2007 Survey of Consumer Finance)

Percentage of Families Saving	1998	2001	2004	2007
No high school diploma	39.5%	38.7%	35.9%	41.6%
High school diploma	53.7%	56.7%	54.0%	51.1%
Some college	56.7%	61.7%	51.0%	53.6%
College degree	65.6%	70.0%	68.3%	68.6%

Exhibit 12-12 shows that households headed by a person with a college education or just a high school diploma represented 68.2% of households in 2007 that saved.

Exhibit 12-12   Percentage of Families in Education Group as a Percentage of Total (Source: 2007 Survey of Consumer Finance)

Percentage of Families	1998	2001	2004	2007
No high school diploma	16.5%	16.0%	14.4%	13.5%
High school diploma	31.9%	31.7%	30.6%	32.9%
Some college	18.5%	18.3%	18.4%	18.4%
College degree	33.2%	34.0%	36.6%	35.3%

The continued shift to an information-based services economy increases the value of intellectual capital. Many of the basic tools needed to participate successfully in the economy are learned in the classroom. Those tools should be refined and enhanced with more education. The statistics show the vast majority of people pursuing more education are rewarded with a much higher level of income. That trend is expected to continue, and any tools that improve the quality, accessibility, and impact of an education should also be rewarded.

The Goal Is to Beat Your Financial Benchmark

Investment professionals often judge their performance on their ability to generate a return on their investments that exceeds a given benchmark. That benchmark is usually a stock market index and the most popular index is the Standard and Poor's 500 Index. More than $1.5 trillion of investments are managed to perform better than this index. It represents about 75% of the value of all public companies headquartered in the United States and includes 500 of the largest companies by market capitalization (shares outstanding times price).

Beating a benchmark probably gets more attention during a bull market than during a bear market. When stock markets are rising, investors naturally like it if their stocks rise more. However, when stock markets are falling, investors are less excited that their stock portfolios outperformed the market because they still lost money.

Most individual investors are not trying to generate returns that outperform a specific stock index. Instead, they are saving and investing for various purposes during the course of their lives. They should develop return expectations based on their financial needs and plans and not on exceeding the return of a stock index that is not necessarily structured with their needs in mind.

One way to reduce company-specific risk is to invest in index funds and ETFs. Index funds are meant to generate returns similar to a given index such as the S&P 500, S&P Mid-Cap 400, the S&P Small-Cap 600, or others. Exhibit 12-13 lists some of the large indexes, their market capitalization, and their performance for 2009.

Exhibit 12-13   Market Capitalization and 2009 Return (Source: Standards & Poor's)

As of 12/31/09	Market Capitalization	Year Performance
DOMESTIC—USA		
S&P 500	$9,927.6 billion	+26.5%
S&P MidCap 400	$ 904.0 billion	+37.4%
S&P SmallCap 600	$ 401.7 billion	+25.6%
GLOBAL		
S&P Global 1200	$21,370.1 billion	+31.7%

Index funds help investors reduce company-specific risk through diversification. ETFs enable an investor to reduce company-specific risk, while focusing their investment on a certain segment of the market. ETFs also enable an investor to invest in commodities, fixed income, and international markets. Index funds and ETFs are usually a lower cost way of investing than active mutual funds. As with any financial instrument, understanding it or working with a professional is critical.

As you structure your financial portfolio, keep in mind your personal needs and wants, which will help you define your financial goals. Ultimately, the goal of a financial plan is best developed after making a personal financial assessment, understanding one's risk appetite, and developing a personal cash flow statement and balance sheet. When that goal is established, focus on beating it and not a stock or other financial index. That is your personal financial benchmark; not some arbitrary financial index used to measure the performance of part of the financial market.

While creating your personal financial benchmark keep in mind several secular trends highlighted in this book. They suggest structural shifts in the global economy and significant potential headwinds that equity markets should face in the coming years.

The structural shifts highlighted start with the global economic mix. Less and less of it will come from what has been known as the developed world. More should come from the developing economies, especially China, India, and Brazil. With these changes should also come changes in the political environment. Compared to the global economy following World War II until early into the past decade, this economic shift represents a fundamental change of the economic playing field, and we believe necessitates more of a global approach and certainly awareness for the investor.

Next to the structural shifts is the phase of the equity markets. The U.S. equity markets entered a structural bear market in 2000. The Japanese equity markets entered one at the very end of 1989, while the European markets, like the U.S. markets, started a structural bear market in 2000. Both were structural bear markets preceded by structural bull markets triggered by a change in the political structure to enable the end of an era of inflation. Partially offsetting these structural bear markets are structural bull markets in many of the emerging markets. These markets have benefitted from strong growth prospects and increasingly open economies. One of the keys to future market direction will be the direction of economic control: Will it trend toward being more disbursed or increasingly more controlled? If the emerging markets follow the recent lead of most of the developed world, it will be more controlled. The alternative is for leaders of the developed world to embrace the foundation of the successful economic structures of their more robust growth periods and make economic decision-making more disbursed. The latter road is the one leading to a sustained bull market, while the former leads to a continuation of the structural bear market, weak economic growth, and less political stability.

Finally, there is the prospect of deleveraging. History shows the vast majority of past periods of deleveraging were, at best, disappointing. Many were disruptive. The unfortunate reality is leverage is a force that eventually must be addressed. The longer it is ignored, the more painful or risky its remedy. Unwinding leverage, deleveraging, requires less spending by the leveraged one. In the economy, the disciplines and methods to address leverage in the private sector are straightforward and typically bring quick involvement on the part of the lenders. The public sector does not face the same constraints. Its citizens, other investors, and institutions of other countries are its lenders and the rationalization of too much debt has most often been addressed by debasing a currency, defaulting, significant austerity, or a combination of the three. Growing the economy faster than debt to deleverage has rarely been done.

The U.S. economy is in the beginning part of the deleveraging process. Nonfinancial corporate America long ago began to deleverage. The process included reducing debt and reducing open-ended commitments including pensions and other retirement benefits. One part of nonfinancial corporate America facing the prospect of deleveraging is the commercial real estate business, which we believe accounts for well under 10% of the debt outstanding.

The deleveraging process has already begun for the Household sector and the Financials sector. For the Household sector, the most critical element in a successful deleveraging will be job and wage growth, while the deleveraging of the Financials sector should involve reintermediation, recapitalization, and rationalization.

The greatest risk from deleveraging is tied to the public sector. The structure for deleveraging is not as well developed and its magnitude dwarfs the challenge facing the private sector. The potential for volatile slow growth environment is high, as is another decade of modest equity returns. Capital preservation should be goal number one.

Endnotes

[1] Solomon, C. "Why Poor People Win the Lottery," http://articles.moneycentral.msn.com/RetirementandWills/RetireEarly/WhyPoorPeopleWinTheLottery.aspx, accessed June 22, 2010.

INDEX

FINANCIAL TIMES

In an increasingly competitive world, it is quality
of thinking that gives an edge—an idea that opens new
doors, a technique that solves a problem, or an insight
that simply helps make sense of it all.

We work with leading authors in the various arenas
of business and finance to bring cutting-edge thinking
and best-learning practices to a global market.

It is our goal to create world-class print publications
and electronic products that give readers
knowledge and understanding that can then be
applied, whether studying or at work.

To find out more about our business
products, you can visit us at www.ftpress.com.